Young Learner English Language Policy and International Perspectives

Edited by Janet Enever, Jayne Moon and Uma Raman

Published by
Garnet Publishing Ltd.
8 Southern Court
South Street
Reading RG1 4QS, UK
www.garneteducation.com

This edition first published 2009

British Library Cataloguing-in-Publication Data
A Catalogue record for this book is available from the British Library.

ISBN: 978 1 90109 523 4

Production

Project Coordinator:	Hans Mol
Editorial team:	Kate Brown, James Croft
Design and layout:	Dany Awwad, Rita Kilzi

Printed and bound in Great Britain by Cambrian Printers Ltd, Aberystwyth, Wales.

Contents

Innovations, experiments, projects

Foreword

If you are one of the many ministries of education or professionals grappling with the issues of whether to or how to effectively introduce early foreign language learning, this collection of papers – the proceedings from the Bangalore conference on Teaching English to Young Learners (TEYL) – is essential reading.

The conference and these proceedings capture the insights of a truly international group of speakers at a crucial point in time, when early foreign language policies are just beginning to take effect and the success stories and problem areas are emerging. These insights offer us the opportunity to compare emerging results and identify areas for further research and evaluation. The summary of the conference themes by Jayne Moon and Janet Enever serves as an excellent introduction to the opportunities and challenges involved, challenges, which we know from our work with ministries across the world, are of prime importance to all countries looking at ways of preparing their children for life in a globalized world.

The conference was a successful and rewarding collaboration between IATEFL and the British Council and I would like to thank Jayne Moon, Janet Enever and the IATEFL Young Learners Special Interest Group for making it happen. Thanks are also due to all those participants who shared their experiences and helped to take forward our understanding of how early language learning policy can be effectively designed and implemented.

Barbara Hewitt, Director of Research and Consultancy, British Council

Introduction: The Way Forward: Learning from International Experience of Teaching English to Young Learners (TEYL), Regional Institute of English, Bangalore, India, 3–6 January 2008

The papers included in this collection are a selection from those presented at the conference held in Bangalore, India, in January 2008. A first in the field of Primary ELT policy research, this conference was organized by the IATEFL Young Learners Special Interest Group, in partnership with the British Council, with the aim of providing a forum for discussion and debate on the process of policy design and implementation.

The Bangalore conference, 'The Way Forward: Learning from International Experience of TEYL', grew out of the organizers' concerns that there is often insufficient guidance available to decision-makers at Ministry level regarding the policy and practical implications of an early start. The last three to four decades have seen a huge expansion in TEYL programmes across the world, mainly in response to the impact of rapid globalization. This is allied to the perceived importance of English, which is beginning to have a significant impact on policy decisions, increasingly from pre-Primary upwards, with far-reaching implications for teachers, learners and resources.

It was felt that a conference targeted at experts and key decision-makers within the educational process would allow sharing and dissemination of experience in implementing English programmes for children in the state school sector internationally. This in turn, it was hoped, would widen perspectives and influence future policy. The conference was organized, therefore, around a series of case studies that presented a description and analysis of various aspects of policy and state school provision for TEYL in individual countries. This was complemented by presentations on specific innovations, experiments or projects (which were not nationally implemented) within the state or private sector with regard to teaching English to children.

The papers included in these proceedings were all presented at the conference. They represent the two foci mentioned above. The first section contains country case studies and the second section contains accounts of innovations, experiments or small-scale projects. In each section, papers are arranged alphabetically by author.

The two main sections are preceded by an article that draws on and summarizes some of the rich diversity of themes and issues arising out of many of the presentations at the conference. This article also includes a summary of recommendations for policy-makers that arose out of an online discussion held shortly after the conference.

The conference was truly international, with speakers representing 26 different countries from North and South America, Africa, the Middle East, Europe and Asia. Unfortunately not all the presenters at the conference submitted written summaries, however

PowerPoint™ presentations for some of these, not included in this symposium, can be found on the conference website at http://www.primaryeltconference.org.

The conference title 'Learning from International Experience' is intended both to highlight the international nature of the trend towards teaching English earlier in schools and to indicate that a strong theme of the conference was to build on a number of initiatives in recent years. These include, for example, research and practitioner conferences in Europe; a newly established regional Primary project in South East Asia; an increase in the number of policy-makers at national level seeking guidance on how effectively to introduce an earlier start to the teaching of English in schools and the rapid growth in development of international research in this field.

As editors, we would like to thank members of IATEFL and the YL SIG committee who helped to make both the conference and this publication a reality. We would specially like to thank the British Council for their generous support and the Regional Institute for English in South India (RIESI), which so excellently hosted the event. We hope the papers included in this volume will both stimulate discussion and encourage much needed further research in this developing field.

Jayne Moon, Janet Enever and Uma Raman
September 2008

New global contexts for teaching Primary ELT: Change and challenge

Janet Enever, Institute for the Study of European Transformations, London Metropolitan University, UK

Jayne Moon, Primary ELT and Teacher Education Consultant, Leeds, UK

Almost unnoticed in the latter years of the twentieth century, English crept into the Primary school curriculum, steadily edging its way downward to a point where, in 2008, it is frequently to be found included at the very start of the compulsory school curriculum. Contexts vary, resulting in its introduction as a second, additional or sometimes distinctively *foreign* language to which school children need to become acclimatized and in which they need to gain fluency. However, despite the very rapid growth in the perceived importance of this language, we have yet to clarify the priorities for formulating effective language policies, for designing appropriate programmes of implementation and for meeting the very real challenge of ensuring that policy is effectively and sustainably implemented within the daily practice of classrooms.

In this paper, we identify three persistent themes that thread through many of the conference presentations, papers included in this symposium, and studies so far conducted in this area. They can be categorized into those that:

- consider the impact of specifically global factors on policy decisions and classroom practices;

- explore the challenges of policy and its implementation, including the need to ensure that age-appropriate and adequate provision is made for inclusive policies at national level;

- explore broader and more local language issues and their impact on policy.

In the final section of this paper, we include an appendix with a draft set of recommendations, based on an online discussion among some conference participants, which might provide a template for policy-makers in planning, shaping and refining their future national provision.

Impact of global processes on Teaching English to Young Learner (TEYL) policy and practice

In this section, we will consider a number of issues related to the impact of global processes on TEYL policy and practice – a theme prominent in many of the conference papers, to which this chapter provides an introduction.

First, it is important to acknowledge the extent to which a substantial shift of economic power from public to private, from the state to the market, can now be identified globally (Schugurensky and Davidson-Harden, 2003). This is a consequence of the continuing neo-liberalist strategy of the 'free market' global economy moving towards increased economic liberalization via corporations, governments and international organizations such as the International Monetary Fund (IMF), the World Trade Organization (WTO) and the World Bank (WB). In this process, new pan-regional groupings have emerged such as the Association of East Asian Nations (ASEAN), the North American Free Trade Association (NAFTA) and the European Union (EU), seeking to gain and maintain a viable economic position within an increasingly globalized economic space. This neo-liberalist tendency has led countries such as China, Korea, Japan and Vietnam to 'open up' to increased international interactions in the past few years. In turn, this has contributed to creating an increased demand for English as the language of choice for international communication, given its current status as a global language or lingua franca (Crystal, 1997, quoted in Nunan, 2003). National decisions to choose English as the language for international interaction may also be identified as politically motivated where English is increasingly seen as a generic skill, according to Graddol (2008), leading governments to lower the starting age with the aim of building strong English proficiency levels for human resource development.

The decision to lower the starting age in many of the countries represented at the Bangalore Young Learners policy conference seems to have been based on two main assumptions: that younger children are better at learning/find it easier (Nunan, 2003: 605) and that a longer period of learning leads to higher proficiency by the end of schooling. Some of these assumptions are still contested in academic circles (Singleton and Ryan, 2004: 227), while others are dangerously over-simplified in public rhetoric (Marinova-Todd, Marshall and Snow, 2001). Uncritical acceptance of the view that 'early is better' under all circumstances can lead to hasty policy decisions to begin early, with huge implications for national resources.

While there are strong downward international pressures on governments, at the same time there is also a strong upward pressure from parents nationally on governments for their children to learn English from an earlier age because of perceived social and economic benefits, for example, as a symbol of a better life, or as providing increased social mobility and enhanced status (as reported by Ghatage, İnal, Kapur and Lee, this volume). Gupta (2004: 268) reports that these benefits are increasingly perceived by the workforce as the impact of global influences trickles down through the economy to such contexts as call centres, modern shopping malls, international brand fast food outlets and trade fairs.

Another way in which we can increasingly see the impact of global processes on TEYL policy and practice is in school curricula and approaches to the teaching and learning adopted. The perceived need for a workforce that is more entrepreneurial, more flexible and capable of lifelong learning in the new, more global, technologized and post-industrial economies is leading governments to reform curricula in order to respond to these new challenges. Linguistic skills, knowledge of other languages, and the new literacy skills demanded by new technologies (Cameron, 2002; Block and Cameron, 2002; Street, 1999) are increasingly viewed as what Bourdieu (1997: 47) has identified as valuable 'linguistic capital'. This is also having an impact on Primary education and the learning of other languages, as illustrated in the latest TEYL Primary curriculum, which represents something of a paradigm shift towards more learner-centred approaches, learner autonomy, critical thinking skills and communication skills (as reported by Al-Zedjali and Etherton, İnal, Kapur, and Lee and Wang, this volume). Some countries have also introduced Language 1 (L1) and Language 2 (L2) literacy skills simultaneously (e.g., Hong Kong, Oman, Malaysia and the Maldives).

Global vs local

Although a discussion about globalization often implies that there is a direct transmission of ideas in one direction, this is by no means the case in practice. Many writers point to the dynamic interplay between global and local issues (e.g., Butler, this volume; Block and Cameron, 2002; Pennycook, 2008; Robertson and Dale, 2002: 29). One area in which this can be seen in TEYL is with regard to communication skills. Due to the perceived need for communication skills in an increasingly globalized world economy, these skills, in particular, are now given greater prominence in YL curriculum (as reported by Wang, Lee, İnal and Kuchah, this volume). This focus on communication skills development has tended to lead to the adoption of various versions of the Communicative Language Teaching (CLT) approach in teaching – an approach originally devised for teaching adult EFL classes in commercially-oriented organizations in the UK, North America, Canada, Australia and New Zealand (colloquially known as the BANA countries in EFL contexts) (Holliday, 1994). Cameron (2002: 81) suggests that this approach tends to give prominence to oral skills based on western-oriented and increasingly standardized norms of interaction and interpersonal communication that have become more prominent in the workplace with the rise of service industries worldwide. However, this model of communication is often not fully understood, particularly in its interpretation and relevance for the teaching of a foreign language to young children in state school classrooms. The consequence may be reinterpretation and adaptation to suit local conditions, which may lead to quite different learning outcomes (as reported by Butler, this volume) or realizations in ways which take account of local cultural norms and values (Phan Le Ha, 2004). Several of the contributors to this volume allude to the difficulties faced by teachers in implementing CLT approaches (e.g., Hoque, Inal, Mathew and Pani, and Wang, this volume) though none considered them insurmountable or questioned the relevance of the model. The increasing discussion in the professional literature of notions like 'appropriate methodology' (Holliday, 1994); 'the importance of social context' (Bax, 2003 and Coleman, 1996); calls for 'third way pedagogies' (Pennycook, 2008); and for 'cultural mediation' (Ellis, 1996) suggest that local responses have influenced global academic discussions about CLT.

The notion of the interplay between the local and the global may also lead to different outcomes in different places. This is well illustrated by Butler (this volume) with regard to the challenge, faced by many countries, of the need to have Primary teachers proficient in English. In comparing the responses of Japan, Korea and Taiwan to this challenge, she notes that Japan has sought out native speaker (NS) teachers, while Korea and Taiwan have provided intensive language training and overseas courses for their teachers, though Taiwan is now beginning to make use of NS teachers and Korea is beginning to employ non-native speaker (NNS) teachers from Bangladesh, India, Pakistan, Russia and the Philippines (Scott Marchant, 2008: 4). Countries also respond differently to the challenge of improving English language proficiency in schools. Poland is introducing an official start (with a choice of English or German) from Grade 1; Croatia introduced an official start from Grade 1 in 2003 (with a choice of English, German, French or Italian – though English is overwhelmingly the first choice); China and Korea have mandated an official start from Grade 3 (with pilot projects from Grade 1 in urban centres such as Beijing and Shanghai (as reported by Wang et al., this volume); whereas Vietnam and Indonesia (as reported by Chodijah, 2008) have chosen to make English optional at Primary levels.

Finally, we consider the role of the private sector within this globalized education context and its impact on national policy and practice. Both the private language school sector and the private Primary/Secondary school sector have been quick to perceive market opportunities created by global events and influences and to respond to parental demand for English at Primary level (Mattheou, 1997: 5) and even pre-Primary levels (Bayyurt and Alptekin, 2000: 312), in many cases 'forcing' the state to introduce English at Primary level or to lower the starting age. In some reported cases, this has led to an 'overheating' of the private sector (as reported by Lee, this volume) and the costs to middle-class parents are now becoming a political issue (e.g., in Korea). In India, Bangladesh (Mathew and Pani, and Hoque, this volume) and other places, this challenging interplay between global and local forces is currently resulting in many English-medium schools contributing to furthering the gap between the 'haves' and 'have-nots' of society. Their linguistic advantages are regarded as highly desirable yet unattainable by the vast majority because most are in the private sector and their affordability is beyond reach.

While issues in the private educational sector are clearly complex, in some cases they can be viewed as positive. In many situations, private schools are viewed as providing 'quality' education in contrast to underfunded mass education in the state sector with large classes and poorly qualified teachers (as reported by Mathew and Pani, Gimenez, Hoque this volume, and Chodijah, 2008), which may 'push' governments to take affirmative action and improve access and quality. Even the perception that private schools are out of the reach of poor parents may be changing, with many types of private school opening, such as in rural and urban areas of India where Kumar (quoted in LaDousa, 2007: 140) reports of 'poorer parents' willing to make sacrifices so that their children can hopefully get a slightly better education. Kumar (quoted in LaDousa, 2007: 142) also makes the interesting point that paying for education, even if amounts are small, gives poorer parents some sense of control or say in their children's education. Despite these positive aspects, Kumar argues that there remain concerns about the role of the private sector, which is largely unregulated and by no means always of a high standard (also reported by Gimenez, this volume). Increasing inequalities of access may in turn place political pressure on state governments, leading to unprincipled and hasty decisions.

Challenges of implementing policy

The impact of the global processes outlined in the above section has introduced a very real challenge to the processes of policy implementation. This section reviews the evidence and explores the extent to which political will is reinforced by the provision of sufficient appropriate training and resources for effective implementation. Here, planning and programmes for implementation appear to differ greatly across the world, ranging from the official 'encouragement' for an early start enshrined in policy documents in Hungary, yet currently unsupported by national provision of additional training and resources (as reported by Nikolov, this volume), to the planned pilot phase introduction of English from Grade 1 in designated urban regions of China, supported by a comprehensive training programme and monitored by a research and evaluation team (as reported by Wang, this volume).

Evidently, the design of implementation programmes is likely always to be dependent on both political will and available national investment. However, the many different models reported in this volume appear more strongly to reflect both particular national histories of managing educational change and the multiplicity of new challenges implicit in introducing FL learning across a whole state system from an early age. Consistently, familiar themes arise in many countries – a consequence of continuing national and international uncertainties regarding effective programme design for this age group. The central themes include: optimal start age, language choices, teacher quality, class size, curriculum and assessment design, equity of provision, continuity across school phases and resource needs. A short summary of evidence for each of these themes is provided here, with reference to relevant papers in this collection.

Optimal start age

Several countries represented have mandated TEYL Primary programmes starting at mid-Primary level (often Grade 3 or 4), but allow regional and local authorities flexibility to begin earlier according to demand. This leads to a great deal of variation in provision and subsequent problems for transitions at the official grade of starting (any time between one and three years later) and Secondary level (as reported by Butler, Gimenez, Lee, Lefever, Mathew and Pani, Nikolov and Wang et al., this volume). In Europe the prevailing trend has been to introduce mandatory programmes from age 6–7 years, heavily promoted by a 'strong recommendation' from the EU policy group that the first foreign language should be introduced from the early Primary or pre-school phase (as reported by Enever et al., this volume). This earlier start policy may offer a stronger potential for equality of provision for all, providing adequate teacher professional development is also made available.

Teacher quality

A widely reported problem is the gap between the supply of qualified TEYL teachers and the demand for them as programmes expand (reported by Chodijah, 2008; Kgwadi, 2008; Enever et al., Gimenez, Kgwadi, Kuchah, Lee, Lefever, Mathew and Pani, and Wang, this volume). The lack of qualified teachers means that countries frequently have to rely on teachers who are not trained to teach TEYL, including Primary class teachers and others who might not have qualifications appropriate for teaching younger children, such as Secondary trained teachers, graduates, and teachers of other subjects. This clearly will have an impact on outcomes and suggests that countries have to be more realistic in their expectations of what can be achieved. Very few countries represented already had specialized pre-service TEYL training courses in place, but many were proposing to implement such courses in the future as awareness of the link between teacher quality and outcomes at Primary level is becoming more apparent. The wide gap between supply and demand suggests that expansion of TEYL has often not been adequately prepared for.

Class size

There is huge variation in class size across and within country contexts. Smaller class sizes generally are found in Europe. For example, both Poland and Hungary traditionally have divided classes for language learning, often resulting in teaching groups of no more than 15 learners. In contrast, much larger classes seem to be the norm in Asia and Africa. For example, in Bangladesh, Cameroon, China, India and Indonesia, class sizes of 50 or more are frequently to be found. Class size and classroom organization tends to affect the teacher's willingness and ability to use more activity-based, interactive methods typically associated with the communicative approaches and YL methods and may have an impact on the level of proficiency that can be achieved in these contexts.

Curriculum and assessment design

In a number of countries, it appears that stated curriculum aims and guidelines are not necessarily being implemented as intended. Reportedly, in Bangladesh, Turkey, India and Hungary (see, respectively, Hoque, İnal, Kirköz, Mathew and Pani, and Nikolov, this volume) many teachers still use what are seen as more traditional formal grammar-focused approaches despite the fact that official curricula are promoting more communicative, activity-oriented approaches suitable for YL. Much of the difficulty experienced by teachers in introducing a strong oracy focus for early foreign language learners may be traced back to the effect of formal public exams at the end of Primary school within some school systems. In a number of countries it appears that teachers, parents and children are collectively so focused on getting through the exam that it proves difficult to implement innovative new programmes successfully (as reported by Hoque, İnal and Samantray, this volume). The washback effect of an exam focus tends to trickle down into lower classes where teachers start to prepare children in advance so become less willing to spend time on more interactive spoken activities. There are a large number of additional issues related to local contextual factors and conditions for learning which clearly have a significant impact on implementation of TEYL programmes. Some are common to many countries, while others are unique to particular contexts. These are further elaborated in individual papers included in this volume.

Resource provision

Notable in a number of papers are the wide gaps in choices regarding resource needs for this rapidly developing area of Primary education. Decisions at national level are sometimes related to an individual country's wealth, but sometimes simply to centralized policy-making processes that aim to plan for the future in resource provision. Hence, a number of countries reported the use of technology and multimedia in TEYL as fairly standard practice, though this was by no means uniform across the countries represented. These countries included Taiwan, Korea, China and Malaysia (as reported, respectively, by Butler, Lee, Wang, Yaacob and Gardner, this volume). In some cases, it may be viewed as a way of compensating for underqualified teachers or those with low proficiency; it is also seen as a way of supporting and training them (Korea), while in China the use of CD-ROMs as a replacement for the course book is seen as a more effective visual aid when teaching larger classes. In contrast to the Chinese solution, England is now rapidly introducing interactive whiteboards (IWBs) to Primary schools as an essential teaching aid in the creation of a multimedia-based platform for learning. However, there are clearly dangers of the technology driving the teaching and reducing the teacher to a mere operative (as reported by Yaacob and Gardner, this volume) and of management underestimating the degree of training required. Kumar (quoted in LaDousa, 2007: 148) also raises the issue of how seductive computer software programmes are for children regardless of their educational quality, which may result in a tendency to downgrade the status and role of the teacher, particularly in contexts like India where there is a dearth of good quality textbooks and resources. Nevertheless, if programmes are well conceived, the use of technology can also be seen as a boon in large southern hemisphere countries such as Nigeria and India, with limited resources and where the use of interactive radio programmes for in-service training can transcend distance and provide a quality service for teachers (as reported by Moh and Dutt et al., this volume). The key question for the future evaluation of these new environments for learning will be an understanding of the extent to which they enhance the learning experience.

Equity of TEYL provision

Given the above-outlined difficulties experienced in the introduction of early foreign language learning in many state school systems, it is unsurprising to note also that countries are increasingly concerned about children's access to TEYL and the equity of provision, with frequent reports of large differences in access and in quality of provision between rural and urban areas, between geographical areas and between different urban schools. Particularly noted in papers by Butler, Kapur, Lee, Nikolov and Wang (this volume) and Chodijah (2008), this is corroborated by Nunan's survey data from countries in the Asia Pacific region in 2003. The demand for English is identified here as exacerbating the problem (Nunan, 2003: 605). It appears that some governments are beginning to take measures to try and increase provision, for example in Korea, through English camps and English villages (Lee, this volume); Taiwan, where young military recruits can do their service teaching English in remote areas (Butler, this volume); India, through lowering the starting age in many States (Kapur, this volume); India and Nigeria, with the development of interactive radio training for teachers (Dutt et al., Moh, this volume, respectively). Nevertheless, the challenges for public education are immense, leading to the gaps in provision increasingly being filled by the private sector and non-governmental organizations (NGOs).

Continuity across school phases

Linked to the above concerns about achieving equity of provision is the challenge of also ensuring continuity of provision as children transfer from one class to the next, or from Primary to Secondary school. The relatively recent introduction of Primary languages teaching is often not fully acknowledged by the Secondary school (or even the next class), resulting in insufficient recognition of prior learning and a tendency almost to 'start from the beginning' again (Edelenbos, Johnstone and Kubanek, 2006: 24). Few countries have yet established a cohesive curriculum outline in foreign languages, ensuring a cumulative programme of provision for each phase of schooling.

Dynamic interplay between top-down and bottom-up

Reports from different countries indicate that though the trend is for nationwide top-down policy-driven TEYL programmes (as reported by Lee, Al-Zedjali and Etherton, and Wang, this volume), there is also some evidence of a more grass-roots, bottom-up participation by civil society, for example in Cameroon where a local teachers' group (CAMELTA) has been active in supporting teachers (see Kuchah, this volume); in Bangladesh, where many NGOs are increasingly involved in basic education provision, including English (see Hoque, this volume); and in Taiwan, where teachers are involved as mentors in helping other teachers implement the new curriculum (see Chern, this volume). Evidence from the outcomes of policy implementation utilizing either a top-down or bottom-up model suggests that alone, neither is likely to be a recipe for success. Johnstone (this volume) argues convincingly that implementation on a national scale is unlikely to be effective in the absence of a top-down strategy. However, the range of challenges outlined above seems to suggest that a combination of both top-down and bottom-up procedures is necessary if such a large-scale educational change is to become fully embedded within a national system.

Language issues and policy

This final section of the Introduction focuses on more locally based factors impacting specifically on the choices of languages to be taught and to language choice in classroom instruction. Here again, we consider the interplay between national and local perspectives and the additional layering of influence currently observable as an outcome of global pressures.

Use of Language 1 (L1) and English through English

Many countries report that TEYL teachers often use more L1 in TEYL classrooms than is desirable, suggesting either that teaching English through English is the desired norm or at least that conducting the greater part of the foreign language lesson in the L1 should be avoided. Studies mentioning this feature include those by Chern, Lee, Lefever and Nikolov (this volume). This seems to be a particular issue in foreign language contexts where education authorities sometimes stipulate that English should be taught through English in order presumably to increase exposure (as reported in Lee, this volume). In reality, many TEYL teachers make frequent use of L1, influenced by factors such as their own level of proficiency and confidence; their ability to adjust their language to the children's level and support children adequately; large class sizes; and their concern that children should understand. There seems to be insufficient understanding by policy-makers and educators of the complexity of language use in the YL classroom where the L1 can be viewed as an initial resource for children to draw on and where teachers need guidance if their use of language in the classroom is to be more principled and planned (Cameron, 2001: 213). The use of L1 may be viewed rather differently in multilingual contexts. For example, in India, official policy appears to support the use of L1 or other known languages in the classroom as a resource to help children acquire the new language (English) (as reported in Kapur, this volume) in the early stages. The danger, of course, with teachers of low proficiency is that the use of L1 becomes the preferred strategy.

English as threat vs English as bridge

Some concerns about the possible threat to national identity and language accompanying the move to an earlier start for English are evident. For example, Oman's reformed curriculum strongly emphasizes and promotes Omani culture and the Arabic language (as reported in Al-Zedjali and Etherton, this volume). Similarly, the Korean public is reportedly concerned about the effect on children's L1 if English starts earlier (as reported in Lee, this volume). Prabhu (this volume) warns of the possible danger to local languages if English starts too early, and argues that English should be an addition to a child's repertoire of languages not a substitution for their L1/home language. However, in contrast Rajuan and Michael (this volume) report how English is seen as a neutral language in Israel, which may enable Palestinians and Jews to bridge the cultural divide. Such viewpoints echo the continuing debate regarding the current position of English globally and concerns expressed over perceived potential of a decline in the importance of or a lower status for other languages. As indicated by Graddol (2006), given the historical patterns of continuous shift and change in both the status and spread of local, national and supranational languages it is difficult to predict the likely future importance of English or any other language. Nonetheless, at local levels these concerns are influencing many policy decisions.

Dilemma of language choice in multilingual societies

Multilingual countries face many dilemmas in choosing the medium of instruction at Primary level, depending on whether they choose the child's mother tongue, which may not have wide currency outside local communities; a regional language with wider currency; or an international language such as English. In the choice of English it may well be that teachers lack proficiency, thus creating barriers to understanding subject content. One reported case is that of Cameroon, where English and French are the two main second languages with which Cameroonians affiliate, depending on whether they come from the area previously colonized by the British or French (see Kuchah, this volume). This has led to polarization along anglophone-francophone rather than ethnic lines. Recent legal and policy changes have given equal status to both languages and have also led to the teaching of French as a subject in anglophone schools and English in francophone schools, which in turn has lead to more positive attitudes to each language. The context of South Africa presents a different linguistic history and thus a language policy with a strong social dimension enshrining a choice of 11 officially recognized languages (including English) with the aim of promoting respect for all languages; communication across ethnic lines; and in order to reflect multilingualism as a norm (as reported in Kgwadi, 2008). Policy also supports children being able to learn through their home/mother language as well as learning two additional languages. In practice, however, English is chosen as the preferred medium of instruction by parents in black areas even though local teachers do not have adequate English proficiency. Recent evidence (Chick 2002: 475) indicates that these children are doubly disadvantaged throughout their basic education. Like South Africa, India has also adopted a multilingual three language policy to address the challenges of their linguistic situation, involving learning through the mother tongue or a regional language, with English being chosen as a second or third language in most state schools. The majority of poorer children learn in state-run, regional-medium schools with English as a subject. As teachers in these schools tend to have the lowest levels of English proficiency among the four types of Indian school (as reported in Kapur, this volume), children may well be further disadvantaged over those in English-medium schools. The current increase in demand for learning English in India similarly may result in a limited application of the language policy, as reported in South Africa (Kgwadi, 2008).

Language choices

At whatever age a second or foreign language is introduced in schools, a contemporary theme of policy-makers across the world is the decision regarding which language to introduce first. For some, the priority is to choose the language that is currently perceived to give the greatest future economic advantage (e.g., English in China, Italy and Korea). For others, the priority is a language choice that will help to maintain social cohesion within the country (Cameroon and South Africa) or with neighbouring countries (e.g., English or German in Poland and Hungary). Other groupings have prioritized regional/national bilingualism (e.g., French and English in Cameroon; Spanish and Catalan in the Catalonian region of Spain at kindergarten level, with the addition of English from age six). The debate relating to economic advantage versus social cohesion is particularly strong in England where currently there is no obvious first choice of foreign language. The unpredictability of future language needs (for a country where English is predominantly the first language) has resulted in a decision to devolve language choices to the level of the individual school, allowing them to respond to local needs and preferences.

Conclusion

This Introduction has summarized many of the key challenges faced in the introduction of early foreign language learning in state school systems today. Driving policy forward is the view that by introducing a foreign languages early, future generations will be better equipped to communicate locally, regionally and globally. The real process of embedding such policies securely at national and local levels has perhaps only just begun and hence our knowledge of how this might be achieved is limited. Published research is also limited in the field of critical policy studies relevant to the first few years of foreign language learning in Primary education. Nevertheless, we would assert, albeit tentatively, that the studies published in this volume have shed much light on this area. Drawing on these findings we consider that it is now possible to identify some initial indicators of how effective policy has come to be designed and implemented.

First, we note that those projects which were reported as successful appeared to have a number of characteristics. Without exception, these included collaboration between different stakeholders such as the local education authorities, teachers, headteachers and local radio stations, as reported in both Nigeria and China (see Moh and Wang, this volume). In some cases support from an external agency (such as the British Council for the Nigerian teacher radio programme) was identified. In others, strong support for teachers proved to be a key factor, as reported in Argentina, China, Nigeria and Taiwan (see respectively, Corradi, Wang, Moh and Chern, this volume), or building on existing reforms, as in Oman (see Al-Zedjali and Etherton, this volume). Elsewhere, studies identified the importance of giving teachers tools to be more independent (see Dutt et al., Wang et al., this volume) and of investment in the training of teachers and trainers (see Chern, this volume).

Secondly, we can note reports of the wider outcomes of successful project implementation on the broader school curriculum. Such outcomes as the development of early positive attitudes to learning English are particularly identified in Croatia, China and Iceland (as reported in Enever et al., Wang, Lefever this volume). Evidence of high levels of language awareness is reported in Argentina (see Corradi, this volume). Increasing evidence of the wider knowledge of English even among adults is evident in the community in Maharasthra, India (see Ghatage, this volume). Improved L1 and L2 literacy is evident in Oman (see Al-Zedjali and Etherton, this volume). The positive impact of English learning on other subject learning is reported in China (see Wang, this volume).

Mostly, the studies of policy and practice reported on here relate to decisions made within the past ten years or so for the introduction of FL learning from the early phases of state Primary school systems. To achieve optimal frameworks for the effective implementation of policies will clearly take some time yet, but we hope this Introduction has provided some sense of how much has already been achieved and what still remains to be clarified. We hope that readers of the studies included in this volume will be encouraged to take up further research and evaluation opportunities to extend our understandings further.

References

Bax, S. (2003). Bringing context and methodology together. *ELT Journal* 57, 295-296.

Bayyurt, Y. and Alptekin, C. (2000). EFL Curriculum Design for Turkish Young Learners in Bilingual School Contexts. In Moon, J. and Nikolov, M. (eds) (2000) *Research into Teaching English to Young Learners. International Perspectives.* Pécs: University Press.

Block, D. and Cameron, D. (eds) (2002). *Globalization and Language Teaching.* London: Routledge.

Bourdieu, P. (1997). The forms of capital. In Halsey, A.H., Lauder, H., Brown, P., and Stuart Wells, A. (eds) *Education, Culture, Economy and Society* (pp. 46-58). Oxford: Oxford University Press.

Cameron, L. (2001). *Teaching Languages to Young Learners.* Cambridge: Cambridge University Press.

Cameron, D. (2002). Globalization and the teaching of 'communication skills'. In Block, D. and Cameron, D. (eds) (2002) *Globalization and Language Teaching* (pp. 67-82). London: Routledge.

Chick, J.K. (2002). Constructing a multicultural national identity: South African classrooms as sites of struggle between competing discourses. *Journal of Multilingual and Multicultural Development* 23 (6), 462-478.

Chodijah, I. (2008). English in Primary School: Gem in the Mud. Paper presented at the Bangalore Conference 'The Way Forward: Learning from International Experience of TEYL', 3–6 January 2008. Bangalore, India: RIESI.

Coleman, H. (1996) (ed.). *Society and the Language Classroom.* Cambridge: Cambridge University Press.

Edelenbos, P., Johnstone, R. and Kubanek, A. (2006). The main pedagogical principles underlying the teaching of languages to very young learners. Languages for the children of Europe: Published Research, Good Practice and Main Principles. *Final Report of the EAC 89/04, Lot 1 Study.* European Commission, Brussels: Education and Culture, Culture and Communication, Multilingualism Policy. Available at http://ec.europa.eu.education/languages/pdf/doc425_en.pdf

Ellis, G. (1996). How culturally appropriate is the communicative approach? *ELT Journal* 50 (3), 213-218.

Graddol, D. (2006). *English Next.* British Council.

Graddol, D. (2008). How TEYL is changing the world. Paper presented at the Bangalore Conference, 'The Way Forward: Learning from International Experience of TEYL', 3–6 January 2008. Bangalore, India: RIESI.

Gupta, D. (2004). CLT in India: context and methodology come together. *ELT Journal* 58 (3), 266-269.

Holliday, A. (1994). *Appropriate Methodology and Social Context.* Cambridge: Cambridge University Press.

Kgwadi, B. (2008). Teaching of English to young learners in South African schools: Subject and Policy implementation paper at the Bangalore Conference 'The Way Forward: Learning from International Experience of TEYL', 3–6 January 2008. Bangalore, India: RIESI.

LaDousa, C. (2007). Liberalization, privatization, modernization and schooling in India: an interview with Krishna Kumar. *Globalization, Societies and Education* 5 (2), 137-152.

Marinova-Todd, S.H., Marshall, D.B and Snow, C.E. (2001). Missing the point: a response to Hyltenstam and Abrahamsson. *TESOL Quarterly* 35 (1), 171-176.

Mattheou, D. (1997). Living in the Global Village. Problems, Policies and Prospects of Foreign Language Teaching in the Primary School. In Karavas-Doukas, K. and Rea-Dickens, P. (eds) *The Teaching of Foreign Languages in European Primary School. Evaluating Innovations and Establishing Reseach Priorities* (pp. 3-8). Conference Proceedings, 20–24 April 1997. University of Warwick.

Nunan, D. (2003). The Impact of English as a Global Language on Educational Policies and Practices in the Asia-Pacific Region. *TESOL Quarterly* 37 (4), 589-597.

Pennycook, A. (2008). Changing Practices in Global ELT. Plenary Paper presented at the 42nd Annual International IATEFL Conference, 7–11 April 2008.

Phan Le Ha (2004). University classrooms in Vietnam: contesting the stereotypes. *ELT Journal* 58(1), 50-57.

Robertson, S.L. and Dale, R. (2002). The Varying Effects of Regional Organizations as Subjects of Globalization of Education. *Comparative Education Review* 46 (1), 10-36.

Schugurensky, D. and Davidson-Harden, A. (2003). From Cordoba to Washington: WTO/GATS and Latin American Education. *Globalization, Societies and Education* 1 (3), 321-357.

Scott Marchant, J. (2008). Korean bulldozer hits EFL. *EL Gazette* 342 (July), 4.

Singleton, D. and Ryan, L. (2004). *Language Acquisition: The Age Factor.* Clevedon, UK: Multilingual Matters.

Street, B. (1999). *Multiple Literacies and Multi-Lingual Society.* Watford, UK: National Association for Language Development in the Curriculum (NALDIC).

Appendix

Recommendations for policy development and implementation: Introducing English as a second/foreign language in Primary schools

1. 'The earlier the better' is not automatically true in all situations.

2. Evidence suggests that hastily implemented early start policies may be ineffective.

3. To ensure quality and sustainability over time, a planned and phased introduction is important.

4. The likelihood of sustainability is much increased if planning and implementation is both a top-down and a bottom-up process. For implementation to become effective, schools, parents and local communities need to be involved, together with national, regional and local project teams.

5. Key factors in achieving quality and sustainability include:

    5.1 Trained Primary teachers with pedagogical skills in teaching English as a second/foreign language to younger Primary-aged children.

    5.2 Teachers with a minimum competency level in English of B1 level (as described by the Common European Framework of Reference for Languages)

    5.3 Age-appropriate and culturally appropriate teaching materials are vital.

    5.4 Substantial institutional support for the initiative is needed.

    5.5 Ongoing local workshops/training should be provided to support teachers in developing skills over time.

    5.6 A phased introduction may be more effective – starting with the upper Primary then gradually extending to the lower Primary years.

6. Initial regional piloting projects can provide important insights and understanding of the necessary conditions and offer opportunities to accumulate experience in teacher supply and training. Such experience will help to identify key issues for successful large scale implementation.

7. As one part of the implementation process, a research study to monitor and evaluate the process should be set up. Findings will enable the formulation of workable guidelines for sustainable implementation.

8. Communication networks should be established between Primary and Secondary schools and their related support services (local advisers, teacher education colleges, etc.). These cross-phase clusters should work together to ensure that continuity of learning is provided across the transition phase – a frequently identified point of weakness in learning programmes.

9. Primary teachers' workload responsibilities should be addressed to ensure that teachers have both the time and the space to reflect on their own practices and work collaboratively to solve new problems.

10. National policy-makers should make a clear and realistic appraisal of the role of English in the Primary curriculum in relation to the future needs of the workforce and to the contextual realities for current provision.

11. Given the length of time needed to develop proficiency and age-appropriate teaching skills, sufficient and continuing funding will be vital in achieving and maintaining quality of provision.

12. Education reform needs time. Quality cannot be achieved overnight.

Contributors

Prof. Yuko Goto Butler, University of Pennsylvania, USA

Prof. Won Key Lee, Seoul National University of Education, Korea

Prof. Wang Qiang, Beijing Normal University, China

Wendy Arnold, IATEFL YL SIG, UK

Dr Janet Enever, London Metropolitan University, UK

Dr Sheena Gardner, University of Birmingham, UK

Dr Telma Gimenez, Universidade Estadual de Londrina, Brazil

Dr Samúel Lefever, Iceland University of Education, Iceland

Jayne Moon, Primary ELT and Teacher Education Consultant, Leeds, UK

Teaching English to young learners: The influence of global and local factors

Yuko Goto Butler, Graduate School of Education, University of Pennsylvania, USA

Introduction

In recent years, there have been a number of global changes that have exerted an impact on language-in-education policies in various countries (Block and Cameron, 2002). One of the most notable examples has been the introduction of English as a foreign language at Primary schools (referred to as EFLPS hereafter) as English has spread as a means of wider communication. Case studies have revealed, however, that many nations have encountered a number of challenges in implementing EFLPS. Some challenges have been commonly observed across multiple countries, whereas others are specific to local contexts. Policy decisions in some cases have been made based on a series of 'assumptions', or by directly importing popular ideologies and methods from English-speaking countries but without giving sufficient attention to their own local factors. In such cases, we need to re-examine and reinterpret popular ideologies and methods in order to make sense of them in their respective local contexts.

In this paper, I draw from the experiences of various EFLPS implementations in East Asia to illustrate the complicated ways in which both global and local factors influence EFLPS implementations. This paper is based on the experiences of three East Asian countries that I have worked with closely, namely, South Korea, Taiwan and Japan. Among the various challenges that these countries have encountered with EFLPS, I focus on the following three to illustrate the interactions between global and local factors:

1. accounting for diversity while providing equal access;

2. hiring native English-speaking teachers versus training local teachers; and

3. the use of popular ELT methods and their adaptation to local contexts.

Challenge 1: Accounting for diversity while providing equal access

Globally, as the role of English as a communication tool has become increasingly important, acquiring a high level of communicative competency in English has become a major goal of English education worldwide. The varying degrees of the impact of globalization and increasing mobility have brought about diversity within and across nations. This in turn has driven a diversity of needs among learners based on their region, socioeconomic status (SES), linguistic background and so forth.

In East Asia, English serves a number of purposes. In addition to its use as a tool for communication, English has taken on another important role within various educational systems, namely, as a barometer of academic achievement. English has become a high stake academic subject; obtaining good scores on English tests has become a critically important means of advancing to higher education (e.g., Choi, 2007; Butler and Iino, 2005). As a result, parents, learners and local politicians are sensitive about any discrepancies in access to English education. Thus, FLPS implementations in East Asia have to be evaluated keeping these two important roles in mind. While policy-makers may attempt to provide equal access to English for all of the children in their respective educational systems, they also have to pay close attention to the increasingly diverse needs of their learners.

The three East Asian countries under consideration in this paper have taken different approaches towards dealing with this dilemma (Table 1 summarizes the EFLPS policies in each of the three countries). The Japanese government allowed local governments and individual schools to introduce English at their own choosing. The policy has been to introduce English as a non-academic foreign language that provides cultural exposure. The government has granted local governments and schools a tremendous amount of autonomy in this regard. In contrast to the Japanese government's approach, the Korean government opted for much stronger oversight and introduced English at Primary schools in a highly uniform way.

Regardless of the course set by the central government, all three countries have experienced a number of problems. In Japan, EFLPS have struggled to accommodate the diverse needs of learners, and tremendous differences in practice have raised serious concerns with respect to equal access to English language education (Butler, 2007a). In Korea and Taiwan, the official introduction of EFLPS appears to have escalated the household expenses associated with English lessons outside of schools. Teachers have already begun observing substantial achievement gaps among Primary school learners according to their parents' SES and by region due to the differing levels of private English lessons available to learners outside of their schools. The Korean government's effort to create English-only speaking spaces within the country (so-called 'English villages') was partially motivated by the desire to provide the opportunity to be exposed to English outside of school to all the learners regardless of socioeconomic background. However, the effect of such efforts has been questioned (Kim, 2006). The Taiwanese

	Korea	Taiwan	Japan
Government initiative	Strong central government initiative	General guidelines set by the central government but with some allowance for local choice	Based on local choice
Form of introduction	As an academic subject	As an academic subject	Can be introduced as part of a curriculum to facilitate international understanding
Date officially introduced	1997: nationwide	1998: selected areas 2001: nationwide	2002: introduced based on individual school choice; 2007: a proposal was accepted to mandate English education at the 5th and 6th grade levels (possibly starting from 2010)
Target grade levels (2007)	From 3rd to 6th	3rd grade and up nationwide (from 1st grade in select areas)	Varies from school to school
Number of lesson hours (2007)	3rd and 4th grades: 34 lessons per year 5th and 6th grades: 78 lessons per year (40 minutes per lesson)	72 lessons per year (40 minutes per lesson)	Varies from school to school
Curriculum	Detailed guidelines regarding when and what to teach under the 7th National curriculum	Suggested guidelines regarding when and what to teach are recommended by the central government	No official guidelines
Textbooks and materials	One textbook for each grade approved by the government	Multiple textbooks approved by the government; teachers can choose from among these textbooks	No specifically approved textbooks; teachers can use books and materials that they feel are appropriate

English teachers	Primarily regular homeroom teachers	Various types of teachers are allowed to teach	Various types of teachers are allowed to teach
In-service professional development	Initially 120 hours of in-service training organized by the government was required/various training opportunities at the local level	Training programs organized by local boards of education and private institutions/MOE initiated professional development systems including Seeded Teachers (selected experienced teachers) and Instructional Consulting team	Short-term training is mainly offered by local governments and private institutions but is not mandatory
Native speakers (NSs) in public schools	Not many so far but increasing in number	Not many so far but increasing in number	Many NSs employed but their abilities and their recruitment processes vary

Table 1: *Comparison of English language education at the elementary school level in Korea, Taiwan and Japan (2007)*

Note: Adapted from Butler (2004: 248-249)

government imposed restrictions on English-only kindergartens as one way to mitigate such differences, but this does not appear to have stopped enthusiastic parents from finding other means to give their children a head-start in learning English before beginning formal English instruction at Primary schools.

In sum, EFLPS implementations such as those in Japan, Korea and Taiwan have found it challenging to provide equal access to English education for all of their students while still meeting their diverse needs. In this process, the private sector has had a tremendous influence over the students' English learning, and thus the impact of the private sector on such educational initiatives cannot be ignored.

Challenge 2: Hiring native English-speaking teachers versus training local teachers

In introducing English at Primary schools, one of the more pressing concerns is how best to secure teachers for English classes. Global trends have made people believe that communicative skills, and oral communicative skills in particular, are very important. High proficiency has been highlighted as a critical component of qualified teachers, and in turn native English speakers (NSs) are often preferred as English teachers by teachers, parents and administrators in many parts of the world (e.g., Kamhi-Stein, 2004; Llurda, 2005). At the local level in East Asia, public discourse has shown a very high degree of concern regarding the English proficiency among Primary school teachers. Indeed, local teachers do not appear to have enough confidence to conduct English lessons (Butler, 2004), and their low confidence also appears to be related to their reliance on NSs at Primary schools (Butler, 2007b). Young learners themselves wish to have teachers who are confident in their use of English (Butler, 2007c). Under such circumstances, policies have focused on two different strategies for securing teachers: one has been to recruit NSs, while the other has been to train local teachers.

The three East Asian countries cited herein have taken different approaches towards securing teachers. Both Korea and Taiwan, where English has been implemented as a mandatory academic subject, initially focused on training local teachers. In Japan, on the other hand, systematic training programs for local teachers have rarely been offered (at least up to January 2008) whereas many NSs have been recruited. While training local teachers is a pressing issue in each of the three countries, the limited time and resources available for training local teachers has often been an obstacle to doing so. Regional gaps in teacher quality are also a major concern. The governments have taken various strategies to overcome such limitations, including the Taiwanese government's policy of sending young Taiwanese males who have been educated in English-speaking countries to rural areas as a substitute for fulfilling their military service obligations (known as English Education Military Substitutes) (Wu, 2007).

Recruiting NSs has been a challenge for all three countries. On the one hand, there is substantial demand for NS teachers. On the other hand, there are only a limited number of potentially qualified NSs who are interested in teaching in East Asia. Since many countries have begun aggressively hiring NSs, the extent to which countries can secure qualified NSs increasingly depends on how much salary such countries can afford to pay them. This will eventually create an 'NS teacher divide' according to the economic power of each nation or region.

One of the challenges that comes up both in hiring NSs and in training local teachers appears to be our limited understanding of specifically what teacher qualifications are necessary to effectively teach English at Primary schools. The identification of such qualifications depends on a number of factors, including who is best qualified to teach English (homeroom teachers, local English teachers, or NSs), the goals of teaching English at Primary schools, the role of NSs in English teaching, financial availability and so forth.

Challenge 3: Importing popular ELT methods and adapting them to local contexts

According to Cameron (2002), as globalization progresses, what is considered to constitute 'good communication' is globally determined. This idealized good communication is not culturally neutral; a particular style of speaking is favored and thus has been adopted in various English teaching practices. Thus, certain types of ELT methodologies have gained popularity worldwide, including Communicative Language Teaching (CLT), task-based instruction and so forth. Moreover, teachers have been asked to adopt various related concepts, including learner-centered teaching, the use of authentic materials, activities and so forth, by their respective educational policies. However, if these methods are employed locally, reinterpretation and adaptation are usually indispensable if teachers also wish to account for the influence of various local factors.

In an earlier cross-national study (Butler, 2005), teachers in each of the three countries discussed herein mentioned that while they employed suggested 'communicative activities' such as games, songs, role-playing activities and so forth, they were unsure of the purpose and effectiveness of these activities. By employing a multivocal method (Tobin, Wu and Davidson, 1989) in which multiple observers were invited to interpret such practices across each of the three countries, it became clear that teachers struggled to adapt such activities in light of the goals and expectations of EFLPS and their respective teaching environments. The teachers often had different motives for employing the same suggested activities. Even if the learners exhibit similar observable behaviors in a given activity, according to Activity Theory (e.g., Lantolf, 2000), they are considered to be engaging in qualitatively different 'activities'. This may eventually lead to different outcomes as far as learning is concerned. In other words, employing a suggested communicative activity itself does not necessarily mean that the same learning takes place.

The difficulties that teachers in the study faced appeared to arise in part as a result of our limited understanding of what 'communicative abilities' means to non-native speakers. Accordingly, what constitutes 'teaching for communicative purposes' in a foreign language for young learners has yet to be clearly understood. A number of concepts related to 'teaching for communicative purposes' such as learner-centered teaching, the use of authentic materials, and information-gaps have gained in popularity among teachers and policy-makers in East Asia, and yet this has happened without the meaning of such concepts being fully examined in the light of local contexts and without such concepts having been fully explained to teachers.

Conclusion

This paper illustrated how global and local factors influence the implementation of English at the Primary school level. I provided three examples of the types of challenges that have arisen across Korea, Taiwan and Japan. Both global and local factors influence policy decisions and their implementation in very complex ways. While the education policies in the three countries discussed herein faced certain common challenges, they also entailed different views towards EFLPS and frequently incorporated different approaches within their respective local contexts. Directly importing popular ELT methodologies does not seem to work well without making major adjustments to account for the local educational contexts. Indeed, successful implementations do not appear to be possible without giving serious consideration to local factors.

References

Block, D. and Cameron, D. (eds) (2002). Globalization and Language Teaching. London: Routledge.

Butler, Y.G. (2004). What level of English proficiency do elementary school teachers need to attain in order to teach EFL?: Case studies from Korea, Taiwan and Japan. *TESOL Quarterly* 38 (2), 245-278.

Butler, Y.G. (2005). Comparative perspectives towards communicative activities among elementary school teachers in South Korea, Japan and Taiwan. *Language Teaching Research* 9 (4), 423-446.

Butler, Y.G. (2007a). Foreign language education at elementary schools in Japan: Searching for solutions amidst growing diversification. *Current Issues in Language Planning* 8 (2), 129-147.

Butler, Y.G. (2007b). Factors associated with the notion that native speakers are the ideal language teachers: An examination of elementary school teachers in Japan. *JALT Journal* 29 (1), 7-40.

Butler, Y.G. (2007c). How are non-native English speaking teachers perceived by young learners? *TESOL Quarterly* 41 (4), 731-755.

Butler, Y.G. and Iino, M. (2005). Current Japanese reforms in English language education: The 2003 'Action Plan'. *Language Policy* 4 (1), 25-45

Cameron, D. (2002). Globalization and the teaching of 'communication skills'. In Block, D. and Cameron, D. (eds.), *Globalization and Language Teaching* (pp. 67-82). London: Routledge.

Choi, Y.H. (2007). The history and policy of English language education in Korea. In Choi, Y.H. and Spolsky, B. (eds.), *English Education in Asia: History and Policies* (pp. 33-66). Seoul: Asia TEFL.

Kamhi-Stein, L.D. (ed.) (2004). *Learning and Teaching from Experience*. Ann Arbor, MI: The University of Michigan Press.

Kim, M-Y. (2006). 'English villages' in South Korea: what do they really promote? *NNEST Newsletter* 8 (2).

Lantolf, J.P. (ed.) (2000). *Sociocultural Theory and Second Language Learning*. Oxford: Oxford University Press.

Llurda, E. (ed.) (2005). *Non-native Language Teachers*. New York: Springer.

Tobin, J.J., Wu, D.Y.H. and Davidson, D.H. (1989). *Preschool in Three Cultures: Japan, China and the United States*. New Heaven, CT: Yale University Press.

Wu, M.H. (2007). Incorporating compulsory military service in English education in Taiwan: Issues of teacher recruitment in EFL context. *The Journal of Asia TEFL* 4 (1), 173-194.

An early start: What are the key conditions for generalized success?

Richard Johnstone, University of Stirling, Scotland

The Bangalore conference provided an opportunity to meet colleagues from different continents, reflecting a rich diversity of backgrounds and first languages but all with a common interest in the early learning of additional languages. For most of those attending the conference, the main additional language with which they are professionally concerned is English. However, my talk was not intended to focus on English alone but rather on the early learning of additional languages in general. The present article is not intended as a direct account of my talk, since I elaborate somewhat on a number of points that were made only briefly during the talk. In addition, having sat in on many other excellent presentations, I thought it right that my article should be influenced by insights and issues that had arisen during the conference, some of which were indicated in my concluding remarks as the conference came to its end.

The title of my talk asks the question: 'What are the key conditions for generalized success?', so I should begin by saying a brief word about 'generalized', 'conditions' and 'key'.

'Generalized', 'conditions' and 'key'

The notion of 'generalized success' is important, because it implies achieving success not only with expert teachers working in favourable circumstances but also with 'ordinary' teachers working in 'ordinary' circumstances, which may be far from ideal. In my view, for this to happen, planning and support at various levels, including national and desirably international levels, is likely to be necessary.

The notion of 'conditions' is not intended in any absolute sense, as in 'Unless all of the following conditions are met in full, there is no chance of success'. In fact, I do not speculate on what it means to 'meet' a condition 'in full'. In the present article, by 'conditions' I mean areas of activity on which it is desirable to focus. If progress can be made in as many of these areas as possible, then the chances of generalized success are improved. Moreover, a strong element of interpretation is required, in that not every country, region, school or teacher is at the same point of development. It is therefore important to ask oneself in what areas things are going reasonably well and in what areas further development is needed. The answers will vary considerably from one context to the next.

Nonetheless, despite the enormous diversity of contexts which early language learning (ELL) encounters and the consequent need for diversity of approach, my own experience as a researcher and as an observer of ELL in many different countries does suggest that certain conditions are particularly important, possibly across all national and cultural contexts – hence my use of the term 'key' to identify what to one person at least seems particularly common and important.

Large-scale policy developments: essential but with potential drawbacks

I would go so far as to say that for success in ELL to be generalized there has to be a significant amount of large-scale policy development at national level (or at least at regional level within a country). I do not see ELL becoming successfully generalized if the approach is entirely 'bottom-up' – that is, left to the initiative of individual schools and teachers.

Large-scale policy planning undoubtedly has brought major benefits to the implementation of ELL. Among these are: firstly, the high status that ELL thereby receives – an important consideration not only in the minds of pupils, parents, teachers and senior management staff in schools, but also for the wider public; secondly, the additional resources that are often made available in order to ensure that the public policy attains some level of measured success; thirdly, the professional development that teachers may receive, in order to prepare them for implementing the ELL policy; fourthly, the impetus towards collaboration across schools and in many cases across national borders, for example, enabling teachers in different countries to share experiences; fifthly, the links with broader educational thinking and policies that are affecting schools at the same time, since ELL is of course by no means the only policy-related initiative happening in education; and finally, the possible (though not certain) association with funded research and evaluation, since Ministries are often keen to receive an independent perspective on how the new policy is progressing. Taken together, these are substantial advantages.

On the other hand, large-scale policy developments can show potential drawbacks. Among these are: firstly, that the ELL policy may be based on rather dubious assumptions (e.g., I have heard one highly eminent politician claim that young beginners are inherently superior to older beginners when it comes to learning an additional language – at best, this is only partly true); secondly, the policy development may offer a 'quick fix' but national priorities in education can often change, and the supply of teachers and other resources may begin to diminish, so the development may lose momentum and even head towards unsustainability (I have seen clear signs of this in more than one country); thirdly, the policy may be too 'different' from the current practice and thinking of busy teachers, and instead of the teachers accommodating themselves to the new policy, the new policy may become distorted in order to fit the teachers' existing approach, and so not much may be gained. Alternatively, the policy may be too speculative and not sufficiently grounded in the good practices that good teachers are in fact already implementing; and finally, the new policy may promote an over-standardized model of teaching, implicitly discouraging alternative approaches involving teachers' own local knowledge, initiative and creativity.

A preliminary conclusion then is that the above potential drawbacks in large-scale ELL policy development need to be taken into account, in order to ensure that it gains strength as it moves forward. The Blondin et al. (1998) review of ELL across Member States of the European Union, and its more recent follow-up by Edelenbos et al. (2006), show that much remains to be achieved.

Third wave of international ELL development

It is worth bearing in mind that the early learning of additional languages in pre-school or school education is now in its third wave of international development in fairly recent times. The first wave began in the 1960s but in a number of countries, including the UK, had completely lost momentum by the mid-1970s. The second wave began in the mid-1980s or early 1990s in many different countries across the world. In Europe it was strongly supported by the European Commission and the Council of Europe, both of which put in place large numbers of conferences, seminars and networks, which enabled ELL teachers from different countries to make contact and share experiences. The third wave is with us here and now, with countries such as China, South Korea, Taiwan and of course India (host to the Bangalore conference) adding enormously to the numbers of young learners involved and enabling ELL to project itself increasingly as a truly global phenomenon and as possibly the world's biggest policy development in education. Thus, meeting 'the conditions for generalized success' becomes an awesome challenge.

Characteristics of young and older language beginners

Before reflecting further on what the conditions for generalized success might be, it is appropriate to consider what early learners of an additional language are like. In particular, we need to consider the 'age factor' in respect of the 'critical period hypothesis' (CPH), or the extent to which young beginners are more predisposed (or less predisposed) to the acquisition of an additional language than are older beginners. In this connection, three hypotheses are outlined by Singleton (1989), based on a detailed consideration of published research: 'younger = better', 'older = better', 'younger = better in the long run and under certain circumstances', and he cautiously comes down in favour of the third of these. Singleton is right to be cautious, because the published research does not leave us with a clear picture. Marinova-Todd, et al. (2000) claim that of 35 fairly recent studies, 14 seem to offer support for the CPH while 21 suggest the opposite. Writing also in 2000, Scovel claims 'It should be borne in mind that, given the conflicting evidence and contrasting viewpoints that still exist, parents, educational institutions, and/or ministries of education should be exceedingly cautious about translating what they read about the CPH research into personal practice or public policy' (Scovel, 2000: 220).

My own review of the implications of the age factor for language policy (Johnstone, 2002) reaches a similar conclusion to that of Singleton. In other words, ELL can be a very good thing but it is vitally important to ensure that it is set in a supportive context. I agree with the wise words of Stern, expressed as long ago as 1976, who argued that it is misleading to force a choice between early and late language learning. On the contrary, Stern argues, each age brings its own particular advantages and disadvantages. He claims that in the sixties (the 'First Wave' of ELL to which I have already referred), the mistake was to assume that miracles would happen simply by starting young. These miracles did not happen, but he goes on to argue that starting late is not the answer either.

What potential advantages arise from teaching an additional language to young beginners aged (say) five?

My review lists a number of possible advantages that young beginners may have over older beginners. Space does not allow these to be discussed in detail but briefly they include: relative ease in acquiring the sound system of the additional language; less likely to be 'language anxious'; more time overall is available; a range of acquisitional processes can come into play over time, ranging from intuitive to analytical; their cognitive, linguistic, emotional, social, intercultural awareness and skills can be extended to help them form an identity that is bound to be different from the identity of those who begin later at (say) the age of 11 or 12 because in their case many components of their identity are already in an advanced state of formation.

However, the advantages do not all lie with young beginners, for older beginners undoubtedly do have certain things in their favour. Among these are: a more sophisticated conceptual map of the world (so that in their case it may be that a L2 word is new for them but the concept behind the new word is already known, whereas the younger beginner may have to learn not only the L2 word but also the unknown concept behind the word); more experience in handling the discourse of conversations, presentations, reports and other language activities, and so greater adeptness, for example, in negotiating meaning, because they know better how to interact; greater likelihood of having developed a wider range of strategies for learning such as note-taking, using reference materials and revising.

Overall, an advantage of an early start is that in principle at least it allows young beginners to exploit such advantages as they possess, but in addition, as they become older, to make use of the advantages that older learners possess. So, over time, both sets of advantages are available to those making the early start, whereas only the second set of advantages is available to those beginning later. To my mind, this is a compelling argument in favour of ELL, provided that the key conditions for its success can be put in place.

Four different models of ELL

In order to identify appropriate conditions for success, it is important to take account of the particular model of ELL that is being implemented in a particular school or group of schools. The recent review of ELL across Europe by Edelenbos, et al. (2006) identifies four different models:

- roughly one hour per week, based on a given course or set of materials;

- roughly one hour per week, based on a more flexible approach that seeks to embed the additional language in other areas of the curriculum, such as small bits of science, mathematics, or geography;

- a 'language awareness' approach which seeks to sensitize children to languages in general, with particular attention to the variety of languages that are actually used in the local community;

- immersion or bilingual education, in which children learn a significant part of their curriculum through the medium of the additional language, with a correspondingly large increase in the time made available over the other three models.

The first two models are by far the most common forms of ELL. In some countries they are called MLPS (Modern Languages at Primary School) and in others FLES (Foreign Languages at Elementary School). MLPS models can have a variety of starting points (ranging from age four to age eleven) but tend to have certain characteristics in common. These are:

- a fairly limited amount of time per week (in many cases less than one hour);

- teachers in many cases being generalist Primary school teachers (often teaching the entire curriculum to their pupils) rather than specialist language teachers;

- teachers possessing a proficiency in the additional language that falls far short of being that of a native-speaker or even a highly fluent speaker of the language.

MLPS teachers are therefore generally very busy people with lots of important things to do, in addition to helping their pupils learn an additional language. In this respect, I am not referring exclusively to my own country, Scotland. On the contrary, the state of affairs that I have described is widespread across many countries. Moreover, the amount of continuing professional development (CPD) training and support that many such teachers receive may be limited, whether because it is not available or because they may have pressing CPD needs in other areas of their overall teaching and MLPS may not be top of the priority list for CPD in a particular school or region.

An indication of the outcomes which the above model of MLPS was yielding by the late 1990s is given by the review of published research findings prepared by Blondin, et al. (1998), which embraced ELL in pre-Primary and Primary school education across all member states of the European Union. The review found that pupils' attitudes were generally positive. Pupils found the experience of learning an additional language to be enjoyable. However, the review also found that the pupils' measured achievements seemed relatively modest, with only limited evidence, for example, that beginning at Primary school conferred a clear advantage over beginning at Secondary school when it came to assessed performance in listening, speaking, reading or writing. In speaking, very little evidence was found of pupils having developed a competence that would enable them to create their own new utterances in keeping with rules of grammar that they had internalized. Instead, most utterances seemed to be of the 'learnt by heart' variety.

At this point one might ask: Is it reasonable to expect more, given the characteristics of the MLPS model? In other words, maybe the problem lies with the model itself, rather than with any major deficiencies in its implementation? Certainly, when compared with the much more powerful model of immersion (even in its comparatively weaker form of 'early partial' rather than the stronger form of 'early total' immersion), the MLPS model is clearly low on two vitally important factors, namely 'time' and 'intensity'. As regards 'time', the Blondin review points out that in one particular city an MLPS model consisted of 400 hours of L2 teaching from Year 1 to the end of Year 4 Primary (in fact, by most MLPS standards this is a lot), whereas in the same city a bilingual education project over these same Years 1-4 committed 1,700 hours to the L2 – a massive difference. As regards 'intensity', any immersion model inevitably scores higher than any MLPS model, in that in immersion pupils are challenged not only to learn the additional language but also to learn vitally important subject matter through the medium of that language – a big challenge, but one with which many children in fact cope well.

It is widely agreed that immersion leads to very different outcomes from MLPS in the case of young learners. This is not the place for elaborating on these in detail, but those wishing to read more may consult García and Baker (2007) and Johnstone (2001). Suffice for the moment to indicate that immersion can lead to fluent and confident use of the L2, with particularly impressive levels of listening comprehension, with no evident loss of the subject-knowledge that has been acquired through the immersion language. At the same time though, experience over many years in Canada and elsewhere shows that careful attention needs to be paid to the classroom processes of immersion education, with a clearly established need for periodic focus on form as well as on meaning, or as Kowal and Swain (1997) put it, on syntactic as well as on semantic processing, if learners are to become accurate as well as fluent and confident.

However, the fact that immersion leads to more impressive linguistic and content outcomes than MLPS does not mean that MLPS should simply go out of business. In very large numbers of cases it is the only practical option and indeed there are many cases across the world in which, despite the limitations of the model, an impressive degree of success is achieved.

What makes a difference

Earlier I indicated that the term 'conditions' was not intended absolutely but in the sense of areas in which it is desirable to focus, in order to make a difference. Below, I set out a number of areas on which it is desirable to focus and which I believe are likely to be common across different contexts. These have been written mainly with MLPS in mind as the most common form of ELL but are intended to apply to immersion models also.

Early start	An early start is in principle advantageous, because it allows a longer time overall for learning; it allows children to learn naturally as young children but then to learn more analytically as older children as they grow up; as such, it gives learners the opportunity to integrate and further develop these different sorts of learning experience.
(Inter) National policy and support	The evidence strongly suggests that the desirable early languages learning initiatives across whole regions and countries could not prevail if left only or mainly to schools and individual teachers. Some form of national or international support is necessary. Initiatives in Europe have benefited greatly from the support of the European Commission and the Council of Europe. The contribution of agencies such as the British Council (and similar bodies for other languages) has also been decisive. In Spain, for example, there has been excellent collaboration between the British Council and the Spanish Ministry for Education in establishing an impressive national early bilingual education project, as presented at the Bangalore conference. The major contribution of the IATEFL SIG for Young Learners, which organized the Bangalore conference, should also be acknowledged, in bringing together valuable insights and experiences from different parts of the world. At national level, Ministries of Education or regional authorities have a major role to play in catering for an adequate supply of well-trained teachers to meet the major increase in demand that arises from lowering the starting age, as well as in helping MLPS teachers raise their levels of confidence and competence in using the additional language in class, so as to provide the sorts of input and interaction that will stimulate the development of their young pupils' emerging capacities in the additional language they are learning. The national approach to teacher support in Taiwan as described at the conference seemed particularly impressive. However, major questions remain in many countries as to whether the level of support is adequate not only to get an initiative off the ground but to sustain it in the long term. Hence, the importance of long-term planning, going well beyond a 'quick fix'.

Outcomes and models	Language-related outcomes are strongly dependent on the particular model of languages education curriculum adopted. It is therefore extremely important to be clear about which model of ELL is being implemented, what processes of teaching and learning seem to go well with it, and what sorts of outcome may reasonably be expected. Simply to assume that all will be well just because the starting age has been lowered is a recipe for confusion. At the conference a particularly impressive example was given of how China has developed different levels of proficiency in relation to the particular model of ELL implemented, which levels describe proficiency with considerable specificity, down to the number of words that might be expected per level. Clarity of this sort is in my estimation a very good thing both for teachers and for pupils.
Continuity	It helps greatly if there is an agreed strategy for continuity from one year to the next and into Secondary schooling, in which experiences gained in one year are known, accepted and further developed in subsequent years. An outstanding example of continuity is provided by Chesterton, et al. (2004) who report on a major initiative in New South Wales, Australia, in which Primary and Secondary schools acting in partnership agreed a coherent five-year curriculum that took pupils along a range of planned pathways from the final stages of Primary through the initial stages of Secondary.
Motivation	Initial motivation in young learners seems mainly to be intrinsic, based on enjoyment, interest, curiosity and self-awareness, rather than integrative, instrumental or extrinsic. While it makes good sense with very young learners to exploit the 'fun' side of intrinsic motivation through games, songs, playacting and 'doing things', it is important to develop the 'self-awareness' side of intrinsic motivation too, so that children become motivated through realizing that they are becoming successful learners of their additional language and taking pleasure in this. My visit to Croatia in the mid-1990s showed this phenomenon most clearly.
Local languages	There is value in taking account of such languages as children bring to school with them (including different first languages and dialects) and those languages that are used locally by different ethno-linguistic communities. This can go well with a 'language awareness' approach, which to my mind should not be a substitute for, or in competition with, the early learning of one particular language. The two should go together, because language awareness is enhanced at least as much through reflecting on one's ongoing attempts over time to learn a particular language as it is through being sensitized to a variety of languages. Both are important ingredients in the language education of children.

Language and cognitive development	Children progress through a sequence of stages in their internalized language development, at differing rates. This, however, is not akin to climbing a ladder (i.e., always going upwards), because progress in certain areas, e.g., fluency, can for a while mean fossilization or even regression in others, e.g., accuracy or range, and vice-versa. There is value in helping children progress beyond prefabricated utterances, and some initial evidence has accumulated on how this might be achieved, e.g., importance of children receiving feedback which may be positive (encouragement) or may be corrective, to help them further refine their underlying language system. This feedback may be supplied by teachers, other adults, other children or by the particular child him- or herself. In the past, the notion of 'aptitude' has often been viewed as fixed (e.g., an 'able' or 'less able' child). However, this is misleading, since 'aptitude' may be developed through Primary school education, especially in the area of metalinguistic awareness and sensitivity to sound. It is therefore important to develop not only the visible skills of communication but also the underlying qualities that go with aptitude, so that this will develop with the impact of the education each child receives. In their spontaneous play, young children show a tendency to notice, play with and practise features of linguistic form as well as meaning, suggesting the onset of implicit metalinguistic knowledge – something on which classroom pedagogy at Primary school should desirably build. There is also considerable value in introducing children to stories, not only because of their appeal to children's imagination but also because they help children internalize a narrative discourse structure.
Early reading, writing and grammar	There is value in introducing reading and writing at an early stage, rather than concentrating solely on listening and speaking. A visit I made to Croatia in the mid-90s offered the most advanced and successful methodology for ELL I have thus far seen anywhere. It included children aged seven or eight learning grammatical concepts in their foreign language (which might be French, German, English or Italian), derived from their first language (in most cases, Croatian), and also learning to read and write from an early age. As such, more or less from the start they were learning to develop a strong underlying knowledge system and at the same time to express this through all four communication skills of listening, speaking, reading and writing. This contradicted the widespread view that, in ELL, children should concentrate on listening and speaking and should not be asked to develop an analytical knowledge of language. This approach helped the children to think analytically and strategically, in order to monitor their own learning, and also encouraged the sort of self-awareness that I have mentioned in the section on motivation.

Technology-mediated learning	There is high potential value in technology-mediated learning and use, though at present there is relatively little evidence of this in ELL. In my view, the greatest value lies in putting Primary schools in one country in touch with Primary schools in another. In Scotland I have seen children aged 5-6 whose L1 is English, who live in a non-Gaelic-speaking part of Scotland and who on their parents' wishes are receiving their Primary school education largely through the medium of Scottish Gaelic, engaged in video-conferencing interaction with children of the same age who live on one of the islands where Gaelic is spoken. The new technologies offer exciting possibilities for joint projects on a wide range of topics relevant to any Primary school curriculum, involving teachers and possibly parents as well as pupils themselves, and creating new sorts of opportunity for intercultural learning and multilingual or L2 communication. It is worth noting that with the rapid rise of English as major language of global communication, there is no absolute need for the new-technology links necessarily to be with schools in an English-speaking country. Children and staff in (say) Spanish or Italian Primary schools might well engage on joint projects with children and staff in (say) India or China or Taiwan or South Korea, with English as the main language of interaction, since all the children would be learning English as an additional language, but with opportunities for introducing some elements of each national language as part of the emerging linguistic and intercultural awareness of children across the networks as a whole.

The list set out above can only make these key points briefly – in fact, each section of the list is a significant research field in its own right – but this has to suffice for present purposes as an initial pointer. The list is derived in part from the recent large-scale survey for the European Commission by Peter Edelenbos, Angelika Kubanek and myself (Edelenbos, et al., 2006), which contains chapters on 'research findings', practitioners' views of 'good practice' and experts' views of 'basic principles'. My own responsibility within the group was largely in the area of 'research findings', and the above list draws mainly on this area. I have chosen not to crowd the list with bibliographical references, but the survey referred to above is available online and contains an extensive bibliography, which covers many of the points in this list. The list additionally draws on wider research, reading and visiting over a number of years and also on excellent insights gained from others during the admirable Bangalore conference.

References

Blondin, C., Candelier, M., Edelenbos, P., Johnstone, R.M., Kubanek-German, A. and Taeschner, T. (1998). *Foreign Languages in Primary and Pre-school Education. A Review of Recent Research within the European Union*. London: CILT.

Chesterton, P., Steigler-Peters, S., Moran, W. and Piccioli, M.T. (2004). Developing sustainable learning pathways: an Australian initiative. *Language, Culture and Curriculum* 17 (1), 48–57.

Edelenbos, P., Johnstone, R.M. and Kubanek, A. (2006). The main pedagogical principles underlying the teaching of languages to very young learners. Languages for the children of Europe: Published Research, Good Practice and Main Principles. *Final Report of the EAC 89/04, Lot 1 Study*. European Commission, Brussels: Education and Culture, Culture and Communication, Multilingualism Policy. Available at http://ec.europa.eu.education/languages/pdf/doc425_en.pdf

García, O. and Baker, C. (2007). *Bilingual Education: An Introductory Reader*. Clevedon, UK: Multilingual Matters.

Johnstone, R.M. (2001). Immersion in a second or additional language at school: evidence from international research. Report for the Scottish Executive Education Department. University of Stirling: Scottish CILT. Available for download from among Scottish CILT's publications at http://www.scilt.stir.ac.uk/publications/

Johnstone, R.M. (2002). Addressing 'the age factor': some implications for languages policy. Guide for the development of Language Education policies in Europe: From Linguistic Diversity to Plurilingual Education. Strasbourg: Council of Europe. Available at http://www.coe.int/t/dg4/linguistic/Source/JohnstoneEN.pdf

Kowal, M. and Swain, M. (1997). From semantic to syntactic processing: How can we promote it in the immersion classroom? In Johnson, K. and Swain, M. (eds) (1997) *Immersion Education: International Perspectives* (pp. 284–310). Cambridge: Cambridge University Press.

Marinova-Todd, S.F., Marshall, D.B. and Snow, C. (2000). Three misconceptions about age and L2 learning. *TESOL Quarterly* 34 (1), 9–31.

Scovel, T. (2000). A critical review of the critical period research. *Annual Review of Applied Linguistics* 20, 213–223.

Singleton, D. (1989). *Language Acquisition: The Age Factor*. Clevedon, UK: Multilingual Matters.

Teaching English to young learners: The promise and the threat

N.S. Prabhu, ELT Consultant, India

A summary of the presentation

There are two broad approaches to second language pedagogy – what Howatt calls the 'natural' and the 'rational'. The former is attempting to make second language learning as similar to first language learning as possible, hoping to achieve similar results, while the latter is teaching a second language in an educationally rational way as done with other school subjects. The former leads to such methods as task-based teaching and comprehensible input, and the latter to procedures like structural progression, controlled repetition, functional syllabuses and purpose-orientation. It is likely that the younger the learners are, the more appropriate or productive the natural approach is, and vice versa.

It is also the case that, broadly speaking, the closer second language learning gets to first language learning, the easier the teaching (and teacher-training) becomes. This is because first language learning takes place without any deliberate teaching: parents and adults have only to act as parents and adults, getting children to understand, think things through and make themselves understood as well as they can; and the activities to be used in second language teaching for young learners (telling stories, giving instructions for physical actions, doing meaning-focused tasks, playing games) are essentially similar in nature (and quite different from, for instance, planned practice).

Against these factors, however, we should consider some possible effects of an early start with English on the linguistic and cultural identities of learners. English is today the world's second language, and we would like this to lead to an enlargement of the linguistic repertoire and cultural horizons of many different communities, not a substitution of English for all or many other languages accompanied by a loss of different cultures. It is likely that the closer the learning of English is to that of the learners' first languages, the greater the risk of English becoming the dominant language, abridging and eventually replacing the use of those first languages.

Introduction of English from Grade 1 in Maharashtra, India

Mrinalini Mukund Ghatage, SNDT Womens' University, Arts and Commerce College for Women, Pune, India

Historical background of Primary education development

Maharashtra was declared as a separate state in 1960. Before that no one system was followed to teach English. In each district, English was introduced at different grades. In 1968, the government decided on the new revised syllabus for Primary education and, in 1972, English was made compulsory from Grades 5 to 10. The state government from its formation on 1st May, 1960 committed itself to the planned development of Primary education. The planning process in the country started in 1951 with the first Five Year Plan. Maharashtra joined this process of socioeconomic development at the planning stage of the third Five Year Plan. During the first Five Year Plan, among the schemes designed to assist the growth of Primary education in the state, an important place was occupied by the scheme relating to the introduction of compulsory Primary education on an organized basis.

Developments in general education all over the world influenced the Indian government's adoption in 1968 of a new education policy recommending learner-centered education. Because of increasing globalization and developments in technology, the world had become closer. English had become the most prominent international language and its importance was growing. In India and in Maharashtra, people had begun to mix English with Marathi in their speech. It was no longer a foreign language. Most of the books available today are in English only. A vast fund of information is now available in English language only. English has become the major language of all books stocked by Maharashtra libraries.

For all these reasons, the importance of English is now understoood by everyone and its attraction is evident. If your English is not good and if you are not confident speaking English, you will find it difficult to keep up and to compete in an increasingly accelerated and globalized marketplace. So keen is the interest in English language and English-medium schools that parents in Maharashtra are admitting their children to English-medium schools, even if they cannot afford the fees. Children deprived of English during their early formative years have found it difficult to pick up the language later on in their lives. Whatever you might want to do, whatever career you might want to venture into, English is important.

Taking all of this into account, the Maharashtra government, in December 1999, decided on the new policy regarding teaching of English. The Government of Maharashtra launched the initiative for the teaching and learning of English in the year 2000-01 from Grade 1 of the vernacular medium. Previously it was taught from Grade 5. Under the terms of the new policy, the following were agreed:

- English teaching will begin from June 2000 at Grade 1.

- In each week, five hours will be allotted.

- The same textbook will be taught from Grades 1 to 4.

Key features of this new policy

- The teaching of English from Grade 1 was introduced because of its importance for contemporary culture and society; the syllabus would seek to reflect this contemporary context.

- English should not be treated simply as a discrete subject, but should be used to develop language skills.

- The four language skills of speaking, listening, reading and writing are to be taught.

- The teaching–learning process would be learner-centred. The learner's active participation and self-study are important.

In addition, the committee recommmended:

- that the books prescribed for Grade 1 be illustrated to engage the learner and encourage self-study;

- that a Teacher's Guide be provided in English and Marathi.

It was emphasized that the following editorial and design principles should be borne in mind for the textbook:

- The language should engage young learners.

- Topics reflect the value of Indian culture should be selected.

- The language and explanation should not offend anybody's caste, race and religion.

- Rubrics should be clear for young learners to follow.

- The font should be bold and big to suit the young readership.

Aims and objectives of teaching English from Grade 1:

- to enable learners to speak in English;

- to make learners aware of the difference between their mother tongue (L1) and English (L2);

- to exploit the learners' competence in L1 to further both L2 and L1 competence;

- to build a sound base in Primary skills.

It was also agreed that above all, English learning should be enjoyable and that learners should be able to meet the following objectives:

- to read and write in English – in particular to be able to recite poems;

- to converse in English, understanding what others are saying and responding confidently;

- to pronounce correctly (listening and repeating sounds accurately)

The textbook

It was proposed that the textbook should be prepared in such a way that any Primary teacher would be able to teach English as a subject in the first grade. No exclusive importance should be attached to any particular English Language Teaching (ELT) methodology. The context of learning should be carefully considered.

It was felt that the design of the textbook should reflect a child-centred approach. Emphasis would be placed on learning English joyfully, through engaging activities. The textbook should present a series of graded activities making wide use of illustration to engage the learner. It should also try to give learners systematic exposure to English that will gradually improve their grasp of the language. The course aims to maintain low anxiety levels for young learners. Teacher guidance is given to support classroom management appropriately for this age group.

For the first time, instructions for the teachers were to be given in the L1 (Marathi). Similarly, pronunciation of the words in the poems was to be represented using familiar orthography to make it easier for parents and guardians. For example, the poem 'Baa baa black sheep' in English script would be transformed into Marathi script (i.e., Devnagari) as 'Baa baa blacak siap'.

Training

Prior to the introduction of English teaching from June 2000, a training programme was conducted for all teachers of Grades 1 to 4. In the course of this training, the teachers practiced speaking English and their knowledge and understanding was further developed.

As all the teachers were of Marathi background, the practice of pronunciation, vocabulary and knowledge of the English language system were emphasized. Their active participation throughout the training sessions was stressed. Teachers were introduced to the sylllabus and the textbook. Information about the full range of teaching aids was given as well as instruction on lesson preparation. All teachers were given the textbook and the Teacher's Guide (in English and Marathi). It was explained that as the learner is young (between five and nine years) more pictures are used in the textbook, and the font is also larger than in the Teacher's Guide. Marathi is also used in the textbook. (The Devnagari Script is used – though the child may not be able to read this script, it can help the teacher and his/her family members to assist the child in reciting and repeating the poems.)

New approaches of teaching and learning

The teaching methods and techniques to be used in class were to be selected for their appropriateness to the learners' age and the milieu in which they are learning. No specific method or theory for ELT would be used. The teacher was given the choice as to which methods and techniques would be used in the class and what language would be useful for daily life following consideration of learners' interests. Use of audio-visual aids such as radio and TV was encouraged. With the help of these aids it was hoped that the students would get practice in correct pronunciation and identify examples of the sentence patterns. They may be used as drills. In most of the schools, in rural areas, audio and video aids were and remain unavailable to teachers and so they were encouraged to be creative and to bring cuttings and pictures for teaching the class. Teachers should conduct different activities to enable learning to take place, for example describing different situations and asking learners to respond appropriately, or doing listening and speaking practice.

In essence, the teacher should use any method or activity that would be useful in promoting fluency in speaking the language and in addressing grammatical mistakes. The overall aim of developing the learners' confidence was stressed.

It was decided by the policy-makers that undue emphasis on grammatically correct language and correcting mistakes should be avoided, otherwise natural language learning would not take place. If the teacher keeps correcting mistakes made by the students then they will lose confidence and lose interest in the subject. The policy expressed the expectation, for example, that learners should not be required necessarily to speak in full sentences but might express themselves in words or gestures.

Prior to this development, English teaching was begun at Grade 5. In this framework no emphasis was given to listening and speaking; rather teaching and learning began with writing the letters of the alphabet, and this without having learnt the sounds of the letters (phonics). More recent research shows, however, that L2 must be taught in the same way that the child learns its mother tongue (L1): the child first listens, then speaks, then reads, and last writes. The following diagram shows which skills were therefore emphasized in the policy.

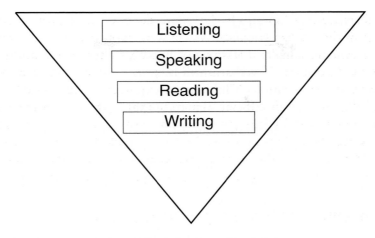

Figure 1: *Triangular graph showing importance of four skills*

At this stage (Grade 1), only the oral skills of listening and speaking are emphasized. Reading and writing skills are not stressed at this level; these skills are developed in the third and fourth grades. As well as showing the relative importance of the skills in the learning process, the diagram also illustrates the coordination and interrelationship of the four skills.

Use of mother tongue (Marathi)

While use of their mother-tongue (Marathi) is natural for learners, the teacher is expected to use Marathi as little as possible, and only when it is really needed. When he/she does use the mother tongue, however, that does not mean that a translation is expected, but no unnecessary explanation should be given in Marathi. The teacher must remember that in most learners' families nobody speaks English and the classroom is the only place where they hear English spoken, so the teacher should make a point of using more English in the class and of encouraging learners to do likewise.

Policy approaches to assessment

In the curriculum, undue stress on evaluation and tests is avoided and the emphasis is instead placed on ascertaining whether the learner has understood whatever is taught in the class. A test may be used for this purpose, which might be done as a group task or individually or both. Throughout Years 6–8 the policy stipulates that tests of spoken English should be conducted. The policy document states that there is no need to keep a formal record of these tests, but teachers are expected to keep record of each learner's progress to aid their self-assessment and help them judge whether any changes to teaching methods are required. These tests must be based on skills taught in class. The teacher can invent any method of evaluation that is suited to both teacher and learner.

Impact of the new policy

This initiative in the teaching and learning of English from Grade 1 in the vernacular medium by the Government of Maharashtra is really a great step in itself because of its importance for future generations. Children are exposed to English from an early age, increasing the likelihood of their being able to use the language confidently in future.

The textbook committee of the Maharashtra Government has conducted a survey reporting that children with no background in English now speak English. For example, the children of maidservants and workers also now use English. I have observed (in my society or at marketplaces) that not only young learners but other family members too are frequently using English words in their daily lives.

Weaknesses in the process of policy implementation

In Maharashtra, English as a subject was introduced from 2000 in Grade 1. In general, teachers have not responded to this change in policy positively and feel that their workload has increased due to the introduction of English at Primary level. It is possible that, with this attitude, teachers may not have given 100 per cent to their ELT.

Many teachers attended the training programme, but subsequent interviews have indicated that most of them feel unable to use what they learnt in the classroom because they think that their own lack of fluency will prevent them from teaching the subject effectively. Although all the teachers are SSC (Grade X) certified with a Diploma in Education (Dip. Ed), they are also all Marathi. They received their own schooling in the vernacular medium only. They do not have confidence in their knowledge of English grammar, and this translates to a lack of confidence when speaking English. In addition, they feel their pronunciation may be inaccurate. They consider that they need further practice to enable them to use it fluently and confidently. Despite all the theoretical knowledge provided, practically it is very difficult for these teachers to teach English. This will definitely be a hindrance in both the teaching and learning process.

Furthermore, learners may only be exposed to English in the school and not at home. If the teacher does not speak English very often in the class, then learners are likely to have insufficient exposure to the language and may choose not to adopt it for communication purposes.

Teachers in rural areas are often unable to use the audio-visual aids and so therefore need to be encouraged to make use of other media, such as cuttings and pictures, to enable learning.

Bibliography

English textbook (2000). Maharashtra State Bureau of Textbook Production and Curriculum Research, Pune.

Rao, D.B. and Khadar, S.A. (2004). *School Education in India*, New Delhi: Discovery Publishing House.

Sharma, R.C. (2002). *National Policy on Education and Programme of Implementation.* Jaipur, India: Mangal Deep Publications.

Teacher training programme information booklet (2000). Educational research and training institute of Maharashtra State, Pune.

Venkataiah, S. (eds) (2002). *Primary Education.* New Delhi, India: Anmol Publications Pvt. Ltd.

English at Primary school level in Brazil: Challenges and perspectives

Telma Gimenez, Universidade Estadual de Londrina, Brazil

Introduction

As the English language becomes a lingua franca in the business world, parents are anxious to have their children learn it. According to Graddol (2006: 89), 'EYL is often not just an educational project, but a political and economic one.' In Brazil, learning a foreign language is compulsory from Grade 5 (average age 10–11). However, due to the increasing importance of English, many private schools have started offering it from age six or earlier. This has created an inequality that is being redressed by some local authorities through the introduction of English in the public school system. In addition to creating greater equality of opportunity, local administrators see English learning as part of a larger strategy to attract foreign investment. However, the introduction of English in Brazilian Primary schools has to be planned carefully and requires the coordinated efforts of educational authorities at both municipal and state levels. As many municipalities in Brazil have started to offer English as part of the Primary school curriculum, these issues have to be managed with care. This paper will focus on perspectives from and challenges faced by Londrina, a city in southern Brazil, as English is integrated into the curriculum starting in 2008.

Firstly, a brief description of the Brazilian educational system and the role of a foreign language within it will be offered and discussed. Then the steps leading to the planning of English Language Teaching (ELT) in Primary schools in Londrina will be presented, together with the challenges faced by the project.

The Brazilian educational system

Brazil is the largest South American country, with an area of 8,514,876,599 km^2 and a population of approximately 184 million people, living in 27 states divided into five regions. The country became independent from Portugal in 1822, from whom the official language was inherited. Basic education is a right established by the Constitution issued in 1988 and demand for state provision for education has been on the increase by a growing young population. Until recently, basic education comprised eight years of schooling (Primary and Secondary), with about 34 million students enrolled in 2006. That period was extended to nine years, a decision that has been only gradually implemented and only partially in many municipalities.

Due largely to the need to expand the number of schools, with a corresponding emphasis on quantity at the expense of quality, many parents have preferred to have their children attend private schools, which have boomed in the last decades due to the poor results by public schools, especially in relation to guaranteeing access to higher education.

Federal, state and local governments share responsibilities in relation to education, with decentralized control of Primary schools by the municipalities, which receive funding according to the number of students enrolled. Official guidelines are issued nationally but each state or even local educational authority can issue their own guidance. Recently, assessment procedures were introduced at Grade 4, Grade 8 and High School, in order to provide a clearer picture of what objectives have been achieved. The results have been quite worrying and quality in education is now considered a major challenge.

ELT in Brazil

The teaching of foreign languages has undergone many changes throughout Brazilian history. As a former colony of Portugal, it suffered from a strong influence of European languages and the prestige associated with them. A more humanist curriculum geared towards the élite incorporated several foreign languages, including Latin and Greek, with objectives largely related to cultural enrichment and access to literature in the target language. However, the modernization of the country also brought the need to develop a curriculum 'for the masses' and foreign language learning determined by community choice, with teaching methodologies largely imported from the US. In the late 1960s, English replaced French as the most popular foreign language in the curriculum both at Primary/Secondary and High School levels.

Although the majority of students take English language lessons in their regular (private and public) schools, both sectors are considered generally ineffective, with language institutes being considered more successful in producing positive outcomes. State-funded schools suffer from many problems, including lack of teaching resources, under-qualified teachers, large classes, unmotivated students and few class hours.

More recently, with the impact of globalization,

> [...] the English language has become an ambiguous symbol in the mind of the average Brazilian. On one hand, it is part and parcel of daily lived reality, appearing on billboards and neon signs, in shop windows and newspaper and magazine ads, and in more restricted discursive spheres, such as information technology and electronic commerce. Most middle- and upper-class Brazilians know that their children must acquire an adequate command of English or they run the risk of missing out on opportunities for better paid jobs offered by multinational corporations. On the other hand, many in Brazil are understandably concerned about the possible negative consequences of the unbridled advance of English into the country's cultural scenario (Rajagopalan and Rajagopalan, 2005: 3).

A recent law passed in 1996, establishes that a foreign language is compulsory at Secondary (age 11+) and High School levels (age 15+), totalling seven years of instruction. That situation may change due to a new law, issued in 2005, that requires Spanish to be compulsory in high schools, a decision that may affect the offer of English classes at that level.

While there are some signals from official authorities that the Spanish language is part of the strategic positioning of Brazil in Latin America, the status of English as a lingua franca for international communication cannot be disregarded. For this reason, there has been a steady increase in the number of language institutes over the last decades, offering ELT courses for all ages.

The private sector has been faster in responding to the demand from parents who are anxious to see their children acquire the language that they believe will improve their children's employability. In this period, many private primary schools started to introduce English as part of their curriculum, further widening the educational attainment gap between the rich and the poor. Although this can be seen as a marketing strategy, it has also pushed the state sector to include English at earlier ages.

Even under such unfavorable conditions as prevail in the state sector, some municipalities are striving to introduce English in Primary schools, as an additional subject in the curriculum. Normally children spend 20 hours a week in school. Out of these 20 hours, 45 minutes is usually dedicated to English, with a heavy focus on vocabulary acquisition. Some schools adopt textbooks but in general teachers produce their own materials.

Due to its introduction as a response to demand rather than part of the required curriculum, there are no official guidelines for teaching of English to young learners (TEYL). Graduates in ELT (with no training in TEYL) are not normally the classroom teachers since they have to have graduated in pedagogy, a course that has no English training, or alternatively need to have a 'licenciatura' with teaching qualifications at high school. TEYL is therefore not part of a national policy but rather the result of local initiatives by government authorities.

For these reasons, any attempt by municipalities to introduce English at Primary level is bound to encounter many obstacles and require careful planning. The city of Londrina, in the south of Brazil, with a population of approximately 500,000 inhabitants, provides a good example of some of those difficulties.

The introduction of English in Primary schools in Londrina

Policy-makers' decisions to include English as part of the education of young people are not always academically justified. Sometimes they are driven by the conclusion that there is nothing else to do but to give in to the pressure from business and the promise of increased employment opportunity. Londrina has a good reputation for being an educational centre, hosting four universities, one of which controls a budget larger than the majority of the cities in the state. However, proficiency in English is still limited and many qualified professionals do not have the necessary command of the language to be able to work in the IT sector, one of the main areas of development. Therefore, in order to put Londrina on the international map, emergency plans, as well as long-term ones, were designed during the last semester of 2007.

For that purpose, language institutes' representatives, educational authorities and business people were invited to a meeting, later to be joined by the largest public university, a private university and the English language teachers' association.

The short-term plan was to design courses to train 1,200 potential workers immediately, combining English and IT skills. The long-term plan involved considering alternative ways of improving the level of English proficiency for those children attending state schools by introducing it at Grade 4, beginning in 2008, with the intention of gradually extending it to earlier years in the future.

A small committee with representatives from the Secretariat of Education, universities, English language teachers' association, and businesspeople was formed. Several alternatives were considered, including the full-scale introduction, but due to budgetary restrictions the phased incorporation of a foreign language in the curriculum was considered the best cautious approach. It was decided that initially it would have project status, with a view to transforming it into an official policy in due course to ensure continuity.

Project: Global Londrina

Initially the project will cover schools in both urban and rural areas, with 5,186 and 543 pupils, respectively, in Grade 4. The total number of pupils at Grades 1–4 is 25,000. Classes normally have 30–35 pupils and 20 class hours per week. The majority of public schools in Brazil are still two-shift schools. Because the local government did not allocate a specific budget for this project, lessons (about 50 minutes per week, 40 hours per year) need to be taught by a specialist teacher, but one who is already part of the staff so there is no need to hire new teachers. This is far from ideal but the only feasible option given the circumstances of the project's implementation.

In order to guide these efforts, a special partnership was created at the local Secretariat of Education, which is leading the project and will be responsible for its implementation and evaluation, involving higher education institutions and the English language teachers' association.

The objectives for TEYL are as follows:

- to expand the social and educational opportunities of students in Londrina through the introduction of English in early years schooling;

- to promote the development of English language skills in the face of increasing demand;

- to develop the knowledge and skills that will facilitate later studies of the English language.

Specific objectives include:

1. Learners having some knowledge of vocabulary and linguistic structures so that they can express:

- their feelings and those of their friends and family;

- their likes and personal preferences, as well as those of their friends and family;

- their ideas about the books they read, the films they watch and the products they consume;

- suggestions for the preservation of wild animals, nature and other locally relevant phenomena.

2. Learners developing a positive relationship with the English language, coming to see it as a means of interpreting and communicating with the world around us.

3. Learners engaging in meaningful, diversified, social learning experiences.

As in many other contexts reported in this publication, English language teachers in Londrina are in general inexperienced in dealing with young learners. For this reason their preparation for this initiative has been one of the committee's main concerns. An emergency course is going to be offered during the planning week before the beginning of the academic year of 2008, focusing mainly on the teaching materials that are being designed especially for the project. Continuing teacher development opportunities will also be offered throughout the year, with the help of partners.

The overall approach of the teaching materials (worksheets) has fictional characters engaged in activities around Londrina and the local area (e.g., students at the local airport, at the local park, etc.). All skills are going to be emphasized. The syllabus is organized around functional speech such as greetings and personal introductions, and using vocabulary such as animals, means of transport, etc. The local partnership at the Secretariat of Education will be responsible for the follow-up work in close interaction with the committee.

Challenges and perspectives

The example of Londrina may be familiar to many educationists working in other contexts where policy-making is done in a dynamic way and not necessarily after careful planning. However, this gives rise to certain challenges:

Challenge 1: Working in an unstable political situation, with elections taking place in October 2008, it will be very important to secure a strong commitment to the continuity of the project.

Challenge 2: Implementation of teacher development plans that are relevant to those teachers who have no previous experience with teaching young learners. Teachers will need emergency as well long-term development activity-based opportunities. In addition, the pedagogy and initial teacher education courses in English traditionally preparing teachers to work in Secondary schools will have to include TEYL as part of their curricula.

Challenge 3: Holding realistic expectations about the outcomes, considering that there will be little exposure to the language (50 minutes per week and 30–35 students per class).

Challenge 4: Adjusting the curriculum as English is gradually introduced into the early years.

Challenge 5: Integrating the curricula both at municipal and state schools, which will require close coordination and liaison between the educational authorities.

Challenge 6: Making sure that educational aims are not overridden by the instrumental needs of businesses.

Some lessons have been learnt from this project so far. One of them is that in contexts where TEYL is not compulsory, the political will needs to be generated, so that the economic case stands a better chance of getting heard. For this reason, close monitoring is necessary to ensure that language teaching is not hijacked by interests other than educational development. In the case of 'Global Londrina', the involvement of multiple actors has been a key factor in creating and implementing the project so that it was possible given the realistic goals established in the light of existing conditions. However, it is important to note that no appropriate funding has been provided or is envisaged in the city budget.

So far, informal comments from parents made to the local office of the Secretariat of Education suggest that they are happy with the idea that their children will have access to English. It is important though not to create unrealistic expectations. The follow-up during 2008 will be essential to make corrections and plan for future implementation at lower grades. Teachers are also enthusiastic and willing to participate and researchers and teacher educators are beginning to show interest in this area.

A combination of enthusiasm and pragmatism in implementing TEYL seems to hold the key to a cautious approach, much needed in an area that is promising but demands true commitment from policy-makers.

References

Graddol, D. (2006). *English Next*. London: British Council.

Rajagopalan, R. and Rajagopalan, C. (2005). The English language in Brazil – a boon or a bane? In Braine, G. (ed.) *Teaching English to the World 2* (pp. 1–10). Mahwah, NJ, USA: Lawrence Erlbaum.

Teaching English in Primary schools in Bangladesh: Competencies and achievements

Shamsul Hoque, BRAC University Institute of Educational Development, Dhaka, Bangladesh

Introduction

This is a case study about teaching English to young learners (TEYL) in the mainstream/state schools in Bangladesh, focusing on the government policy and its implications for the teaching-learning strategy. The study seeks to:

• identify and explain the competencies the young learners are required to acquire;

• investigate the learners' levels of achievement in acquiring those competencies; and

• identify and highlight the lessons from Bangladesh's experience in order to improve TEYL in Bangladesh in future.

Background

Here are some basic facts about the country's education systems that provide a broader context within which the teaching and learning of English takes place:

• Bangladesh has a centralized unitary Primary education system and as such there is no separate/special policy for TEYL.

• English was first officially introduced as a compulsory subject at Primary level from Grade 1 in 1990.

• The starting age for English is 6+.

• The number of years for English at Primary level is five years (Grades 1–5).

• The average number of hours for English per week is 5.30 hours.

- There are over 80,000 Primary schools.

- There are about 300,000 teachers.

- There are about 17 million students in Primary schools.

- The teacher-student ratio is 1:56.

- The general aim for English teaching and learning is that learners will be able to communicate in the language at a simple level (National Curriculum and Textbook Board, 2003).

Competencies

Against this backdrop, a competency-based national curriculum was introduced in the country in 1992. According to the curriculum, the competencies are expressed in terms of language skills, which the learners are required to acquire. There are terminal competencies, which are attainable at the end of Grade 5. These terminal competencies are broken down into a more detailed list, which is distributed among all the Primary grades (1-5). So each grade has a number of grade-wise attainable competencies, based on the terminal competencies. (See Table 1.)

Terminal competencies	Grade-wise attainable competencies				
	Grade 1	Grade 2	Grade 3	Grade 4	Grade 5
Listening: 4	4	4	9	11	12
Speaking: 8	4	4	8	8	8
Reading: 7	5	5	9	12	10
Writing: 10	2	3	9	12	12
Total: 29	15	16	35	43	42

Table 1: *Terminal (at the end of Primary school) and grade-wise (at the end of each grade) attainable competencies*

The Primary textbooks – the *English for Today* series – have been developed on the basis of the curriculum based on these competencies.

Initiatives to implement curricular provision

The need for English has made Bangladeshi people, in general, strongly inclined towards learning English. As a result, a good number of initiatives have been taken in both public and private sectors so as to implement the curriculum successfully.

Initiatives by the government

*   Ministry of Primary and Mass Education (MOPME) has taken a number of initiatives to improve the access and quality of Primary education through programmes on teacher training, materials development, infrastructure development, and assessment. English, as one of the key school subjects, is included in all the subject-specific development programmes. MOPME's various activities are carried out by the different wings and organizations of the ministry, as listed below:

*   Directorate of Primary Education (DPE)

*   Primary Training Institute (PTI) – 54 PTIs

*   Upazila Resource Centre (URC) – 481 URCs)

*   National Academy for Primary Education (NAPE)

*   National Curriculum and Textbook Board (NCTB), Primary Curriculum Wing

At present, all the teaching-learning activities at Primary level are being supported by a big umbrella programme, Primary Education Development Programme II (PEDP II), a five-year $1.8 billion programme, funded jointly by Bangladesh and as many as 11 foreign donors, including The World Bank, the Department for International Development (DfID) and the United Nations Children's Fund (Unicef).

Initiatives by Non-Government Organizations (NGOs)

A number of non-government organizations in the country have a good reputation for providing education, including teaching English to Primary-age, out-of-school children. The following are among the leaders:

*   *Building Resources Across Communities (formerly Bangladesh Rural Advancement Committee) (BRAC)* as an NGO is renowned nationally and internationally for its poverty alleviation, empowerment of the poor (especially rural women and children), education and health programmes. It is currently running over 30,000 special Primary schools in Bangladesh, giving education to about one million children. It has developed its own learning and teacher training materials. It has a strong monitoring and supervision mechanism.

*   *BRAC University Institute of Educational Development (BU-IED)*'s main aim is to assist in improving the quality of the teaching and learning of the key school subjects,

including English, in the mainstream schools. As a step towards achieving this goal, BU-IED has developed a bridging course for the Grade 5 graduates to help them to cope with the Grade 6 textbook. BU-IED has also developed a trial edition of a learning package – supplementary materials for Grade 6 English with user-friendly teacher's guides, student workbooks, etc. Now BU-IED is going to develop learning packages for English for Primary grades. Also the piloting of a BU-IED sandwich training course has shown some really positive impacts.

- *Friends in Village Development Bangladesh (FIVDB)*. To improve the quality of teaching and learning in its own schools, this NGO has developed its own teacher training, monitoring and supervision mechanisms.

All these NGO efforts and activities are also geared to stimulating and enabling pupils to achieve the government competencies. Sometimes such initiatives produce better results because NGOs have less financial constraints and can work independently of the bureaucratic control of the government. Also they can have technical support from experts, both local and international, for developing quality programmes. So their initiatives, usually based on research, are more user-friendly and effective for classroom teaching and learning.

Level of achievements

However, all these initiatives, both government and non-government, do not seem to produce the desired results, as evidenced by research findings and students' performance in both school and national-level exams.

Research findings

To assess students' level of achievements in acquiring the competencies, the BU-IED Research Unit carried out a baseline survey in 2005 with a sample of twenty schools and 318 students in the district of Shariatpur. Table 2 shows the results.

No. of competencies tested		Items tested	% of students achieving competencies
Listening	1	*2 out of 3 MCQs	54%
Reading:	1	2 out of 3 MCQs	71%
	1	2 out of 3 MCQs	
Writing:	1	1 out of 2 Compositions	6.6%
All 4 competencies			4%

Table 2: *Shariatpur Regional Survey: Grade 4 competency achievement in listening, reading and writing*

Four competencies – one from Listening, two from Reading and one from Writing – were tested. There were three multiple choice questions, out of which two had to be answered. The study shows that only 4 per cent of learners achieved all the competencies tested (BU-IED Research Unit, 2005).

Exam results

Three exams – First, Second Terminal, and Annual – are compulsory for each grade in all the mainstream schools. However, the Grade 5 annual exam is called the Completion Exam as it comes at the end of the Primary cycle.

No. of schools	No. of pupils	Grade	Grade
630	22,218	5	54

Table 3: *First Terminal Exams Score (only in reading and writing) in Netrakona District* (Netrakona District Primary Education Office, 2007).

Table 3 above shows the average score out of 100 for the first terminal exam at Grade 5 of pupils in Netrakhona district for reading and writing. It indicates that pupils' achievement level in Netrakhona is quite acceptable, albeit not as great as is hoped. However, the results do not reflect pupils' real learning because the tests were based on the actual content of the textbook, which pupils had memorized and regurgitated to answer the exam questions.

Factors responsible for low achievements

Lack of sound policy decisions and the manner of their implementation in the existing teaching-learning situation are the key factors contributing to the low achievement of pupils at Primary level. The following factors put serious constraints on the effective implementation of TEYL.

Political decisions

English was introduced from Grade 1 as a compulsory subject in the national curriculum in 1990 on the basis of an executive order passed by the Government. However, the decision was not based on the reality of the country's teaching-learning situations. No study was made of how the huge number of teachers needed to implement this order could be trained properly and how suitable materials could be prepared and made available to the seven million new learners in Grades 1 and 2 (before that, English was taught only from Grade 3). In the same way, the Grade 5 Completion Exam was introduced by an executive order of MOPME in 2005. The resources and time involved in conducting this national-level exam effectively were not considered.

These important decisions in TEYL resulted in a huge waste of educational resources, resulting in poor teaching and poor learning. This sorry state of affairs with respect to

English teaching and learning has been compounded by the neglect of the mainstream schools by the upper class, including the politicians, bureaucrats and the businesspeople, who rather than send their children to these schools, send their children abroad or to the English-medium schools within Bangladesh. As a result, these schools are there mainly to cater for the poor parents' children.

Lack of suitable learning materials

The only learning materials for TEYL are the textbooks – the *English for Today* series – centrally produced by NCTB, based on the national competency-based curriculum. There is only one prescribed book per class and all the teaching-learning activities are based on this single textbook.

Usually highly qualified academics, commissioned by the government, with little hands-on experience of Primary-level teaching, lead the textbook-writing committees. As a result, although the books contain some practice in all the four language skills, their content and use of language often does not engage students effectively.

Ineffective classroom teaching

A number of factors are responsible for the current poor, ineffective classroom teaching:

- *Teachers' inadequate academic qualifications:* The academic qualifications of the majority of the teachers are Secondary School Certificate (SSC) and Higher Secondary Certificate (HSC) level. They pass these certificate exams despite getting the bare minimum pass marks in English, because all other subjects are in the mother tongue and they make up the requisite aggregate marks with marks from these subjects. The result is that they come to teach English with little or no English language proficiency of their own.

- *Absence of specialist English teachers:* As there are no teachers designated as subject teachers, there are no English teachers as such in schools – there are only class teachers. They teach all the subjects, without being able to specialize in any subjects.

- *Low pay scale for teachers:* Teaching at Primary level is a deplorably low-paid profession, as evidenced by the National Pay Scale (2005). A teacher's starting salary in a government school is only about US$73 (including rent and medical allowances) per month. It is much lower for non-government schoolteachers. So most teachers are busy trying to make ends meet, disgruntled and consequently often negligent in discharging their professional duties and responsibilities. Consequently, meritorious students completing their SSC/HSC are not interested in joining the teaching profession – they either choose to study in higher education or take up a vocation other than teaching.

- *Inadequate training for teachers:* A one-year INSET at PTIs is compulsory for the teachers. English is included as a paper carrying only 100 marks out of 1200 marks in the exam. There are other refresher courses at URCs, which are mainly pedagogy-based. The training manuals are written mostly in Bangla, which is largely used in the training sessions as well. So the trainee teachers miss out on good opportunities to improve their proficiency in speaking and reading skills.

- Most of the training (both long-term and intensive) takes the form of a one-off event during the teachers' lifetime. As they live in difficult circumstances (see the reference to the low pay scale for teachers above), they do the training mostly for their personal benefit, that is for a pay rise, promotion, etc. (because trained teachers are on a higher scale than their untrained colleagues). Also, they are not interested in whatever training in Communicative Language Teaching (CLT) they are given, as the teaching-learning circumstances prevailing in the schools (together with exam backwash – see below) are good reasons for not applying CLT in the classroom.

- *Lack of proper academic supervision:* A system of academic supervision is in place. Assistant Upazila (sub district) Education Officers (AUEOs), one in each Upazila (totalling 481), have been trained to carry out this professional responsibility. However, in reality, this does not happen. An AUEO supervises 20/25 schools a month in addition to his administrative work. So classroom supervision does not take place regularly and properly. The AUEO is a higher-ranking officer than the teacher and has the authority to report against the teacher. Hence whatever supervision is done tends to be authoritarian and judgmental.

- *Large classes:* Given the weaknesses in our academic supervision and the exam requirements (see below), the teacher is mostly reluctant to take the trouble to involve his class (usually 50+) in pair and group work, which is quite difficult to manage in such a large class. So whatever teaching-learning activity takes place in the classroom, it is almost invariably confined to learning about the content and the language, and not practising the use of the language.

- *Exam backwash:* Too many examinations – two Terminal (the first usually in April and the second in July) and one Annual/Completion Exam (in December) for each grade – are a heavy burden on the pupils. All these exams are like public exams because external bodies (i.e., Upazilas and Districts) administer them.

Exam results are the only educational goal for the majority of the parents, who are poor, mostly illiterate, and generally less educated. So all the teaching-learning strategies and activities used by teachers are geared to getting 'good results' for students in the exams. However, the exam results hardly reflect learners' proficiency in English. Since the exams assess only pupils' reading and writing skills, practice in listening and speaking is often considered a waste of time and as such it is hardly ever done in the classroom, though the textbooks include activities in listening and speaking skills. As a result, reading and writing occupy the most important place both in the exams and in the teaching-learning activities. Reading and writing tests are mostly based on textbook content, which pupils memorize. So most pupils pass the exams in English without acquiring any language skills. Therefore, teachers in this situation can comfortably teach in the grammar-translation method and pupils learn the textbook content and grammar rules by rote.

The first casualty of this type of teaching is young learners' oral proficiency. They do not have to speak English – they need only to read and write and if they venture to speak any English, they have many problems with pronunciation. As a result, their English is hardly intelligible. The teachers' spoken English has many of the same problems. Unfortunately, the learners' writing skills are little more advanced than their speaking skills. They perceive writing to be a matter of writing memorized words and sentences to give answers to the exam questions.

The current situations has far-reaching consequences for future TEYL policy and practice in Bangladesh. The serious weaknesses in the teaching and learning of English at Primary level often hinder pupils from learning English at Secondary and Higher Secondary levels.

Lessons drawn from Bangladesh experience of TEYL

In this section, I will summarize some important lessons from Bangladesh TEYL experience, which must be taken into consideration to implement TEYL successfully in future. Countries with similar socioeconomic and educational backgrounds to Bangladesh might find them worth considering, particularly if they are having a rethink of their own TEYL policy and practice.

Do not politicize teaching English at Primary level. Introduce English at a level, say Grade 3 or even 4, where teaching the subject effectively is possible and let the experts and practitioners make this decision, without allowing the politicians to use implementation of English teaching and learning for their own political motives.

Designate those teachers who teach English as 'English Teachers' so as to allow them to specialize in TEYL and grow professionally.

Recruit better-qualified teachers for teaching English (e.g., BA, BA Hons, MA). One-year of pre-service training in TEFL/TESL must be an essential prerequisite for the appointment of English teachers. Their salary should be raised to attract qualified teachers. If it is difficult to do it in a unitary education system, make provision to give English teachers special allowances.

Train practising English teachers locally in school clusters through short sandwich and refresher courses regularly, say three or four times a year. Introduce a mentoring system – not so-called 'supervision' by officers higher in rank than the teachers.

Introduce a multiple textbook policy, allowing private publishing houses to produce textbooks and supplementary materials. This will reduce NCTB's monopoly of producing all the textbooks for all the mainstream Primary schools in the country. There must be a quality assurance committee at national level to oversee quality.

Firmly establish language testing that will test pupils' proficiency in language skills – not their ability to memorize textbook content. Make sure only trained teachers are appointed to set and mark tests both for school and Board examinations.

Establish fruitful collaboration between Government and NGOs to improve the quality of TEYL in the country. Due to various constraints we have seen earlier, it can be said that the Government alone cannot carry out the huge task of implementing effective TEYL in the country. In the circumstances, the Government should exploit the NGO resources, collaborating with them in all the major TEYL projects and programmes.

Support community-based school ventures. About 17,000 English-medium schools have mushroomed in the county because there is a very high demand for English among people from all walks of life. Unfortunately, most of these schools are not accessible to the people in general, mainly because they all charge high tuition fees (government schools are free). Hence these English-medium schools are not the solution to improving TEYL in the country. In the circumstances, the government as well as the philanthropists, educationists and the rich people in society can help set up community-based English schools/centres throughout the country. Parents will pay for their children's English lessons, according to their ability.

These community-based English schools can initiate and strengthen the process of learning communicative English within the learners' own environment and can help them enter the mainstream schools with a good foundation in English.

Develop a sustainable, permanent system of TEYL. Bangladesh's experience shows that a lot of good work in TEYL is often done by projects, but their benefits are ad hoc. The good work that a project usually achieves does not last long after the project ends.

We greatly emphasize the importance of English for our national development. Yet there is no organization with a separate entity at national or regional level to develop English at Primary level (or at any level) to help meet the need for English. So Bangladesh needs a permanent body, say a National English Language Centre – not a temporary project – to look after its TEYL. The Centre, supported by the Government, can get technical support from a project, if necessary, but will work as an effective autonomous body. TEYL policy and its implementation strategy will be decided by the specialists and the professionals under the auspices of the Centre – not by the generalists and the politicians in power.

References

BU-IED, Researcch Unit (2005). Access and Quality in Primary Education: A Baseline Survey of the Amader School Project of Concern Worldwide. BRAC University Institute of Educational Development, Dhaka, Bangladesh.

District Primary Education Office (2007). Chart showing pupils' average scores in all the schools of Netrakona district.

National Curriculum and Textbook Board (2003). *National Curriculum Document, Part One*, p. 66.

National Pay Scale (2005). *Bangladesh Gazette*, 28 May 2005.

'The early bird catches the worm': The Turkish case

Dilek İnal, Department of English Language Teaching, Istanbul University, Turkey

Introduction

Rapid globalization has equally accelerated the need for communication and a common language to communicate in, which is met by English as a lingua franca. Consequently, research in this field has grown rapidly with students everywhere 'increasing in number and decreasing in age' (Graddol, 2006: 10). Thus, teaching English to young learners has received particular attention, highlighting learner characteristics, questioning the reasons for advocating an early starting age in learning a foreign language and researching the appropriate methodology to be applied in the procedure. Countries around the globe have created their own policies regarding the teaching of English at the Primary level and have found themselves susceptible to changes in the field in an effort to provide the best possible teaching to young learners in their own contexts. The case is no different for Turkey, a country waiting to integrate with the European Union and, thereby, going through a number of important changes.

Given its geographical and cultural position, Turkey has been very cautious in maintaining a balanced stance in its relationships with the East and the West, with which it has assumed a binding role. Throughout its history, Turkey has fully identified itself with the latter, while maintaining access to the East, with which it has a shared cultural history.

Reforms in the Turkish national education system concerning English

Over the course of Turkey's westernization movement, there have been significant reform efforts in education. Although reforms began in the eighteenth and nineteenth centuries during the Ottoman Empire, the most influential ones were seen in the 1920s following the foundation of modern Turkey. Turkish learners were introduced to foreign language courses in Secondary schools in 1924; the first foreign language teacher training department was opened in 1938; the first translation bureaus were founded across the country in the same year (Demircan, 1988). It was in this first decade and a half that the aim of foreign language teaching was observed as enabling the learner to comprehend what is read, utter simple sentences in the foreign tongue, and translate from the foreign language into Turkish – all of which point to an awareness of and a positive attitude towards foreign languages.

The years between 1939, which marked the beginning of the Second World War, and 1972 mark a period in the Turkish history when the foreign policies of the state were noticeably reflected in educational procedures. Competency in a foreign language was first recognized as a benefit by the state in 1939, when civil workers who proved competent in a foreign language were paid extra salaries. In 1941, collaboration with foreign institutions, such as the British Council, United States Information Agency and Fulbright, were started and highly proficient university students became eligible for Fulbright grants (Demircan, 1988). Following alliance with NATO in 1952, the English language was established as the Primary foreign language at Secondary level, followed by German as the second foreign language. In 1955, a new public school type was introduced into mainstream Turkish national education, whose difference was marked by the additional preparatory year of English and which admitted students through an entrance exam. Turkey's first collaboration with the European Council took place in 1968 for coursebook preparation and continued with the revision of language teaching programs in 1972. In 1970, foreign language teaching radio broadcasts were started on the state-owned radio.

This period of about three decades, observed a change in the aim of foreign language teaching, which reflected the role of English as a means to an end and a symbol of better life opportunities, such as better jobs, a better reputation and a privileged social position (Doğançay-Aktuna and Kızıltepe, 2005). Thus, the aim of foreign language teaching in this period was to enable the learner to comprehend what is read and heard, to communicate using complex spoken forms, express in written form what is to be communicated, and prolong interest in the foreign language after graduation from formal schooling – all of which point to an instrumental use of the foreign language.

Developments during the 1980s continued to consolidate the position of English in the Turkish national education system. The increasing spread of English was in no way surprising as the state policies of the 1980s were based on establishing strong political and economic ties with the West. A law related to the teaching of foreign languages at different levels of schooling was passed in 1983, which was followed by the commencement of elective foreign language courses in high schools (nine hours a week) in the same year. In 1984, another public school type was introduced to the system and Anatolian Vocational Schools, where the medium of instruction is English, were opened. Exactly a decade later, yet another public school type appeared and Super High Schools, with an additional preparatory year, were opened for high-achieving students to prepare them better for the imminent university entrance exam (Ekmekçi, 2003).

These developments can be interpreted as the embodiments of the aim of foreign language teaching defined in the 1980s and 1990s as enabling the learner to become proficient in at least one, and preferably more than one, foreign language(s), and to attain that proficiency before the start of higher education. They indicated sensitivity towards multilingualism and a requirement for proficiency in the English language. Thus, by the end of 1990s, English had attained the position of the most popular foreign language for Turkish learners, in spite of the fact that other foreign languages, such as German and French, were not only offered but also encouraged in schools.

The 1997 reform

The year 1997 marked a defining moment in Turkish national education when compulsory Primary education was increased to eight years (from five). This was a step towards meeting the standards of the European Council, whose member states have compulsory education for 10–11 years on average. With this reform movement, it became obligatory for Primary school students to start studying a foreign language – English, in this case – from Grade 4 on (a total of nine years as school starting age is six). Moreover, the preparatory class in Anatolian high schools was removed as the early start at Grade 4 was believed to compensate for that additional year.

The statement regarding the reform made by the Ministry of National Education revealed recognition of the importance of foreign language teaching, underlining the communicative and intercultural aspects of foreign language learning and the need to start early so as to invest in foreign language learning for a longer period of time. Thus, the English curriculum was modified, teacher training programmes at universities were restructured accordingly, in-service training programs were organized and new and communicative course books were written for Primary and Secondary levels of schooling. Regardless of the debates among scholars who advocated opposing positions on 'the earlier the better' issue, this was definitely the beginning of a new era for Turkish national education. Teaching young learners had become an extensively studied field, whose principles and applications were under constant scrutiny. Following the early years of application, studies conducted with teachers in the field revealed that problems had started to appear. A discrepancy between the specified objectives of the curriculum and the specifics of the course books could be detected; teaching time allowed (two lessons a week or 80 minutes) proved insufficient; classes were too crowded to allow actual implementation of the desired methodology; and because the previous teacher training programs did not include courses on teaching young learners, teachers felt inadequately equipped to teach the learner at hand.

Following the 1997 Reform

Various other changes took place following the 1997 Reform, two of which are of considerable importance. First, as of 2002, science and maths courses were no longer studied in English as it became difficult to find content teachers who could teach in

English. Secondly, as of 2005, the English preparatory year required by the Anatolian, Super High and private Secondary schools was abolished in an effort to remove differences in English Language Teaching (ELT) in schools at the same level.

These individual school adjustments and changes aside, the Ministry of National Education instigated a more all-encompassing change in 2003, claiming that there was a pressing need to revise the English curriculum for the Primary school to meet the changing needs of the learners and the challenges of the field. It is stated by the Ministry of National Education in the English Language Curriculum for Primary Education (2006: 16) that the paradigmatic changes in ELT and the process of European and global integrations called for implementations of newer and better approaches and methods in ELT in order to better equip Turkish learners for a future that will align them with others in the West in the political, social and economic arenas.

When interpreted, it can be seen that all these changes reflect a radical re-thinking of educational philosophy in the context of foreign language learning and teaching. First, a shift from teacher-centredness to learner-centredness and a learning process which emphasizes a constructivist view of learning. As an indispensable part of this view, language learning is seen in relation to personal development, which leads to the concept of learner autonomy. Also parts of the language learning process, social and cultural goals need to be recognized, making way for intercultural awareness and competence. Thus, one goal of ELT will be defined as aiming for intercultural speakers who can adapt themselves to different cultural environments with an understanding of cultures other than their own. Finally, highlighting the international position of English language, the teaching aims, methods and assessment need to be based on common criteria as outlined by The Common European Framework of Reference for Languages: Learning, Teaching, Assessment, which became a recommended instrument for the validation of language competences by the European Union Council in 2001.

It was in light of these changes, that academic commissions worked in order to revise the English curriculum for the Primary level. An incremental change was targeted, so the new curriculum for Grade 4 was applied in the academic year of 2006-07 to be followed with the revised curricula for the upper grades in the following years.

The Revised Curriculum of 2006

The revised curriculum for Grade 4 was launched to take into account all the recent paradigmatic changes shaping the context of ELT. The introduction to the curriculum and the curriculum itself reveal that the following have served as guidelines:

- The constructivist approach is recognized as the basis for collaborative and cooperative activities.

- Considerable emphasis is placed on the topic-based approach, with topics selected in a cross-curricular manner.

- The goals and objectives are based on a functional-notional and skill-based syllabus.

- Hands-on activities are suggested for classroom learning.

- The theory of multiple intelligences is taken into consideration in the designing of activities and tasks.

- Criterion-referenced and performance-based alternative assessment devices, such as portfolio assessment, are suggested.

- In line with the concept of learner autonomy, strategy training is included.

- The use of a variety of language teaching materials is encouraged.

- The distinction between language acquisition and language learning is made clear, leading to a better understanding and designing of activities for different age groups.

- More engaging activities, such as songs, riddles, games and craft activities, are utilized for younger groups.

This new curriculum was introduced to students in 33,645 public Primary schools in Turkey (Ministry of National Education Statistics, December 16, 2007).

Survey interviews and discussions conducted with the voluntary participation of 52 teachers of English at Primary level in and around Istanbul a year later revealed the teachers' opinions concerning its efficacy. These can be grouped around the following topics.

Cultural/intercultural awareness

As most teachers have not received training or guidance related to the teaching of cultural issues, the development of intercultural awareness and competence becomes a problematic issue. Teachers report difficulty concerning the integration of cultural matters in the teaching of the language. Moreover, the question of whose culture to teach seems to find its answer in the native speaker culture only. The present position of English as lingua franca and the existence of 'World Englishes', however, calls for a wider understanding of culture, with the inclusion of other cultures in the expanding circle.

Course books

There seems to be a mismatch between the specifics of the curriculum and those of the course books. The skill-based syllabus of the course books does not seem to make room for much strategy training in the early grades, as it claims to have done. Moreover, the theory of multiple intelligences that is underlined as the basis for the diversity of activities and tasks seems to have been represented particularly by two types of intelligences: verbal/linguistic and logical/mathematical. Although there are activities that fit other types of intelligences, they are not presented in a systematic manner.

Teacher beliefs

Most teachers confess to the fact that they adapt a teacher-centred style of teaching, assuming that the learner is naturally passive and turned active only after being stimulated. The teachers often feel that their responsibility to create a classroom atmosphere where the desired behavior is stimulated is influenced by the strong drive to meet the objectives of a criterion-referenced test that the learners will have to take at the end. This, in turn, poses difficulty in moving towards learner and learning-centredness, which entails a focus on the learners' needs in the design of class work and the learners' responsibility for their own actions. Some teachers report that they equate teacher-centredness with authority that they do not want to lose. Thus, the demands of the constructivist approach become hard to meet.

Assessment

Due to centralized, standardized tests that students have to take at the end of Primary (Grade 8) and Secondary schools (Grade 11) in order to continue at the next level (and to enter university), an exam-oriented understanding is also applied to English. Alternative assessment means, such as projects and portfolios, are either beyond schools' experience, or are not trusted by a significant number of teachers.

Resources

Many schools lack adequate resources to make use of a variety of language teaching materials.

On the positive side, the English curriculum for Secondary education is also being revised and the continuity between the two stages of education is being carefully addressed in an effort to remove differences resulting from changes in the quality and quantity of instruction. As Secondary education receives students from both state and private schools, which differ dramatically as far as English instruction is concerned (with more hours of teaching and the recruitment of native speakers of English for most skills courses in the private schools), one can imagine mixed-level problems in the English class. Thus, the English curriculum for the Secondary level is being planned according to the competence levels of The Common European Framework of Reference for Languages: Learning, Teaching, Assessment, adapting a learner-centred approach, making room for different learning styles and pacing learning according to the learners' needs and interests.

Similarly, the Higher Education Board, which is responsible for the studies at university level, initiated curriculum changes to the English language teacher education programs in all state universities. Courses to better equip future teachers of English (such as more courses on teaching young learners and comparative educational systems) have been integrated into the programme. The Ministry of National Education has fully supported and continues to support school collaboration projects with European countries, serving intercultural awareness. In 2006, about 460 partnership projects were submitted from all parts of Turkey.

Although interviews with teachers in the aforementioned survey of 52 Istanbul Primary teachers revealed that portfolio work is beyond teachers' experience, there have been serious efforts to implement the English Language Portfolio at the Primary level. Seminars on using portfolio in language teaching are carried out as part of in-service training for the teachers. In accordance with this, work is continuing on adopting models for the European Language Portfolio. The portfolio model that has been designed for ages 10–14 was piloted in 15 Primary schools across Turkey, all yielding successful results. The model has been accredited by the European Union (National Agency, 12 December 2007).

In conclusion, the new curriculum attempts to reshape ELT at Primary level in an effort to meet the changing needs of learners and invest in their future engagement with English in the best possible manner. It is appreciated that the Ministry of National Education is taking the initiative, recognizing the growing significance of foreign language learning in the global context. It should be noted, however, that no curriculum stands on its own, it comes alive in the hands of teachers who know how to use it, provided with sufficient materials and resources.

References

Demircan, Ö. (1988). Dünden Bugüne Türkiye'de Yabancı Dil (Foreign Language in Turkey – From Past to Present). İstanbul: Remzi Kitabevi.

Doğançay-Aktuna, S. and Kızıltepe, Z. (2005). English in Turkey, World Englishes 24 (2), 253-265.

Ekmekçi, Ö. (2003). Dünden Bugüne Türkiye de Yabancı Dil Eğitimi [Foreign Language Education in Turkey, From Past to Present], in Türk Eğitim Sistemi'nde Yabancı Dil Eğitimi ve Kalite Arayışları [Foreign Language Education in the Turkish Educational System and Search for Quality]. İstanbul: Özel Okullar Derneği.

Graddol, D. (2006). English Next. London: British Council.

Ministry of National Education, English Language Curriculum for Primary Education Grades 4, 5, 6, 7 and 8 (2006). Ankara: Devlet Kitaplığıı Müdürlüğü.

Ministry of National Education Statistics online (2007) http://sgb.meb.gov.tr/istatistik/Kopya_meb_istatistikleri_orgun_egitim_2006_2007detay_ek_dosya.xls (Accessed 16.12.07).

National Agency online (2007) http://www.ua.gov.tr (Accessed 20.12.07)

Teaching English at the Primary level in India: An overview

Kirti Kapur, National Council of Educational Research and Training, New Delhi, India

Introduction

The following paper is based on the position paper of the National Focus Group on Teaching of English and the National Curriculum Framework 2005. Its purpose is to give an overview of the introduction and teaching of English at the Primary level in India.

In India, interest in English is a symbol of people's desire for quality in education, as well as of their desire to participate in national and international life. The opening up of the Indian economy has increased the demand for English-medium schools because people feel that by learning English they will receive better opportunities in life. The introduction of English in India is both a social as well as a political response to people's demand for its introduction in the early years of schooling. The expectation that the system should respond to these demands has resulted in a mushrooming of private English-medium schools. State school systems have started introducing English between Classes 1 to 3. English is in fact being introduced from Class 1 in most of the states in India.

The level of introduction of English is a matter of state policy in India. Since education is a priority of both central and state governments, states have the discretion to introduce English as per their requirements and according to demand. However, they are expected to ensure the availability of material resources and teacher preparedness. The most pressing issue therefore, is developing a sound pedagogy. Given this, we should be able to ensure basic English language proficiency, in about four of the eight years of compulsory education, irrespective of the level of introduction of English (NCERT, 2005: 39). Without sound pedagogy it is not possible to achieve this even if English is introduced from Class 1.

There are a variety of teaching situations prevalent in India. In English-medium private schools, English is introduced from Class 1 and both the teacher and the learner have adequate exposure to the language. In new English-medium schools, English is also introduced from Class 1 due to parental demand but teacher preparedness and the learners' exposure to the language is not up to the mark. In government-aided schools, teachers' proficiency is low and students' exposure to English language is also minimal. In government-run municipal-corporation schools, both the teacher and the learners' exposure to English language is negligible. Furthermore, there can be variations within these types of schools. N.S. Prabhu (1987: 3) suggests that 'typologies of teaching situations … should be seen as an aid to investigating the extent of relevance of a pedagogical proposal.' Hence, we also need to understand how children acquire and use language.

Language teaching and learning lay emphasis on a learner-centered approach. According to Chomsky (1986: 8), children are born with an innate language faculty. This has two important pedagogical consequences. First, if children are given adequate exposure, they acquire new languages with ease. Secondly, the focus in teaching should be more on meaning than on grammar. Linguistic tools can and must play a significant role in developing a child's cognitive abilities. This would be better than teaching normative rules of grammar (NCERT, 2006b: 1).

The National Curriculum Framework 2005 states that the goals for a second-language curriculum are twofold: 'attainment of a basic proficiency, such as is acquired in natural language learning, and the development of language into an instrument for abstract thought and knowledge acquisition through, for example, literacy' (NCERT, 2005: 39). We need to have a holistic approach to language teaching with the objective that the learners are able to use language effectively and meaningfully. They should be able to listen and read with comprehension and should be able to draw inferences. They should also be able to speak with effortless expression and write with coherence.

This argues for an across-the-curriculum approach that breaks down the barriers between English and other subjects, and English and other Indian languages. Therefore, for language learning, an input-rich environment is necessary, in which there is considerable scope for meaningful communication. A curriculum that engenders such teaching practice lays the foundation for spontaneous language learning.

In the initial stages, the aim is to build familiarity with the language so that the child can gain a working knowledge of it. Children develop a natural ability in languages available in their immediate environment. Where English is not a part of the environment, the classroom needs to provide the opportunity for its acquisition in meaningful communicational contexts. A number of researchers (Prabhu, 1987; Krashen, 1985; Elley and Mangubhai, 1983) have shown that language is acquired when attention is focused not on language form, but more on the meaning of the message. The 'burden of languages' is nothing but the 'burden of incomprehension' (NCERT, 2006a: 5). Such a situation arises when language is taught as a set of rules and not as a mode/carrier of coherent textual meaning. The endeavor therefore should be to maintain a balance between comprehension and acquisition of skills. For this, a 'meaningful language-learning environment' is strongly recommended. The importance of this has also been recognized by cognitive theories of learning and language learning.

In India, where a variety of teaching and learning situations prevail, the learner can receive the language input that is appropriate to his/her age outside the classroom as well. The classroom should not be a limiting factor in the acquisition of knowledge of the language. Therefore, the attitude and motivation of learners do play an important role in language learning. At the same time, the attitudes of the teacher and of parents encouraging the learners also contribute to successful language learning. Second/foreign language learning is influenced by certain social psychological variables such as aptitude, intelligence, attitude, motivation and motivational intensity (NCERT, 2006b: 4).

Initially one needs to build the learners' oral and aural familiarity with the language. There is a need for a paradigm shift from rote learning to constructivism. Constructivism is a theory about learning and not a description of teaching. Constructivism's central idea is that human learning is constructed within a specific context. Earlier English Language Teaching (ELT) focused on learning a few sentences by heart. According to the constructivist theory however, we have to create an environment where construction of knowledge can take place. Learners should be provided with meaningful language inputs so that they can build a working knowledge of the language. 'These inputs include textbooks, shared reading of other print materials such as Big Books, class libraries, parallel materials in more than one language and media support in the form of learner magazines, newspapers, columns, radio/audio-video cassettes' (NCERT, 2006a: 6).

For example, story reading can be developed into a classroom methodology. Reading stories aloud, repeated reading, choral reading, story re-telling, shared reading – all these activities build on existing language proficiency because learners are exposed to a common pool of vocabulary and sentences and gradually these words and sentences become part of their spoken language. As the teacher reads, pupils become familiar with the story in spoken language, and the illustrations, and subsequently develop acquaintance with the print code/medium. Pseudo-production and role-play, etc., also help in the development of the language ability of the learner. Repetition coupled with gestures taps into children's physical energy. Total physical response (TPR) where children listen, repeat and physically respond to a song or a rhyme or a set of instructions, sustains the interest of the learners, thereby increasing the degree of language learning (Shin, 2006: 3).

An input-rich communicational environment can also be created by using display charts, poems, stories and children's project work. Other materials include reading cards and very short stories. Learners can be encouraged to bring texts that they enjoy reading such as cartoons, jokes, anecdotes, etc., and for model reading and listening, books with audio cassettes can be used as a resource.

These approaches and methods should be all inclusive and according to the needs, interest, cognitive development and age of the individual learners. The input that the learner receives at the Primary level serves as a base for higher levels at which the teaching of

English aims to develop higher-order skills. The resources that are available to the learners (e.g., the mother tongue, numeracy, conventions, gestures and conjectures, etc.) should therefore be used optimally to reach the target language.

The English language does not stand alone and needs to find its place among other Indian languages (NCERT, 2006a: 3). Every possible effort should be made to build bridges between the languages of home, peer group and neighborhood languages on the one hand and school on the other. It is important that English is not contextualized in a western ambience but is taught through a contextually rich local perspective.

NCERT 2005 states that the mother tongue, when employed as a medium of instruction at the initial stages, can eliminate the linguistic and cultural gaps caused by the difference between the school language and the home language, especially at the Primary level. Education in the mother-tongue will facilitate richer classroom transaction and greater learner participation, yielding better learning outcomes. Every effort therefore must be made to provide adequate facilities for this purpose and a positive attitude towards mother-tongue education must be ensured from all quarters. Use of the mother tongue as the medium of instruction facilitates better cognitive growth, fosters healthier interpersonal communication skills and promotes conceptual clarity (NCERT, 2006b: 15).

Ultimately, 'The aim of English Language Teaching is the creation of multilinguals who can enrich all our languages; this has been an abiding national vision' (NCERT, 2005: 30). 'Multilingualism is constitutive of the Indian identity' (NCERT, 2006b: 20). It promotes social harmony and is a natural phenomenon that relates positively to cognitive flexibility and scholastic achievement. Multilingualism should therefore be given due place in the classroom alongside teaching of English.

Language teaching needs to be multilingual not only in terms of the number of languages offered to children but also in terms of evolving strategies that would use the multilingual classroom as a resource (NCERT, 2006b: 20). The skills that learners acquire in L1 can be used as a resource to develop skills in L2. For example, the instructions given in English are difficult for the learners to comprehend on their own. To get the response in the target language, the instruction for activities and exercises may be given in the native language. Similarly, as the learners can read a simple story in their native language, the same story can be given to them in English to read and they will be able to read it easily with comprehension. The parallel texts referred to here need not be exact translations. In addition, bilingual books and dictionaries can also be used in the classroom.

The first task of the school is to relate the home language to the school language. Thereafter, one or more languages are to be integrated so that one can move into other languages without losing the first. This should result in the maintenance of all languages, each complementing the other(s).

Several recent studies (e.g., Peal and Lambert, 1962; Gardner and Lambert, 1972; Cummins and Swain, 1986) have shown that there is a highly positive relationship between bilingualism, cognitive flexibility and scholastic achievement. Bilingual children are also academically more creative and socially more tolerant. Their wide range of linguistic skills equips them to negotiate different social situations more effectively. There is also substantial evidence to show that bilingual children excel in divergent thinking (NCERT, 2006b: 21). Now that we also know of the positive relationship between multilingualism, cognitive growth and educational achievement, there is every need to promote multilingual education in schools. The multilingual perspective also addresses the dual concerns of language and culture, and applies the pedagogical principle of moving from the known to the unknown, local to global, familiar to unfamiliar.

In this context, the three-language formula (see below) may be seen as an attempt to address the challenges and opportunities of the linguistic situation in India. It is a strategy that should serve as a launching pad for learning more languages. Its primary aim therefore is to promote multilingualism and national harmony. States are therefore encouraged to follow it both in letter and spirit.

The genesis of the three-language formula can be traced to the 1968 National Policy on Education (Ministry of Human Resource Development, 1968: 3-4), which states that:

a) The first language to be studied must be the mother tongue or the regional language.

b) The second language:

   • in Hindi-speaking states, will be some other modern Indian language or English;

   • in non-Hindi-speaking states, will be Hindi or English.

c) The third language:

   • in Hindi-speaking states, will be English or a modern Indian language not studied as the second language;

   • in non-Hindi-speaking states, will be English or a modern Indian language not studied as the second language.

The National Focus Group on Teaching of Indian Languages has observed that by adopting the three-language formula as a strategy, space was created for the study of proximate languages, classical languages, foreign languages and even the mother tongue. NCERT 2005 states that the three-language formula should not be regarded as a goal or a limiting factor in language acquisition, but rather should be looked upon as a launching pad from which to learn more languages.

Another important factor that needs to be looked into is teacher preparation in English at the Primary level. As the teacher is a role model for young learners, the teacher's proficiency in or familiarity with the language is important. Specialist knowledge of grammar or literature is not required but teachers should be proficient in the use of the language. The methods and approaches used by the teacher should be mutually supportive. Teacher education needs to be ongoing, on-site. Both pre-service and in-service teacher training at regular intervals are a must. The role of the teacher is to provide a classroom full of interesting things to encourage learners to construct their own knowledge and give them the ability to explore. The teacher's role is more subtle. The teacher is like a facilitator.

Teaching for successful learning cannot occur without high quality assessment. Assessment, therefore, needs to be integrated with the process of teaching and learning. The greater the integration, the better will be the outcomes of learning. Assessment has to be so designed that it can be used as a powerful means of influencing the quality of what teachers teach and what students learn. Special care should be taken to ensure that it is sensitive to the needs of the learner and that it enables him or her to grow into a responsible and productive citizen. Assessment refers to collecting information on the progress of students' learning using a variety of procedures, and evaluation refers to making judgements on the basis of the information collected. The process and purpose of assessment should shift from merely assigning grades/awarding marks to include constructive feedback and assist with the learners' improvement. Learner-centered teaching should also use assessment as part of the learning process.

In conclusion, in order to bridge the gap between English-medium and regional-medium education, the multilingual and English-across-the-curriculum approach must be kept in mind when teaching English at the Primary level. In regional-medium schools, the learners' first language can be used as a resource to teach English; in English-medium schools other Indian languages should not be neglected, but rather placed on an equal footing.

References

Chomsky, N. (1986). *Knowledge of Language.* New York: Praeger Books.

Cummins, J. and Swain, M. (1986). *Bilingualism in Education.* London: Longman, from National Focus Group on Teaching of Indian Languages (2006), *Position Paper* (p. 21). New Delhi: NCERT.

Elley, W. and Magubhai, F. (1983). The impact of reading on second language learning. *Reading Research Quarterly* 19, 53-67 from National Focus Group on Teaching of English (2006), *Position Paper.* New Delhi: NCERT, 5.

Gardner, R.C. and Lambert, W.E. (1972). *Attitudes and Motivation in Second Language Learning.* Rowley, MA: Newbury House. Publishers from National Focus Group on Teaching of Indian Languages (2006), *Position Paper* (p. 21). New Delhi, India: NCERT,

Krashen, S.D. (1985). *The Input Hypothesis: Issues and Implications.* London and New York: Longman from National Focus Group on Teaching of English, *Position Paper.* New Delhi, India: NCERT, 5.

Ministry of Human Resource Development (1968). *National Policy on Education – 1966* (pp. 3-4). New Delhi: Government of India (Dept of Education).

National Council of Educational Research and Training (NCERT) (2005). *National Curriculum Framework 2005* (pp. 36-40). New Delhi, India: NCERT.

National Council of Educational Research and Training (NCERT) (2006a). National Focus Group on Teaching of English. *Position Paper* (pp. 1-18). New Delhi, India: NCERT.

National Council of Educational Research and Training (NCERT) (2006b) National Focus Group on Teaching of Indian Languages. *Position Paper.* New Delhi, India: NCERT, 14-22, 30-32.

Peal, E. and Lambert, W.E. (1962). The relation of bilingualism to intelligence. *Psychological Monographs* 76. From National Focus Group on Teaching of Indian Languages (2006). *Position Paper* (p. 21). New Delhi, India: NCERT.

Prabhu, N.S. (1987). *Second Language Pedagogy.* New York: Oxford University Press.

Shin, J. (2006). Ten Helpful Ideas for Teaching English to Young Learners. *English Teaching Forum* 2, 2-13. Available at http://exchanges.state.gov/forum/archives/2006/06-44-2.html.

Early bilingualism in Cameroon: Where politics and education meet

Kuchah Kuchah, Ministry of Basic Education, Yaounde, Cameroon

Introduction

This paper sets out to show how early bilingual education in Cameroon has evolved from a purely socio-political choice and is increasingly becoming an educational vision. My purpose is to demonstrate that although the policy governing early bilingualism was and is still mainly political, its educational orientation has and is yielding results that both satisfy the initial political goal for its implementation and what we may call an 'educational' objective. To achieve this purpose, I propose to begin with a brief history of Cameroon so as to situate the reader within the sociocultural and political context in which the educational system has been developed. In doing this, I will be referring mainly to bilingual education in French-medium Primary schools in the hope that the reader will also be able to relate the issues I raise about French in English-medium schools in Cameroon.

Cameroon has a historical relationship with two former colonial powers, France and Britain, following the defeat of Germany, its initial coloniser, in the First World War. Following the war, in 1919, the League of Nations divided Cameroon into two protectorates under France and Britain. The result of this decision by the League of Nations was the emergence of a new Southern Cameroons (governed from Nigeria by the British) and La République du Cameroun (governed by the French). After the independence of French Cameroon in 1961, there arose the need for British Cameroon to also have its own independence. Consequently, the British granted independence on the condition that Southern Cameroons joined the now independent French Cameroon, or Nigeria – ruling out the possibility of an independent state of Southern Cameroon. In February 1961, Southern Cameroons voted to join La République du Cameroun, their former 'brothers', and both parts of Cameroon became known as the Federal Republic of Cameroon. In 1972, they became the United Republic of Cameroon, with a national capital in Yaounde.

These historical relationships inevitably situate Cameroon in a place of linguistic (con)fusion. Although Cameroon at one time had about 256 indigenous languages, English and French were adopted as official languages and languages of instruction in their respective subsystems of education. This political decision to adapt the 'neutral' European languages both for official transactions and for educational purposes eventually proved to be at odds with its initial purpose. Although it avoided a potential conflict over which of the numerous indigenous languages would gain precedence over the others, it created the conditions instead for conflict along francophone-anglophone lines. Ayafor (2005: 124) rightly explains that 'although multiculturalism in terms of ethnic diversity is unexpectedly not yet a problem for national unity, ethnicity along the francophone-anglophone dichotomy is, and has drawn such attention that it threatens national unity more than anything else in the country'.

The political turmoil of the early 90s and a growing feeling of marginalization accompanied by threats of cessation on the part of anglophone Cameroonians, among other factors, necessitated a revision of the constitution of the country in 1996 (Secretariat General of the Presidency of the Republic, 1996). To resolve the linguistic/cultural dichotomy of the country, Paragraph 3 of Article 1 of the 1996 constitution states that 'the official languages of the Republic of Cameroon shall be English and French, both languages having the same status'.

In spite of this decisive ruling, there has never been any accompanying government position on language policy and planning at the broader level. In other words, neither the constitution, nor any other official document, obliges Cameroonians to be bilingual. Nevertheless, it is against the background of this constitutional prescription that a national forum on education held in 1995 resulted in the prescription of a law on education in 1998 stating that 'The State shall institute bilingualism at all levels of education as a factor of national unity and integration' (Ministry of National Education, 1998).

To implement this law, a number of important educational reforms were required, these aimed to define the watershed between the past system and a new more dynamic and inevitably more relevant system, which would help Cameroon take up the challenges of the twenty-first century and solve the major problems plaguing its society. One such reform was the inclusion of English as a subject in French-medium Primary schools and French in English-medium Primary schools in 1997. Later, in 2002, an Inspectorate of Bilingualism was created in the Ministry of National Education and later in the Ministry of Basic Education to define, implement, monitor and assess the teaching/learning of French in English-medium schools and English in French-medium schools. In French-medium schools, this resulted in a reorganization of timetables to include 4 hours and 30 minutes of English per week and the development of an English language syllabus that was implemented progressively from the first year of Primary education. Textbooks were written to meet the new demands of linguistic, cultural and political integration and English became one of the subjects in the end-of-Primary school certificate examination for French-medium schoolchildren.

Models of bilingualism in the school system

As I explained earlier, two subsystems of education, namely the francophone and the anglophone subsystems, coexist in Cameroon with each preserving its distinct methods of evaluation and certificates. To define the nature of bilingual education in Primary schools in Cameroon, it is necessary to understand how both subsystems of education operate. At the level of Primary education, children in both subsystems are expected to spend six years at school before they take the official certificate examinations. The six years are divided into three levels of two years each and the syllabus for each level is organized such that in the first year of each level, pupils are introduced to notions/concepts which are reinforced and extended in the second year. The organizational structure of both subsystems is therefore as follows:

Level	Francophone	Anglophone
One	Section d'Initiation au langage (SIL) Cours Preparatoires (CP)	Class one Class two
Two	Cours Elementaires 1 (CE1) Cours Elementaires 2 (CE2)	Class three Class four
Three	Cours Moyen 1 (CM1) Cours Moyen 2 (CM2)	Class five Class six
Examination	Certificat d'Etudes Primaires (CEP)	First School Leaving Certificate (FSLC)

Table 1

Within this structure, there are three discernable types of bilingualism. The first is in the traditional Primary school, which can either be anglophone or francophone but in which the second official language is taught as a separate subject in the curriculum. For example, in a francophone school, English language will be taught as a second official language. The second type is in the traditional 'bilingual schools', which existed even before the political changes of the early 90s. These are schools where an anglophone subsystem school and a francophone subsystem school coexist in one premises so that children interact in both languages as they play with one another during recreational periods. In this kind of bilingual school, as in the traditional Primary school, the second official language is a subject in the curriculum of both sub-systems. For convenience, English will be called 'Anglais' in the francophone school as opposed to 'English' in Anglophone schools.

The third type of bilingualism that has emerged very recently is what we can call immersion bilingualism. In schools that practice 'immersion' bilingualism, all subjects are taught in English and French irrespective of the linguistic background of the pupils. In each class, there will be an anglophone teacher who follows the anglophone syllabus and a francophone teacher who follows the francophone syllabus and both teachers alternate at a given time of the day or week. Because there is no provision for pupils to be able to sit for both certificate examinations this practice ends in the fifth year of Primary school and parents have to decide whether their children will spend the sixth year in an anglophone class or in a francophone class depending on whether they want to sit for the Certificat d'Études Primaires (CEP) or the First School Leaving Certificate (FSLC).

The syllabus and course books

In francophone schools where English is the second official language, the syllabus is designed to achieve, among other things, the following broad goals:

• to provide learners with the English that they will use at the end of Primary school in daily life requirements;

• to establish a basis for further work in English at Secondary school;

• to expose learners to the other aspects of the English speaking culture;

• *to foster bilingualism and national integration* (my emphasis).

These goals are transmitted in an itemized syllabus which is built on communicative objectives with a basic grammar skeleton, intended to be used to achieve a communicative purpose. The syllabus for CM1, for example, is presented in table 2.

The syllabus further recommends that at the first level of Primary education (SIL and CP) emphasis should be on oral/aural communication, while literacy skills should be gradually introduced after selection and grading in Levels 2 and 3. Teachers are expected to draw learning from real life activities while at the same time employing classroom activities that cater for the cognitive, affective and psychomotor domains of learning.

The policy for course books provides for a maximum of three course books on the official list, but each school selects one course book series to cover all levels. These books may either be published by local or foreign publishers but they must reflect the socio-cultural and religious diversity of Cameroon. The major organizing pattern of course books that have been on the programme so far has been topic-based. What is more, there is a remarkable effort by authors to fulfil government policy to 'train citizens who are firmly rooted in their cultures, but open to the world', by focusing on characters and topics that are not only familiar to learners, but also project the cultures of anglophone Cameroonians.

Communicative objectives	Sample structural focus
Describing or talking about a journey	She caught a bus in the morning.
Talking about one's obligations	We must sweep the classroom.
Asking someone to do something politely	Could you open the window please?
Talking about habitual actions	She plays the guitar everyday.
Talking about one's present actions	He is singing.
Finding out what is wrong with someone	What is the matter with you?
Stating what is wrong with oneself	I have a backache.
Comparing people	He is as fat as/fatter than his friend.
Comparing things	A cow is bigger than a dog.
Predicting outcomes	What will happen if …/next?
Expressing regret	I wish I listened to my parents.
Talking about the past	Jane went to Kumba last night.
Counting things	Up to 100,000 (Maths syllabus).

Table 2

Matters arising

The challenges so far have been that of teacher training for Primary school teachers whose language competency is not only very low, but who are faced with many hours of work in sometimes overcrowded classes. In spite of the appointment of national and provincial pedagogic advisers and the important role of the Cameroon English Language and Literature Teachers' Association in promoting INSET, there are still enormous difficulties emanating from low budgetary allocations for the promotion of bilingualism; the over-politicization of bilingualism at the expense of linguistic considerations; and the absence of a well-defined position on government policy and planning at the broader level.

A crucial challenge has been that of teacher training for Primary school teachers. Since the publication of order No. 21/E/59 of 15th May 1996 organizing the teacher Grade 1 certificate examination (Ministry of National Education, 1996), Primary school teachers have found themselves being asked to teach the second official language irrespective of their mastery of the language. Although it cannot be denied that individual teachers have in isolated cases done an impressive job, the fact remains that basic training of the vast majority of teachers is a national necessity. This is because the conditions for the success of bilingualism are predicated on irrefutable linguistic and educational facts (Hoffmann, 1991). One of these is that language teachers must possess a good grasp of the language they are called upon to teach. Yet in Cameroon, francophone teachers with little or no mastery of English are required to teach all subjects in the curriculum, including English language. The argument for this is that English is part of the curriculum for pre-service training. Yet, there is still no syllabus for English in francophone training colleges; hence each ELT teacher trainer conceives a syllabus relevant to their immediate realities – a situation that cannot be cohesive across the country.

In 2005, the Cameroon English Language and Literature Teachers' Association (CAMELTA) decided to get involved in in-service training for Primary school teachers as a way of bridging the gap that existed between Primary and Secondary ELT. With over 500 of its total 2,500 members coming from Primary schools, CAMELTA has been able to run workshops at national and provincial levels on ELT issues in Primary schools. However, these workshops focus on pedagogy and practice and do not address the fundamental linguistic difficulty of francophone Primary school teachers. The need to provide remedial English language classes to these teachers is therefore imperative if we are to make bilingualism a reality in our Primary school system.

The difficulties raised above do not, however, undermine the prevailing upbeat attitude of both parents and pupils towards anglophones and anglophone cultures. Indeed, there has been a shift in perceptions, at least among schoolchildren and their parents, about what the terms 'anglophone' and 'francophone' refer to. In the past, the term 'anglophone' in Cameroon, for example, had very little to do with knowledge of the English language: an anglophone would be someone coming from the territory of former Southern Cameroons whether or not he/she knew a word of English (Simo-Bobda, 2001). Although this perception is far from being overturned, more and more francophone parents are sending their children to anglophone or immersion bilingual schools and as such are beginning to refer to their own children in such schools as 'anglophones'.

Conclusion

As yet there is no empirical research to prove that early bilingualism has been beneficial to the language development of learners at the Secondary level and beyond. Secondary school teachers agree that young francophone learners come to Secondary school with a better knowledge of English but the truth remains that, at the end of Secondary school, the results have not been better than they were prior to the implementation of early bilingualism. However, it can be argued that at the socio-affective and sociocultural levels, learners and parents are getting more and more tolerant of speakers and cultures of the other official language.

The Cameroonian situation confirms the view that language, culture and politics can work together, and therefore that language policies are, in a sense, political policies. A knowledge of this link is important in determining how much political commitment and action a political system adds to its will. Political commitment, to my mind, means providing the material, financial and institutional framework for implementing, monitoring and evaluating education-related decisions and accepting that teacher associations are important partners, not only in implementing policy but also in defining them.

References

Ayafor, I.M. (2005). Official Bilingualism in Cameroon: Instrumental or Integrative Policy? In Cohen, J., McAlister, K.T., Rolstad, K. and MacSwan, J. (eds) Proceedings of the Fourth International Symposium on Bilingualism. Somerville, MA: Cascadilla Press.

Hoffmann, C. (1991). An Introduction to Bilingualism. London: Longman.

Ministry of National Education (1996). Order No 21/E/59 of 15 May 1996 to organise the Teacher Grade One Certificate Examination.

Ministry of National Education (1998). Law No98/004 of 14 April 1998 to Lay Down Guidelines for Education in Cameroon.

Secretariat General of the Presidency of the Republic (1996). Constitution of the Republic of Cameroon. Yaounde: National Printing Press.

Simo-Bobda, A. (trans) (2001). Varying perceptions of English in Cameroon: A diachronic and synchronic analysis [Internet-Zeitschrift für Kulturwissenschaften] 11. Available at http://www.inst.at/trans/11Nr/bobda11.htm (Accessed 12 February 2008).

Primary English Language Teaching (ELT) in Korea: Bold risks on the national foundation

Won Key Lee, Seoul National University of Education, Korea

Introduction

For many reasons, English education is a major issue in Korean society, hotly contested throughout the whole society. In this paper, I will try to give you some of the background to this debate, as well as the current state of affairs and the future direction of Primary ELT in Korea.

A brief overview of Primary ELT in Korea

Background

In the early 1980s, there was an 'early education movement' that was encouraged by the Ministry of Education (henceforth MOE) as a future-oriented educational policy. The spotlight fell on early English education as one possible early education subject.

In academic circles, a variety of assumptions and hypotheses about early (foreign language) education were discussed and debated, including 'the earlier the better' theory, the 'critical period' hypothesis, the Language Acquisition Device (LAD) hypothesis, and so on. On the basis of these assumptions and hypotheses, which more recent research has rigorously challenged, many people argued that English should start to be taught in the Primary schools.

However, the decisive step was taken in the political sphere. Prior to the late 1980s, Korea was almost a closed society, often branded as the 'Hermit Kingdom'. But in 1986 and 1988, two major international athletic events were held in Korea: The Asian Games in 1986 and the Olympic Games in 1988. After these two international games, Korean society naturally started to open up to the world.

There was also enormous international pressure to open up Korean society. When the General Agreement on Tariffs and Trade (GATT) system was reorganized as the World Trade Organization (WTO) in 1995, fierce international competition was clearly foreseen. This new competition was perceived as a life-or-death threat by the Korean people and the Korean government. To survive this unprecedented threat, the government decided to implement a so-called globalization policy. It was naturally assumed that English would be used as a means of communication in a globalized society.

In terms of natural resources, Korea is deficient; consequently the idea of human resources had a real appeal. Human resource development became the essential strategy for the nation's survival and prosperity. As part of the human resource development policy, it was decided that English should be taught in Primary schools from 1997. This was decided by the president and the government of the time; it was a political decision, not a pedagogical one. In Korean society, as in other societies, politics is everywhere, and big decisions are usually political decisions. This may seem undesirable, but it is inevitable, because if this kind of big policy was approached pedagogically, things might never happen at all.

There were some preparations for the policy to be implemented, but they weren't sufficient. Because preparations were insufficient, the decision to introduce ELT in Primary schools was not greatly welcomed by academics and educationists at that time. There were a number of rationales for the decision. The first rationale was to give every child in Korea an equal opportunity to learn English, whether that child came from an urban area or a rural one, a rich family or a poor one. The second rationale was to improve the Grammar-Translation-based conventional teaching methods of English in Secondary schools, which had turned out to be largely ineffective. The third rationale was to secure the competitiveness of the country in the modern globalized world, and this was probably most important from the point of view of the political decision-makers.

National curriculum and textbook

Korea has a national curriculum for school education. It has acted as a powerful driving force for education as well as acting as a barrier in some aspects of education, such as textbook writing. Primary English textbooks are generally CD-ROM based. The CD-ROM contains most of the textbook contents; dialog, song, chant, game, play, role-play, task, with English native speaker pronunciation. This CD-ROM is meant to work as a teaching aid as well as a teacher-training aid. Even the teachers whose professional training is not sufficient can just play the CD-ROM, and have students follow the CD-ROM. In the meantime, teachers can also learn how to teach English effectively. Recent relevant or supplementary materials developed by highly experienced teachers are being provided to schools and homes directly through the Internet.

Features of the Primary English curriculum

The current national curriculum of Primary English (Ministry of Education, 2000) is distinct from previous ones in that the following three features are strongly emphasized when implementing the curriculum.

The primacy of spoken English

At the beginning stage of Primary ELT, teaching written English was deliberately prohibited, in order to weaken the grammar/translation method that was evaluated as unproductive and ineffective in improving students' spoken English proficiency. The idea was that if teaching written English was officially prohibited from Primary ELT in the beginning stage, teachers could not help teaching spoken English, resulting in students' spoken English improvement. It was also clearly foreseen that without drastic action, the chronic diseases of Korean ELT would never be cured. Those frequently mentioned three chronic diseases were;

- students studying English for examinations and nothing else;

- students studying English by memorizing rules and words, i.e., by rote learning;

- students studying English mainly by reading without speaking (so-called 'Dumb English').

In the current Primary curriculum, the ratio of spoken English to written English is approximately 8 to 2. The policy of establishing the primacy of spoken English has, according to some evaluations, made a very positive change in wide areas of ELT.

Learner-centeredness

Korean students are known to be rather passive, and highly teacher-dependent. They usually want to be spoon-fed and are very used to teacher-centered classrooms as a result. So it is necessary to encourage passive students to take responsibility for their own learning by having them involved in the learning process. So the current curriculum focuses on learner-centered teaching; the best way of teaching is the way students learn best, not the way teachers teach best.

One way in which the national curriculum attempts to inculcate learners with the desire to learn is by explicitly stating a two-pronged aim; in addition to equipping learners with a basic minimum of communicative ability in English, the curriculum stresses that children should be made to feel comfortable with English and that they should discover that English is both easy and fun. As a result, every lesson contains at least two or three 'Let's Play' activities, as well as a song or a chant. Let's Play activities include a variety of task-based activities and games.

Level-based teaching

The average elementary school class size in Korea is about 35 students. So individual differences between students exist inevitably. In spite of many practical difficulties and constraints, the current curriculum pursues level-based teaching to achieve maximum learning. A suggested method of level-based teaching is to form, for instance, ten small groups of three or four (e.g., two low-achievement groups, four mid-achievement groups, and two high-achievement groups), and have each small group perform three different level tasks each during the same period.

At present, there are no clear guidelines for implementing 'level-based teaching' in the national textbook itself, and providing supplementary materials for 'advanced' and 'basic' level learners is largely left to the discretion of the teacher. In the new, revised curriculum, it is very likely that this will be changed.

Some positive and negative effects (since 1997)

The implementation of Primary ELT in Korea has been evaluated as having the following positive and negative effects (Lee, 2007). Turning first to the positive effects, Primary ELT has raised people's awareness that:

- English plays a very important role in modern society.

- Early learning of English is very necessary and beneficial.

- Korea needs to have more globalized perspectives.

- People need to become more open-minded, appreciating other people and other cultures that are different from their own.

We can probably say with some confidence that:

- On average, students' English has improved as they get more opportunities to be exposed to English.

- Children have come to accept learning English as an everyday task, and a life-long endeavor.

On the other hand, there have also been some serious negative effects incurred.

The first negative effect has been the overheating of the private sector education business. High private tuition fees have become a threat to people's living expenses, and this in turn has become a politically sensitive issue.

The second negative effect has been that the English divide between the haves and have-nots, and urban and rural areas, greatly increased. This is a social as well as a political problem. The government worries about this English divide because it has the potential to cause social unrest and threaten national integrity.

The third negative effect has been that the exodus of young children studying English overseas away from their families has increased dramatically in recent years. This has created the phenomena of 'wild goose daddies' in Korea. A 'wild goose daddy' is a father who stays behind in Korea working hard to support a wife and children who are living abroad.

The fourth negative effect has been that there is pressure for ever-earlier starts. At the moment, in many kindergartens English is taught, and even some toddlers are learning English. Recently prenatal English education, which has a very doubtful scientific basis, has become big business. Learning English is necessary and important, but these phenomena seem to indicate a lack of balance, too early can be as bad as too late.

Some of the government's policies and projects

The government has made a variety of efforts to maximize the positive effects and neutralize or minimize the negative effects.

Two national research projects

Two national research projects are being carried out in order to find out the best way of expanding Primary English teaching hours in Primary school.

- The first one concerns a proposal to lower the starting year from the current Primary Year 3 to Primary Year 1.

- The second project concerns a proposal to increase the current teaching hours from one class hour (i.e., 40 minutes) per week to 2–3 class hours for the 3rd and 4th graders, and from two class hours per week to 3–4 class hours for the 5th and 6th graders.

As of early 2008, Korean people's general feelings about lowering the starting year seem quite negative.

English villages/camps

Building and running English villages was a 'pork-barrel' (politically motivated) educational project on the part of certain local government authorities. It is basically a 1–2 week English experience programme. Groups of students reside for one or two weeks in the English villages and are encouraged to use English during their stay. Since there is little or no educational follow up after learners move out of the English village, criticism of this type of project focuses on its high-cost, low-outcome, one-shot business model.

It is hoped that the Korean government will heed at least some of the harsher points of criticism made, either by winding up the more wasteful English villages or else by providing educational follow-up to English village visits.

The English-only city on Jejudo island

In order to minimize the English divide and to curb the overheating of the private sector in English education, as well as to decrease the number of young children going overseas to study English in the early years English, the government has decided to construct an English-only city (of about 1,200 km^2) on Jejudo Island, tens of miles away from the southern-most part of the Korean peninsula. The city is planned to accommodate 15 Primary, middle and high schools (9,000 students per year), in which all the subjects are taught in English, and students are required to use English outside their schools.

EPIK program

EPIK stands for English Program in Korea. This is a national project by which hundreds of English native speakers are invited to local Primary, middle and high schools as full-time teachers. In 2007, it was intended that 500 English native speaking teachers should be invited, but it was not possible to employ enough that were sufficiently qualified. Through this experience, people realized that teachers cannot be made overnight.

The Teaching English through English campaign

The government strongly recommends that Korean English teachers use English as the medium of instruction for at least half of their teaching hours. This campaign has borne some fruit and many teachers of English make it a rule to use English when they teach English, unlike in the past. The ratio of the use of English in the classroom as against L1 is increasing as teacher training develops.

After-school English programmes

Currently the after-school English programme is a really hot issue. This programme is about teaching students English after they finish everyday curricular activities. The government is putting an enormous amount of budget resources into this project, in order to lessen the English divide between the haves and have-nots, and to reduce private sector education expenses.

English educational broadcasting

Following government instruction, the national Educational Broadcasting System has transmitted a special series of English teaching programs, launched in April 2007. The programs are also available through the Internet to home and school classrooms.

Some recommendations for future development

An unchangeable axiom in education is that 'teachers are key players in education'. In Korea, the statement that 'the quality of education cannot exceed that of teachers' is often heard, and widely accepted. This means that the success or failure of education is essentially determined by the quality of the teachers. Therefore more and intensified teacher training is necessary, focusing on two aspects of teacher training:

- making teachers sufficiently proficient in English; and
- training them in teaching methodology.

More and intensified teacher training

The government has made efforts to employ increasing numbers of native-speaking English teachers every year, but there are serious doubts about the role of native-speaking English teachers in school settings.

Recently there has been a new awakening in Korean ELT circles. Korean teachers ask: 'Until when can we rely on the native-speaking English teachers for English Language Teaching? We can't rely on them forever. Korean teachers should take charge of it.'

This means that more intensive domestic teacher training is needed. Now the Ministry of Education and most of the 16 local education authorities are making greater efforts to increase and expand direct teacher training.

Support from outside is also available; for example, the British Council in Korea is making a solid contribution in cooperation with Seoul Metropolitan Education Authority and Seoul National University Education, pursuing and experimenting with a cascade model of teacher training.

On top of the domestic teacher training, many more opportunities for overseas teacher training by native English teacher trainers in all aspects of teacher training are given. Here cascading can also be applied.

More and effective materials and resources

Teachers want to concentrate on teaching. To do this, they require;

- expertly made teaching materials and resources;

- more intensive training in language improvement and methodology;

- models of teaching and assessment.

These teacher needs should be met as quickly as possible.

Conclusion

South Korea is a small country, but it has consistently 'punched above its weight' in industrial development, information technology, shipbuilding, bio-engineering and many other sectors. Perhaps our proudest achievements come in Primary school teaching, where, at least according to the Project for International Student Assessment, South Korea is the only major country consistently in the top three in the central subjects of reading, maths, science and problem-solving.

English has always been our Achilles heel, a serious weakness. However, Primary English Language Teaching has, overall, been surprisingly successful, particularly given the poorly prepared way in which it was introduced just ten years ago. For this we can thank an all round generally good educational infrastructure.

However, we have paid a price: the past ten years have seen a severe English divide that mirrors the national divide between rich and poor and between rural and urban areas; a bloated, over-heated 'bubble' in private education at the national level; wasteful 'pork-barreling' projects in English education at the local level; and, perhaps most tragically, broken families in which the father works in Korea to support a wife and children studying English abroad.

The most worrying aspect of these negative factors is that they threaten the very basis of our success; the support of Korean people for their public education system. In order to ensure that English education not only persists but prevails, we need to make sure that in the future such bold experiments are built, as this one was, on a solid, public, national foundation.

References

Lee, W.K. (2007). *Primary ELT in Korea* (4th edition). Seoul: Moonjin Media.

Ministry of Education (2000). *Curriculum*. Seoul.

'When I wanna be cool ...': English for young learners in Iceland

Samúel Lefever, Iceland University of Education, Reykjavík, Iceland

Introduction

This case study looks at the current situation regarding Primary English Language Teaching (ELT) in Iceland. Iceland is a small country with a population of roughly 300,000. Most of the populace lives in the capital and the rest are spread around the coastline in rural areas and small villages. The native language is Icelandic, an old Germanic language which has changed little over the centuries. Considerable emphasis is placed on foreign language learning at both Primary and Secondary school levels and there is extensive exposure to foreign languages through the media, and in particular, English.

The information presented here is drawn from a number of recent research studies in Iceland which have looked at English programmes at the compulsory school level; teachers' and pupils' attitudes towards English teaching and learning; and the English skills of young learners before formal instruction begins.

The National Curriculum for foreign language teaching at compulsory level was revised in 2005 and reflects the growing interest in English learning in the country. The main emphases are on communicative language teaching and instilling an interest in learning English. English instruction currently begins at Grade 4 (age 9) but schools have the option of introducing the language in younger grades, which is the case in 30 per cent of Primary schools in the country.

A comprehensive evaluation of ELT at the compulsory school level was commissioned by the Ministry of Education and was carried out in 2005-06. Eight schools representing a cross-section of school sizes and rural and urban areas in the country participated in the evaluation. Data was obtained from a number of sources such as school curricula and syllabi, school assessments, teacher and pupil questionnaires, interviews with teachers and classroom observations.

A written questionnaire was given to pupils in Grades 5, 9 and 10 (aged 10–16 years old) and their English teachers. The questionnaires surveyed the pupils' and teachers' attitudes towards the teaching and learning methods and materials used in English instruction. Pupils were also asked to comment on their use of English outside school. Approximately 800 pupils and 23 teachers participated in the survey.

The vast majority of the teachers were certified to teach at the Primary and lower Secondary level but only about one third of the teachers had taken English as their main subject at university (Lefever, 2006). Similar results were found in a nationwide survey of the educational backgrounds of language teachers, conducted by the Ministry of Education in 2006. In that survey, less than half (46 per cent) of the teachers who taught English in Grades 8–10 in 2005 had some form of special training in English. Of those teachers who taught English in Grades 5–7 that year, even fewer (29 per cent) had any special training in English (Ministry of Education, 2006).

The findings of the evaluation showed that both pupils and teachers have very positive attitudes towards English. Almost all of the pupils (97 per cent) felt that it was 'very' or 'quite' important to know English (Lefever, 2006). Over 90 per cent of the pupils stated that English was important to be able to communicate when abroad. A large majority also said it was useful to understand English movies, TV programmes and music, and to read English books and magazines. Most pupils felt that knowing English was important for future study and work. Many pupils stated that English was important for using the Internet. More boys said English was useful for playing computer games – twice as many as girls (see Figure 1).

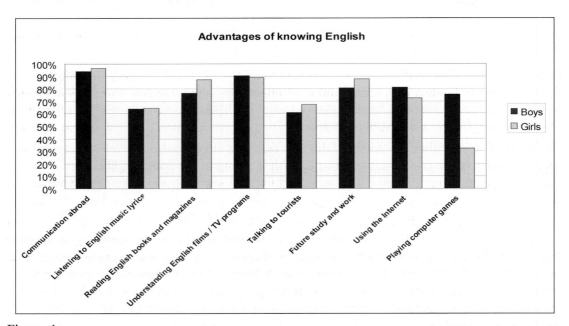

Figure 1

Most pupils said they liked learning English. Younger learners were more positive than older learners, as can be seen in Figure 2. This poses the question of whether the tendency of teenagers to be more negative towards school in general could be the cause of this decline in interest or whether instruction in the older grades is no longer as appealing or motivating as in the earlier grades.

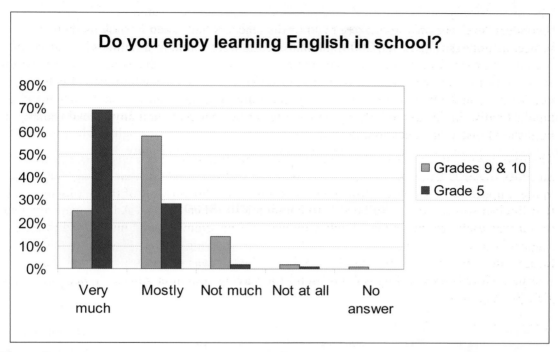

Figure 2

One of the objectives of the questionnaire was to gather information about teaching methods used in English instruction and their effect on pupils' learning. Pupils were given a list of teaching methods and approaches and were asked to rate how much they learned English through their use. The teachers were given a similar list and were asked to rate how much they emphasized the methods in their English teaching.

The teachers' and pupils' responses drew attention to some discrepancies between communicative teaching methods recommended by the National Curriculum and those used in English instruction. Teachers tended to emphasize teaching methods that focused on listening and reading in English, grammar exercises, workbook use, and writing tasks. They put less emphasis on teaching methods that are considered effective in activating students in creative and/or authentic language use, such as speaking activities, using English songs and videos, games, theme work, and computer use. It is interesting to note that pupils tended to rank traditional grammar-translation methods highly. However, teachers said that they did *not* emphasize these methods in their teaching – with the exception of translating from Icelandic into English.

A limitation of the method of questioning may have affected the accuracy of the pupil responses. It was difficult to know whether pupils' answers were a reflection of how often the methods were used in the course of instruction rather than of how helpful they had been in learning English. It is also possible that pupils valued teaching activities that are linked to tests and grades more highly. Additionally, pupils may not have been familiar with all of the methods and thus probably would not be able to rate their helpfulness.

The National Curriculum for English emphasizes the use of English as much as possible during instruction. The teachers and pupils who undertook the questionnaire were asked to estimate the amount of English used by both the teachers and pupils during English lessons. According to their responses, less than half of the pupils in Grades 9 and 10 (44 per cent) reported that their teachers used English 'always' or 'often' during lessons. A fifth of the pupils (21 per cent) said that pupils 'always' or 'often' used English when answering the teacher and only 5 per cent said that pupils 'always' or 'often' used English when talking to one another during lessons. The pupils' responses can be seen in Figure 3.

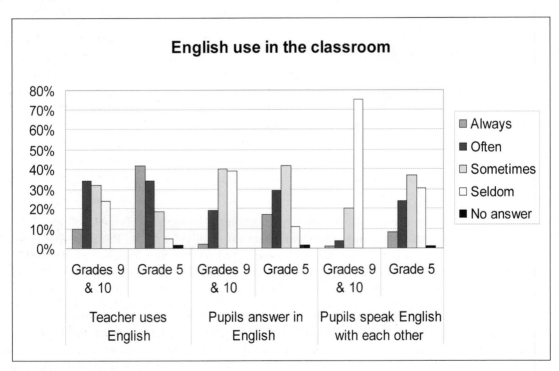

Figure 3

These results seem to indicate that English is not widely used by teachers and even less by pupils during lessons. That said, the situation does seem to be better at Grade 5, at which a greater percentage of pupils reported a greater degree of English use by the teachers and the pupils. Three-quarters of the pupils in Grade 5 (75 per cent) reported that their teachers used English 'always' or 'often' during lessons. Less than half (46 per cent) said that pupils 'always' or 'often' used English when answering the teacher and 32 per cent said that pupils 'always' or 'often' used English when talking to one another during lessons. But once again, it is difficult to know how the pupils interpreted the question. It could be that pupils chose the 'always' possibility if the teacher used *some* English in every lesson rather than *solely* English during the entire lesson.

Pupils were also asked about their use of English outside the classroom. Their responses showed that they have opportunities in several different contexts for authentic use of English outside school. They use English for entertainment and leisure (movies, television, music, books and magazines, and computer games) and for obtaining information (from print media and the Internet).

This evaluation of English teaching at the compulsory level clearly indicates high regard for the English language among young people. It is a status symbol to be able to speak English, as can be seen by the following comment by a boy in Grade 9: 'When I wanna be cool, I speak English.' Children also commented on how exposure to English media is helping them to learn English, for example: 'My English is so good because I watch so many movies – I know some of them by heart' and 'I'm smart, thanks to modern-day TV.'

In recent years, there has been a growing interest in offering English instruction to children at ever-younger ages. This is partly due to the general belief that the younger children begin to learn a new language, the better. Although research does not support this belief (Pinter, 2006), the findings of the programme evaluation indicate that young children in Iceland are generally motivated to learn English and are quick to see the advantages of knowing English in their daily lives (Lefever, 2006). Many of them are learning English on their own, outside the classroom. Parents want their children to learn languages to increase their opportunities for future study and jobs. Both parents and teachers want to cash in on this interest and early learning ability by giving children the opportunity to learn English in school from the very beginning.

With the adoption of the newly revised National Curriculum for foreign languages at Primary level in 2007, the starting age for English instruction in Iceland was lowered from Grade 5 to Grade 4 and guidelines for introducing English in Grades 1–3 were included in the curriculum. The main objectives for English teaching in the youngest grades are to instill a positive interest in learning English, to engage children in active learning and to increase their self-confidence and awareness of English in their environment.

A study done in the spring of 2007 showed that the number of schools in Iceland that begin to teach English before the required grade level has increased from 10 per cent in 2002 to 30 per cent in 2007 (Lefever, 2007). The amount of teaching offered per week was generally from 1/2–1 lesson a week in Grades 1 and 2 and two lessons a week in Grades 3 and 4. In a few schools, the instruction was broken down into shorter lessons, for example, 15-minute lessons two or three times a week.

The teachers who participated in the survey were asked to describe their English teaching. Over 60 per cent of the teachers said they used conventional whole-group instruction for teaching English. Some teachers used other approaches such as rotating centres or stations, theme teaching, or integrating English with other subjects. Most teachers said they focused primarily on spoken English and the use of songs and games. Others placed emphasis on vocabulary and listening to English.

There were no locally produced teaching materials for teaching English in these grades so teachers collected learning materials from a variety of sources, such as the Internet, course books used in other countries, teacher resourse books and children's books in English. Many teachers produced their own worksheets and exercises.

Teachers were also asked to describe how they assessed children's English learning. The majority did not use formal assessment; instead they reported using ongoing assessment or portfolios. Many of them based their assessment on the children's participation and their work over the course of the winter. A few teachers said they used written tests, often end-of-term tests, to assess children's learning.

Using English in the classroom was clearly a challenge for many teachers, especially those who had not been specially trained as English teachers. Although many teachers recognized the importance of speaking English in the classroom, more than half said they used English less than 40 per cent of the time during lessons.

The results of this study showed that in most cases, English instruction in the youngest grades is in the hands of the homeroom (class) teacher. There are certain advantages with this arrangement; the teacher knows the pupils well and is likely to have more flexibility in fitting English into the daily teaching and integrating it with other subjects. However, almost two-thirds of the teachers who were surveyed had received no special training in teaching English. Only a few of the teachers had received training in teaching English to young learners in the form of in-service workshops.

As mentioned earlier, many children in Iceland are learning English on their own, informally, outside the classroom. In a study carried out in 2005, children from Grades 4 and 5 in eight schools around the country, who had received very little or no prior instruction in English, were tested on their English comprehension and communication skills (Torfadóttir, Ragnarsdóttir and Lefever, 2006). The children were asked to complete a set of English listening tasks based on an international test of English for young learners and intended for use after 100–175 hours of formal instruction. The outcome was surprisingly high – an average of over 70 per cent correct answers. There was no significant difference between genders or ages or location of the schools. The results suggest that most children have acquired basic English skills by the age of 9 without any formal English teaching. This is likely to be at least partly due to their significant exposure to English in their daily environment, for example through media sources.

In addition, a small-scale study was conducted to determine the children's ability to take part in basic conversations in English. Twenty children from the larger study volunteered to meet individually with the researcher and speak with him in English. Although the participants were not a representative sample, the study gave insight into the communicative abilities of Icelandic children in this age group. Pictures of familiar scenes were used to elicit speech from the children and they were also asked to talk about familiar topics such as family, hobbies and pets. The findings showed that most participants could successfully engage in simple conversation and that language mistakes did not impede comprehension or communication. Some participants showed high levels of communicative competence in English, responding without hesitation and appropriately.

The following are examples of the children's spoken responses when asked to describe what was happening in a series of pictures. The meaning is clear despite some language mistakes.

> *Boy in grade 4:* Ehh, the monkey takes his hat and put it on his head. He is crying and his mother takes up banana and give the monkey and the monkey give his mother the hat again.

> *Girl in grade 5:* Uh, huh. And then one of the monkey gets angry and takes his cap and then Ben starts to cry and his mother gives the monkey banana and get the cap back and then Ben is happy.

The next example shows how the child expanded upon the topic and used advanced grammar:

> *Researcher:* Do you have a pet?

> *Boy in Grade 5:* Yeah, I have three cats and four kittens. Once I had two frogs and one fish but one of the frogs, uhh, jumped in the . . ., in the water and smashed up but the other one just died.

Conclusions

Based on the research studies reported here it can be said that the conditions for learning English in Iceland are very favourable. Children are highly motivated to learn English and have plentiful access to English in their daily environment. Parents, teachers and school policy-makers are also positive about providing children with an early start in learning English. However, the current situation in Iceland has some serious weaknesses. In many schools there is a discrepancy between communicative teaching methods recommended by the National Curriculum and those used in English instruction. More focus is needed on spoken communication, using English during lessons, and using teaching methods that 'activate' the learners and give them greater opportunity to use English for fun and creative use.

Another weakness is the teachers' lack of training. Most teachers do not have training in teaching English, particularly in teaching English to young learners, and they do not feel confident in using English in the classroom, despite recognizing the importance of doing so.

There seems to be a serious lack of understanding on the part of school policy-makers in regard to the special needs of young learners and English teaching. This is at odds with the growing demand for more and earlier English instruction in the schools. More emphasis needs to be placed on preparing teachers and schools for these important changes. Teachers need to be provided with opportunities for in-service training and for improving their

English skills. They also need to be given the time to prepare the teaching and choose appropriate materials and approaches. Schools need to be more flexible in terms of timetabling and integrating English learning with other subjects. In short, more attention needs to be given to programme development. If children are to reap the benefits of receiving an early start in English and to continue to progress throughout their school careers, schools in Iceland must foster and support ELT to a greater degree than is currently the case.

References

Lefever, S. (2006). English Language Teaching in Icelandic compulsory schools. *Málfríður* 22 (2), 9-12.

Lefever, S. (2007). Putting the cart before the horse – English instruction in grades 1–4. *Málfríður* 23 (2), 24-8.

Ministry of Education (2006). Menntun dönsku-, ensku-, og íslenskukennara í grunnskólum 2005-2006 [Educational backgrounds of Danish, English and Icelandic teachers at the compulsory level 2005-2006].

Pinter, A. (2006). *Teaching Young Language Learners*. Oxford: Oxford University Press.

Torfadóttir, A., Ragnarsdóttir, B. and Lefever, S. (2006). Enskukunnátta barna í 4. og 5. bekk grunnskólans – Hvað kunna þau? [English skills of children in Grades 4 and 5]. Reykjavík: Iceland University of Education Research Institute.

Issues in the implementation of Teaching English for Young Learners (TEYL): A case study of two states of India

Rama Mathew, Department of Education, Delhi University, Delhi

Susmita Pani, English Language Teaching Institute, Bhubaneswar, India

Background

English has been part of India's education system for more than a century. Because of its more recent growth as a global language, English proficiency has become an even greater asset as it not only encourages upward social mobility at home but also opens the door to numerous opportunities abroad. Although English-medium education addresses this need to a large extent, the majority of students in government schools that have vernacular languages as their medium of instruction suffer from poorer access, since until recently, they studied English as a subject only from Class V or VI depending on the state they were in. Thus the gap between those who could afford good English-medium education and those who could not has been wide. The National Knowledge Commission's report (Pitroda, 2006: 1) explicitly recognised this when it said that although 'English has been part of our education system for more than a century … [it] is beyond the reach of most of our young people, which makes for highly unequal access'. More recently, agencies, including those of state and central governments, have responded to this unprecedented demand for English by introducing it in the early classes. The National Curriculum Framework (NCF) (2005) designed a new English curriculum for Class I onwards for schools at the national level, while state governments introduced English as a subject from very early classes in regional-medium schools (i.e., from Class I in many states) according to their own curriculum requirements. Although it seems that the issue of equal access has now been addressed in policy, the question of its effective implementation (i.e., whether English is being taught properly and by qualified and competent teachers in government schools in different states) has not been examined so far.

This paper examines if and to what extent the objectives of TEYL and equal access are achieved in reality. Specifically it looks at the following aspects:

- teachers' profiles: their qualifications, language competence and professional competence; their attitude to English and to English Language Teaching;

- the kind of textbooks and other materials used for teaching English;

- classroom processes/learning experiences that students are exposed to; and

- learners' language proficiency.

The paper presents data on these factors from selected government schools in two states: Orissa and Delhi. Interviews with teachers, classroom observations, informal and tests for assessing the language proficiency of students were used to gather data, rather than simply the analysis of textbooks. This article presents a summary of the findings from these sources and analyzes the main constraints that hinder the achievement of the aims of the TEYL programme.

The TEYL scene in Orissa

This study was carried out in Orissa – a state in the Eastern part of India where English is introduced in Class III in the regional-medium schools. A new book *My English Book* is in use, which was prepared keeping the NCF 2005 in mind. This study examined 29 rural, semi-urban and urban schools. Data were collected by administering a questionnaire to 29 teachers at Class III and observing classes followed by interviews.

Teacher profile

The typical teacher interviewed for this study was a graduate with a Certificate in Teaching and up to five years teaching experience. Teachers showed varying degrees of proficiency in English; some of the teachers held the entire interview discussion in English (20 per cent), some got others to fill in their questionnaires (50 per cent); others wrote the questionnaire using low-level English (30 per cent). Their classroom use of English was generally restricted to simple instructions, using words and sentences from the textbook. The teachers themselves seemed to be aware of this problem and expressed a desire to improve their English, especially their pronunciation. Some even went as far as saying that they were the reason for learners' failure to learn English.

Most of the teachers themselves favoured an early introduction of English for some of the following reasons:

- 'helps learn with almost no pressure';

- 'proficiency will be better';

- 'will not be afraid of English';

- 'if children from English-medium schools can learn, why not our children?'.

Some teachers even went as far as introducing English a year earlier, reasoning that it would help learners cope with English better in Class III. However, there were still a few who perceived that the lack of competence on the part of teachers as well as learners was a stumbling block to the degree to which language policy could be implemented.

Textbook

The new book introduced in Class III, *My English Book*, is published by the Government of Orissa. The introduction to the book specifies that its purpose is to develop the language skills of the learners through rhymes, stories and colourful pictures. The book starts with familiar words like: 'bat', 'ice cream', 'jug', 'fan', etc. There is opportunity to practise the different language skills and the book is well graded. Some methodology is built into this book through the instructions which, as seen in classroom observation, are strictly followed by around 50 per cent of teachers. Teachers' reactions to the book have been both positive and negative, but positive responses outweigh the negative.

The lack of availability of books at the early, entry stage (i.e., Class III) proved to be a major problem in carrying out this study. In one block, out of 33 schools, ten had not got the new books and five schools had less than five books per class. In some schools, even in urban areas, English was still being taught from Class II using material from the old book and learners did not have access to textbooks.

Classroom processes

What learners did: The following are some of the things that the learners did in the classes observed:

- They copied from the blackboard, wrote new words on the blackboard, as well as answers to questions.

- They read words from the book, or flashcards, or off a blackboard.

- They listened and did Total Physical Response (TPR) activities.

- They listened to questions and responded with simple sentences of 'This is . . .' construction.

- They gave the meanings of words in the mother tongue.

- They listened and repeated rhymes, individual words, and sentences.

Use of the textbook: The majority of the teachers taught exactly according to the textbook. Some of them went beyond the textbook, adding their own examples; new steps for a given activity; asking learners to tell a given story in the mother tongue as well as by using flashcards.

Use of mother tongue: The mother tongue was used for instruction and classroom management in all the classes. It was also used to explain the content of the book in 60 per cent of the classes. In less than 50 per cent of classes, teachers used the mother tongue to correct error.

Classroom interaction types: The bulk of the classroom interactions were of the T→SS type followed by S→SS. The second type of interaction took place when a designated student worked as a substitute teacher. Contrary to expectations, learners in more than half the classes had as much or greater opportunity to talk than the teacher, albeit in a very restricted way, often involving reading aloud or repeating sentences. Most of the language produced was imitative in nature. In some classes, even when learners repeated what the teacher said, the teacher repeated along with them.

Teacher's attitude to error: A variety of error correction techniques were recorded in the classes observed. During interviews some of the teachers said that immediate correction was always necessary, while others said that they took care in advance to avoid learners making mistakes. Some of the teachers felt that teacher correction should only be done after peer correction. This was also observed in actual classroom situations.

In general, teachers asked for training. They were eager to improve themselves – surprisingly, even those teachers near retirement. All the teachers asked for demonstration lessons and teachers' books. Interestingly, all the effectively taught classes had one thing in common: the positive, upbeat attitude and personality of the teacher.

The TEYL scene in Delhi

The study in Delhi, like the study in Orissa, was carried out in regional-medium schools where English is introduced in Class I and a new set of textbooks have been in use since 2003. The 18 schools covered in this study were both urban and semi-urban schools. Data were collected from 12 observed classes, questionnaires from 25 teachers and interviews with 15 teachers.

Teacher profile

Teachers' qualifications range from the two-year certificate course in teaching offered by the District Institute of Education and Training, to the four-year Bachelor's Degree in Elementary Education (BEIEd), and even the BEd for Secondary level. Quite a few teachers are pursuing part-time MEd qualification. However, none of these courses specifically equip teachers with ESL pedagogy at the Elementary (Primary) level.

Teachers feel that children should be taught English at the Primary level; in fact, many of them say that it should be introduced from the nursery classes. They are, in fact, not aware that introducing English from earlier classes requires that they provide children with a lot of exposure, which they cannot give, given their low competence in the language. Their language proficiency ranges from quite poor to very good. They do not have any opportunity to participate in inset programmes that focus on ESL pedagogy and express a strong desire to attend such programmes.

Textbooks

Teachers feel that the textbooks introduced in 2003, although better than the earlier books, contain long and difficult texts. Children often cannot understand these and the books do not help with pedagogy and activities that actively engage the learner. Teachers need to modify the exercises/tasks, which takes time and is something that not all teachers are equipped to do. As a result, they have to just 'teach' the textbook, which involves reading aloud, with a lot of translation and explanation. To quote a teacher:

> These books are better than previous books from the point of view of pictures and classroom activities. The book is full of knowledge, but the level is very high as the students' background knowledge of English is very poor.

Classroom processes

Teachers in the schools who participated in this study normally do not use English to teach English: they read out parts of a text that is to be taught from the prescribed Reader and explain it in Hindi. Texts are also read aloud by students whose pronunciation is perceived to be acceptable. Not all students have their textbooks with them when this activity takes place. Normal classroom conversation takes place mostly in Hindi, even when teachers are quite comfortable with English; it is not used in natural conversations since teachers believe that students will not understand it. Explanation in simple language, examples, easier words, and comparisons are all devices used in Hindi to get the text across to students. Students also expect their teachers to do this; good teaching is defined in terms of how well the teacher can explain the meaning of the text so that it becomes accessible to them. As regards writing, the teacher gives ready-made letters, short compositions, etc., that students copy and memorize for exam purposes. Use of English in the classroom is generally restricted to words and routine expressions such as 'keep quiet' or 'open your books'. Students also use standard expressions such as 'May I come in Ma'm', 'May I go to drink water?' A lot of repetitive and mechanical practice of grammatical structures and vocabulary was also observed, as the following excerpt from Class V illustrates:

T: Now I'll ask you about fruit. Which fruits do you like? *(T points at a student.)* Don't take too much time.

S: Orange. *(T looks at the next one.)*

S: Madam ji banana ji. *('ji' is a Hindi prefix or suffix added to show respect.)*

S: Madam ji strawberry ji.

T: Don't say like this: Madam ji banana *ji (imitates them)*. Say, 'I like …'

S: I like orange … *(This continues till the bell rings.)*

Most teachers reveal in actual practice a negative attitude about the ability of poor children to learn in general and to learn English in particular. The following is just an example:

> The teacher tells a story in Hindi with barely a few words in English which were wrongly pronounced, for example, 'thrusty' for thirsty, scribbles a word or two on the blackboard

which are not readable, draws some pictures which again are indecipherable. When he can't proceed, turns to me and says, *Maine bataya na inko kuch nahin ata hai? Inke dimag me to mitti bhari hai.* (I told you they don't know anything? They have mud in their head.) The Class VI children know the story and are not excited by it.

Students' language proficiency

A study conducted earlier by Kunnan and Mathew (2006) aimed to assess students' reading and writing abilities with unseen materials. It did this with the intention of moving away from achievement to proficiency testing for two grade levels (Class V and VIII). Achievement testing, especially in the Indian context, refers to testing the content of prescribed texts for English, which is therefore largely memory-based, while proficiency testing refers to testing of reading, writing, speaking and listening skills in unrehearsed contexts.

Twelve tasks were administered in six government schools in Delhi for which the sample size ranged from 60–220 for different tasks. It was found that:

- They could do very low-level scanning (i.e., they could pick out the sentence which had the same key words as the question).

- They related questions in the task to themselves or were unable to apply a set of given criteria or parameters available in the text to answer the question. For example, given the context 'Your school is organizing an inter-school competition in cricket for children in junior schools in Delhi…', the question, 'Suppose that your brother is studying in Class X, can he take part in the competition? Why?' led to answers such as: 'No, I'm in Class V' or 'No, he has Board exams, he has to study.'

- The idea of reading instructions and understanding what is required was alien to them. This, coupled with the unfamiliarity with the test format, does not allow proficiency assessment. Talking to students in simple English or Hindi in a reassuring manner, however, indicates that the tasks are not totally inaccessible to them. They can answer in Hindi, in single words, broken sentences (often a mixture of English and Hindi), or orally in English, which clearly shows that they can handle the tasks.

- They can attempt tasks that require them to take a position. Although they cannot demonstrate this through writing, they can talk about it in English in an interactive mode with a lot of support/scaffolding from the teacher; they can write with reasonable competence in Hindi.

Issues and concerns

This case study of two states points to the following issues and concerns:

- Textbooks have been introduced in a hurry; in fact, in Orissa, many are not even aware of the new resources, and in Delhi, even though the books are in use, their implications are not clear to the teachers.

- In Delhi, teachers with a BEIEd appear to be making the class activity-oriented, but BEd training does not equip them for this: neither qualification is oriented to teaching ESL, let alone to young learners.

- Teachers' attitudes to disadvantaged learners are negative and vitiates the situation further. Many think that without home support, students cannot learn a language, and that their language learning ability itself is poor.

- Teacher proficiency is low in both states. Therefore there is a strong need to help teachers develop proficiency and, in so doing, confidence.

- No ESL teacher-orientation programmes are available to teachers in Delhi. In Orissa, training programmes are being conducted but are limited in number, as mentioned earlier. There is very little ongoing support for teaching and the need for training in TEYL is strongly felt in both the study samples.

- Training programmes would have to focus on attitudinal change, proficiency and pedagogical principles, in that order.

References

Kunnan, A.J. and Mathew, R. (2006). English language exams reform project in India: From achievement to proficiency testing. Paper presented at the Language Testing Research Colloquium, Melbourne.

National Curriculum Framework (2005). New Delhi: National Council of Educational Research and Training.

Pitroda, S. (2006). Letter to PM. Recommendations of National Knowledge Commission on languages. India. Available at http://knowledgecommission.gov.in/downloads/recommendations/LanguageLetterPM.pdf Accessed on 24 January 2007.

The dream and the reality of early programmes in Hungary

Marianne Nikolov, University of Pécs, Hungary

Introduction

This chapter discusses how variety in early modern foreign language (MFL) programmes contributes to processes and outcomes in a specific educational context. The case study of Hungary demonstrates that a lack of curricular guidelines for lower Primary years has resulted in a wide range of practices and a strong streaming tradition in which most young learners are taught by retrained teachers from Russian. The chapter draws on empirical studies, large-scale quantitative and smaller-scale qualitative research to show controversial trends. The main point is that English cannot be discussed in isolation, but only in relation to other target languages.

The context

Foreign languages (FLs) in the lower Primary years have been part of official curricula for decades in Hungary. Until 1989, Russian used to be mandatory for all learners from Grade 4 (age 9) and languages of ethnic minorities, most importantly German, were also available. An early start was hoped to ensure success in learning Russian; however, the history of over 40 years of mainly ineffective Russian teaching has proved that an early start by itself will not guarantee proficiency. Since the political changes of 1989, two MFLs have competed with one another: German, traditionally the most valuable MFL in the region, and English, with the latter becoming increasingly widely taught and gaining a higher prestige over the course of the past decade (Nikolov, 2000). No MFL has been mandatory since 1989: students and their parents decide what language(s) they want to learn in the light of what schools offer.

Another important feature of the educational system is a strong tradition of streaming learners into classes and groups according to their abilities; more able students are taught in specialized classes where they are given more intensive as well as better quality education. Competition is also a characteristic of schools, as they receive government funding on a per capita basis. As English and German have been seen as important to ensure good opportunities in Secondary and Tertiary education and in the job market, schools try to attract more students by offering these languages. Over the years, the pattern of German *and* English has transformed into English *or* German, where some students are offered both, and others only one. This phenomenon is made more complex by the reality that English is the language most in demand; thus, not all children can gain access to it, as all teachers need to keep their jobs. As the figures in Table 1 show, the changes are dramatic; the ratio of English learners in 1989 was 4.5 per cent, whereas in 2007 it reached 64 per cent. The percentages for German and Russian have changed from 5.7 and 90 per cent to 35 and 0.2 per cent, respectively.

Year	English	German	Russian	Total
1989/1990	33,120 (4.5%)	41.889 (5.7%)	665,218 (90%)	735,564
1990/1991	130,663 (16%)	186,017 (22%)	485,002 (59%)	821,555
1995/1996	277,404 (43%)	346,460 (53%)	12,661 (2%)	650,223
2001/2002	336,642 (54%)	275,652 (44%)	3,538 (0.6%)	625,730
2006/2007	369,211 (64%)	201,008 (35%)	1,081 (0.2%)	577,195

Table 1: *Number of students learning English, German and Russian in recent past and today in Grades 1–8 (%)* (Statistical Yearbook of Education 2006/2007, pp. 24–26)

The first early English programme starting at Grade 1 (age 6) was launched in 1977 at a Primary school affiliated to the University of Pécs, where I used to teach students over an eight-year period (see Nikolov, 2002a). Since the mid-1990s, more and more schools have offered early language learning opportunities before the mandatory start at Grade 4. To illustrate how many young learners study an MFL in the lower Primary grades, Table 2 includes figures and percentages for the 2004–05 school year. As can be seen, one fifth of first graders, almost a third of second graders, and nearly half of third graders learn an MFL before it is mandatory. However, only 88 per cent start at the mandatory age prescribed in the Hungarian National Core Curriculum. This means that although many children have access before the mandatory age, 12 per cent do not start learning any MFL in Grade 4, either small villages have no teachers, or they are diagnosed with learning disabilities.

Grade	Number	Ratio (%)
Grade 1	22,093	20%
Grade 2	28,278	26%
Grade 3	53,923	48%
Grade 4	101,195	88%

Table 2: *Number and ratio (%) of pupils learning a foreign language in 2004/05* (Ministry of Education, 2004: 3)

Curriculum

The Hungarian National Core Curriculum (2003) is controversial. It prescribes an MFL from Grade 4 for all learners, but allows schools to launch an earlier programme in any of the first three grades depending on what parents want and schools can afford. No curricular achievement targets are specified for the first three years, but the ministry has proposed some guidelines (Ministry of Education, Hungary, 2004). Although both these guidelines and the curricular goals and achievement targets set for Primary schools between Grades 4 and 8 are realistic and the suggested methodology is in line with young learners' needs and abilities, the outcomes of early MFL programmes vary to a great extent and classroom practice often reflects different processes from those that the curriculum and the guidelines promote.

The main problems centre around the variety of provision in schools, reflecting local power relationships and parents' socio-economic status; the strong streaming tradition; and a wide range of classroom practices (ranging from age-appropriate techniques to grammar-translation extremes), reflecting huge differences in teachers' competencies, motivation, beliefs and practices, in turn reflected in learners' proficiency over time.

In addition to the issues of the age of starting and of how many years are devoted to learning an MFL, the number of weekly classes devoted to MFL study deserves discussion. The National Core Curriculum prescribes a minimum of three 45-minute classes a week from Grade 4. Table 3 shows that about 23 per cent of the children surveyed studied English in fewer than three classes (i.e., one or two). This is understandable, as in the first three grades this is the typical frequency. The statistical report groups together data for weekly classes of between three and five, and the majority (68 per cent) belong in this category. However, it is also clear that about nine per cent studied English in more than five classes a week (double or higher than the prescribed frequency), showing what a wide range of provision characterizes schools.

Classes per week:	<3	3-5	>5	Total
Number of students:	87,216	248,658	31,810	367,684
%:	23	68	9	100

Table 3: *Number of Primary-school students learning English in 2004-05* (Jelentés a közoktatásról 2006, Table 5.23)

To summarize data related to time devoted to early language study, about half of learners start an MFL before age nine, the age prescribed in official documents, and in comparison with European countries, weekly exposure is high. To illustrate the scale of time spent learning an MFL in Hungarian state education, according to *Key data on teaching languages at school in Europe* (Eurydice, 2005: 74), in Denmark students have 510 MFL classes in six years; in Finland and Sweden, they study an MFL for six or nine years in 456-80 hours; in Austria, for nine years, in 630 hours; whereas in Hungary the minimal exposure is nine years in 984 classes in small groups (Vágó, 2007).

Some additional features also need to be pointed out, while European documents suggest teaching two MFLs from very early on, in Hungary, a child's abilities and parental pressure determine if the child studies one or two languages – or none at all. In addition, normal school classes are split into two groups of 8–16 learners for MFL classes to allow learners to interact more and to make MFL learning more efficient. This rule has been applied for decades and used to be applied in Russian classes as well. As a result, large resources are devoted to MFL teaching compared to other school subjects and the results are controversial. In some schools, most learners become independent users in two MFLs, whereas in others they are exempt from learning any.

The prestige of the teaching profession is low in Hungarian society; the younger the learners, the lower the prestige of the job. Teachers of young learners need less education than their colleagues in upper Primary and Secondary schools. Finally, Hungarian school achievements have been characterized by the largest differences across schools and groups in schools in the PISA studies, and the educational system fails to counterbalance them over time.

Transition

In addition to the problems outlined above, transfer across the school system presents a major challenge, as the variety of factors in Primary schools (in number of years, weekly classes, materials, quality of teaching) make it difficult for both upper Primary and Secondary schools to base their teaching on what students can do. To show the complexity of the problem, let us examine how students are distributed in Grade 9 (age 14–15) at different Secondary schools according to the number of years they studied an MFL in Primary school. As the figures in Table 4 indicate, seven per cent of students at vocational schools (the least academic ones), never learnt a language. The ratio of students at grammar schools, comprehensive, and vocational schools varies; the better the school, the more probable it is that students studied an MFL at Primary school for a longer period of time. All students in the category of 6–8 years were exposed to more years of study than the mandatory five years: a total of 53 per cent, according to official statistics.

Years of study/ Type of school (%)	0	1-3	4-5	6-8
Grammar	0.8	2.3	34.0	62.9
Comprehensive	1.3	2.9	42.4	53.4
Vocational	7.0	7.3	48.1	37.6
Total	2.4	3.7	40.7	53.1

Table 4: *Length of FL, study at Primary schools (in years) in 2003/04 in Grade 9* (Jelentés a közoktatásról, 2006, Table 5.28)

A large-scale survey involving all Grade 9 students (Vágó, 2007) found that two-thirds of all students either could not continue the MFL they studied for years or they were false beginners. A qualitative study on unsuccessful adult language learners explored transition from the learners' perspective (Nikolov, 2001); the lack of continuity decreased students' self-confidence and language learning motivation. To summarize, the potential benefits of an early start are often lost and transition is a serious challenge for language learners.

As Secondary schools fail to build on what students can do, the Ministry of Education launched a special programme, called the 'Year of Intensive Language Learning', in the 2004–05 academic year. In this intensive project, students learn one or two MFLs in 12–18 hours a week and this gap year increases their Secondary studies to five years. Without going into the details, the existence of the programme itself is an explicit criticism of Primary-school MFL education. On the one hand, there is too much variety in eight-year Primary schools, on the other, Secondary schools do not build on what students know and how they learn and a lack of trust is typical. Quite controversially, the variety of the system works against the success of an early start.

Outcomes of early foreign language programmes

The benefits of early exposure to English are obvious for the few exceptional students whose motivation to study the language over many years is maintained and whose proficiency is continually developed. I have experienced as an assessor in competitions for sixth and eighth graders that a few students perform at native-like level. However, results of studies involving nationally representative samples show discouraging results in MFL proficiency. One way of examining how efficient early programmes are is to examine the relationship between the length of time in years devoted to language study and students' performances on proficiency tests. Such correlation studies have been conducted in recent years in Hungary.

In a recent study on Hungarian sixth graders' aptitude, motivation and achievement in English (Kiss and Nikolov, 2005), involving 419 learners, the number of hours invested in learning English explained 8.5 per cent of variance in learners' performances, where hours included not only classes taught at school but also extracurricular exposure. Aptitude, however, explained over 20 per cent and motivation 8 per cent of the variation in the results. These figures indicate that the cognitive contribution seems to be the strongest.

In a large national survey conducted in 2003 of sixth and tenth graders learning English and German, relationships were calculated not only for proficiency scores and years of language study, but also for students' socio-economic status (SES), parents' education, weekly classes, and extracurricular tuition (Nikolov and Józsa, 2006: 221). Two of these variables were responsible for significant differences in the ratio of explained variance between the two languages: students' SES and the number of weekly classes. Parental education by itself, however, explained the largest ratio of variance (see Table 5).

Independent variables	Year 6		Year 10	
	English	German	English	German
Parents' education (SES)	25	18	24	17
Weekly classes	13	10	14	13
Years of language study	3	3	4	4
Private tuition	ns	ns	2	2
Variance explained (%)	41	31	44	36

Table 5: *Regression analysis with developmental level of language skills as dependent variable ($r\beta\%$)*

The two time-related variables offered by schools (years of study and frequency of weekly classes) together explained less of the variance than learners' socio-economic status. The data on the length of language study is particularly disappointing from the perspective of early start programmes, as they do not seem to contribute to success in the long run in a very significant way. Findings of other studies shed light on the reasons.

Looking at classrooms

A large-scale study assessed nationally representative samples of sixth graders. Besides their proficiency in English and German, their attitudes and motivation were also examined: attitudes towards the FL and its study; their intrinsic, instrumental, integrative and successive motives; and the classroom level were explored. In the students' opinion, their parents are highly motivated for their children to learn English or German, and learners also think that knowing a FL will be useful. They quite like both English and German and claim to be interested in the speakers of both languages. Thus, most students' general attitudes and their instrumental as well as integrative motivation were highly favourable (Nikolov, 2003). However, a high ratio of students did not find the classes challenging enough or failed to reach the expected level, reporting anxiety in class. The majority found their teachers prepared, enthusiastic and pedagogically sound, but teachers' explanations were often unclear.

Learners were asked to indicate how often certain typically applied activities were used. The results indicated that traditional form-focused activities inherited from the audio-lingual and grammar-translation methods tended to characterize sixth graders' foreign language classes in both languages. The most frequent way of meaning-making was translation. Reading out texts, answering teachers' questions in a lockstep fashion, and completing grammar exercises and tests were among the typical activities despite the widespread use of communicative course materials indicated in the background questionnaire data. Playful activities, free conversations, role-plays, pair and group work were the least frequent in both English and German classes. Age-appropriate task types, pictures, video and visual support were relatively infrequent; playful activities, free talk, stories and working in pairs and groups were at the bottom of the frequency list. Teachers emphasized reading aloud, translation and grammar exercises, though these are explicitly excluded from curricular achievement targets, and methodology books also argue against them.

The same list was also used to explore learners' attitudes towards the activities and motivation to participate in them. A reciprocal relationship was found between the frequency of activities and students' attitudes towards them: the least frequent activities were the most popular, whereas the more often applied ones tended to be disliked. Videos, listening tasks, games, pair and group work, and tasks involving some creativity and physical movement featured high on learners' lists of liked activities. The least popular classroom tasks included everything related to assessment.

To ensure triangulation, some qualitative studies also explored lower-Primary classrooms (Bors, Lugossy and Nikolov, 2001; Nikolov, 1999, 2001, 2002b). Although these studies involved convenience samples and involved only learners of English, the findings are in line with what the surveys indicate. In many classrooms, teachers' practices reflect contrastive and behaviourist beliefs, and classroom processes fail to support young learners' initially positive attitudes, language learning motivation, and development in English. Also, the strategies children are encouraged to apply are not age appropriate. Teachers tend to use the mother tongue, as they are insecure in English and do not trust learners. Many of the teachers observed and interviewed are unhappy about having to teach young learners and wish they could do 'real' teaching with older students.

To sum up, research into early language programmes in Hungary shows that an early start by itself is not enough. Several conditions should be met (for a list of these conditions see Nikolov, 2000: 43) to ensure that the realistic aim, as articulated in policy and curriculum documents, of boosting young learners' affective, cognitive and linguistic abilities can be achieved. There is much evidence of good practice; however, my concern is with the large numbers of young language learners for whom an early start is not as beneficial an experience as it could and should be.

References

Bors, L., Lugossy, R. and Nikolov, M. (2001). Az angol nyelv oktatásának átfogó értékelése pécsi általános iskolákban [A comprehensive study of teaching English in Pécs Primary schools]. *Iskolakultúra* 11 (4), 73-88.

Eurydice – European Commission, Brussels (2005). *Key data on teaching languages at school in Europe.*

Jelentés a közoktatásról 2006 [A report on state education]. Accessed 7 December 2007 from http://www.oki.hu/oldal.php?tipus=cikk&kod=Jelentes2006-15_tartalom#abra_5.11

Kiss, C. and Nikolov, M. (2005). Developing, piloting and validating an instrument to measure young learners' aptitude. *Language Learning* 55 (1), 99-150.

Ministry of Education, Hungary (2004). *Ajánlások az általános iskola első három osztályában folyó idegennyelv-oktatás eredményesebbé tételére* [Recommendations for making FL education more successful in Grades 1-3] (2004). Accessed 27 December 2007 from http://www.okm.gov.hu/main.php?folderID=710&articleID=4195&ctag=articlelist&iid=1.

National Core Curriculum [Nemzeti alaptanterv] (2003). Budapest: Oktatási Minisztérium.

Nikolov, M. (1999). Natural born speakers of English: Code switching in pair- and group-work in Hungarian Primary schools. In Rixon, S. (ed.) *Young Learners of English: Some Research Perspectives* (pp. 72-88). London: Longman.

Nikolov, M. (2000). Teaching foreign languages to young learners in Hungary. In Nikolov, M. and Curtain, H. (eds) *An Early Start: Young Learners and Modern Languages in Europe and Beyond.* Strasbourg: Council of Europe.

Nikolov, M. (2001). A study of unsuccessful language learners. In Z. Dörnyei and Schmidt, R. (eds) *Motivation and Second Language Acquisition* (pp. 149-170). Honolulu, HI: The University of Hawaii, Second Language Teaching and Curriculum Center.

Nikolov, M. (2002a). *Issues in English Language Education.* Bern: Peter Lang AG.

Nikolov, M. (2002b). What do teachers of young learners claim and do? An empirical study of their claims and practices. Paper presented at the Dijete i Jezik Danas/Child and Language Today. 2nd International Conference, Osijek, Croatia.

Nikolov, M. (2003). Angolul és németül tanuló diákok nyelvtanulási attitüdje és motivációja [Attitudes and motivation of learners of English and German]. *Iskolakultúra* 13 (8), 61-73.

Nikolov, M. and Józsa, K. (2006). Relationships between language achievements in English and German and classroom-related variables. In Nikolov, M. and Horváth, J. (eds), *UPRT 2006: Empirical Studies in English Applied Linguistics* (pp. 197-224). Pécs: Lingua Franca Csoport, PTE.

Statistical Yearbook of Education 2006/2007 (2006). Budapest: Oktatási és Kulturális Minisztérium.

Vágó, I. (2007). Nyelvtanulási útjak Magyarországon [Language learning paths in Hungary]. In Vágó Irén (szerk), *Fókuszban a nyelvtanulás* [Focusing on language learning] (pp. 137-174). Budapest: Oktatáskutató és Fejlesztő Intézet.

Acknowledgement

I am grateful to Jaynee Moon and Janet Enever for encouraging me to participate in the conference and I thank the IATEFL Young Learners SIG for the generous grant allowing me to do so.

Primary EFL in China: From policy to classroom practice

Wang Qiang, Centre for Foreign Language Education and Teacher Education, Beijing Normal University, China

Introduction

Since the 1990s, there has been a rapid global expansion of programmes for Teaching English to Young Learners (TEYL). As Graddol (2006) points out, improving the proficiency of English has become one of the national strategies for many governments to respond to the more globalized world. To meet the challenges of joining the World Trade Organization (WTO) and increasing openness to the outside world, which require high quality personnel with a high degree of English proficiency, the Chinese government, in 2001, made the decision to promote English as a foreign language in Primary schools with learner-centredness as one of its main goals. Along with the national policy, a rapid expansion of Primary English began in China.

By the end of 2007, the policy had been in existence for more than six years. This paper attempts to examine the government policies on TEYL and how they have been implemented and tries to answer the following questions:

1. What educational approaches and requirements have been advocated in the national curriculum for TEYL?

2. How has the policy with respect to Primary English been put into practice?

    *   What are the current provisional conditions for TEYL in China?

    *   How have teachers been supplied? What are their qualifications?

    *   What kind of teaching approaches have been taken?

    *   What are teachers' attitudes towards and perceptions of learner-centredness?

- What difficulties have been recognized by Primary teachers?

- What features of classroom practices can be identified?

The paper is divided into four parts. Part I introduces the national policy on Primary English with regard to curriculum goals, teaching standards, teaching materials, teaching methods, and assessment strategies, along with the policy on teacher supply. Part II focuses on the current provision of TEYL in China including scale of provision, selection of course books, general teaching contexts, assessment practices, teacher qualifications and supply routes. Part III presents teachers' attitudes towards learner-centredness, their reported teaching approaches, and perceived difficulties based on a large-scale survey of 1,000 Primary English teachers carried out between 2004 and 2005. Part IV discusses some typical features of classroom practices derived from 18 lessons demonstrating good practices observed in 2005. Finally, challenges facing TEYL in China are discussed.

1. The national policy on Primary English

According to the national policy on Primary English (The Ministry of Education (MOE) Document, 2001), the provision of English should start from Grade 3 (age 8–9) first in cities, then counties, gradually moving to towns and villages, with a minimum of 80 minutes a week. The MOE requires that each province work out its own strategic plans for the provision of Primary English in terms of beginning age, time allocation, and planning for teacher training. Along with the policy on Primary English, the government issued a teaching requirement for Primary English in early 2001 as a first step to regulating and guiding the teaching of Primary English. At the same time, a new National English Curriculum (NECS) for the twenty-first century was designed and began to be piloted incrementally from 2001, until it went nationwide in 2005. NECS makes Primary English an integral part of the curriculum within the nine-year compulsory education that connects to the senior high school English curriculum.

1.1 Goals, standards and methods

The overall goal of NECS is to develop students' comprehensive language competence by making learning a process during which students develop language proficiency, form positive attitudes, improve thinking skills, increase cross-cultural awareness and learn to use learning strategies that will gradually equip them to become independent learners. The main task for the English curriculum innovation reflects a shift from overemphasizing the transmission mode of teaching grammar and vocabulary, to the development of students' overall ability in language use, with emphases on activating students' interests in learning, relating the course content to the students' life experiences, promoting cooperation among students and advocating learning by doing (Ministry of Education, 2001). The framework of strands in the English curriculum for the Primary phase is designed as follows with specific can-do statements given for each strand (Wang, 2003):

Level 1 (Grades 3 and 4)	Level 2 (Grades 5 and 6)
➢ Listen and do ➢ Speak and sing ➢ Play and act ➢ Read and write ➢ Audio and visual	➢ Listening ➢ Speaking ➢ Reading ➢ Writing ➢ Play and act; audio and visual

Although NECS does not enforce any specific teaching method, the performance descriptors designate a change in methodology that clearly reflects an activity-based approach, encouraging teachers to provide opportunities for children to learn the language through a playful and happy experience.

1.2 Policy on teaching materials and assessment

All textbooks for use in Primary schools are required to pass reviews by the National Textbook Review Committee, MOE. Textbooks that pass reviews can then be recommended to schools. Up to now, more than 30 Primary textbook titles have passed reviews and are now in use in different parts of China. Most of them are joint-venture productions between a Chinese publisher and a foreign publisher. Straight import of foreign textbooks is not allowed in schools. It is also stated in NECS that the assessment for Primary English should be consistent with the overall goals of NECS for enhancing children's overall development and teachers' effectiveness in teaching. Formative assessment is promoted whereas examination-oriented assessment is not encouraged for Primary schools (Wang, 2003).

1.3 Teacher supply policy

The immediate challenge facing Primary English is the supply of qualified teachers. Chinese Primary teachers are all specialists who only teach their own respective subjects. They used to be qualified by completing a two-year special training on a chosen subject from a two-year teacher-training school, but in recent years, there has been an upgraded qualification requirement for Primary teachers to have a three-year teacher-training certificate at college level. However, as English has not been a required subject in the national curriculum in the past, very few specialized foreign language teaching programmes are offered by teacher-training colleges. To promote English in Primary schools, the MOE requires that educational departments at all levels resolve to take effective measures to help train Primary English teachers. Since 2001, a number of pre-service and in-service courses have been set up to meet the needs of expanding Primary English nationwide.

2. Current provision of TEYL

Along with the national policy, each province has taken measures to ensure a gradual provision of English as a foreign language in Primary schools from Grade 3. Large cities such as Beijing, Shanghai, Guangzhou, Chengdu and Shenzhen, where English had been offered at Grade 4 or 5 from the early 1990s (age 10–11), began to lower the provision of English to Grade 1 (age 6). Since 2001, Primary English has expanded rapidly throughout the country, from 6.7 per cent in 2000 to 62.1 per cent in 2006. Some major cities, such as Beijing, Shanghai, Guangzhou, Shenzhen and Tianjin, have reached 100 per cent. As a result, the number of Primary English teachers increased from 80,000 in 2000 to nearly 500,000 in 2006 (Cao, 2007).

2.1 Teacher supply routes

Besides a very small number of teachers who graduated from English departments of teacher-training colleges, teacher supply has mainly taken four routes:

1. graduates majoring in English from colleges other than teacher-training colleges or universities with no special training in TEYL;

2. experienced Primary teachers, originally teaching other subjects but made redundant due to falling birth rates, asked to transfer to teach English after taking some short training courses (from two weeks to a few months);

3. graduates who hold a college degree or certificate other than English (non-English majors) with some proof of English proficiency but with no special training in TEYL;

4. 'walking' or shared teachers – for those schools that have difficulty hiring their own English teachers.

Obviously, the main concerns regarding teacher supply are first whether these teachers have the necessary language proficiency and second whether they have proper training in teaching young learners.

2.2 General teaching contexts in Primary schools

A survey of 1,000 Primary EFL teachers carried out between 2004 and 2005 in seven provinces provided a picture of the current teaching situation in the Primary sector (Wang, 2007). Data showed that the Primary English profession was comprised in the main of female teachers in a ratio of 92.5 per cent women to 7.5 per cent men. The age groups fell between 69.7 per cent in their 20s and 26.7 per cent in their 30s. In terms of their Primary English teaching experience, 52.5 per cent had less than two years' experience and 24.5 per cent had three to five years' experience. Data also shows that more than 40 per cent of the teachers had a degree other than English. Seventy per cent of the teachers surveyed came from urban schools.

The findings also showed that the teaching contexts where these teachers teach varied greatly, with class size ranging from as large as 120 to as small as 8, with an average of 50. Forty-five per cent of the teachers taught between 4–6 different classes a week; 17 per cent, between 7–9 classes; and 3.8 per cent, 10–12 classes. As regards teaching hours, these varied from a maximum of 22 to a minimum of 2 hours a week with the mean being 16. Nearly 40 per cent of the respondents taught between 15–20 hours a week and 10 per cent taught more than 20 hours. In addition, over 50 per cent of teachers taught across 2-3 grades and 12 teachers taught all 6 grades – possibly the only English teachers in their schools.

3. Teachers' attitudes towards and perceptions of learner-centredness

3.1 Teachers' response to learner-centred ideology

The survey showed that the overall attitude of the teachers towards learner-centredness was overwhelmingly positive (88.9 per cent), while only 5.2 per cent were doubtful or reserved, with another 5.9 per cent holding a paradoxical view – welcoming the idea but feeling it was difficult to implement it.

3.2 Teachers' reported teaching approaches

In the survey, teachers were invited to assess their own approaches to teaching. A scale was given with teacher-centredness at one end and learner-centredness at the other. Along the continuum were seven boxes which listed, from left to right: teacher-centred, largely teacher-centred, somewhat teacher-centred, between teacher-centred and learner-centred, somewhat learner-centred, largely learner-centred, and finally, learner-centred. The respondents were asked to tick the box that most accurately represented their own approach to teaching. Out of 1,000 respondents, only four teachers (0.4 per cent) reported that they were fully teacher-centred, while at the other end, 50 teachers (5 per cent) were fully learner-centred. The rest chose a position between the two extremes. When these teachers were again presented with teacher-centredness, learner-centredness and teacher-directed learner-centred (TDLC) approaches and asked to decide which approach they most preferred, a majority of them (81.7 per cent) chose TDLC. The following were some explanations given for taking the TDLC approach:

> We should not take to extremes in whatever we do. It is the same with teaching. Proper teacher guidance is necessary for a learner-centred classroom (No. 595).

> Teacher-direction is good for controlling teaching objectives, while learner-centredness is good for activating pupils' motivation and interests in learning (No. 570).

> Classroom teaching consists of two major aspects (teaching and learning); neither aspect should be neglected (No. 360).

> The teacher must have the capability to manage the class. It should be managed like a prose – loose in form but not in spirit. Only in this way, can he/she achieve what he/she intends to do (No. 776).

3.3 Teachers' perceptions of their roles in the classroom

In the survey, a list of 17 teacher roles was given and teachers were asked to decide which roles they believed they should play and which they thought they played well. The findings showed that over 70 per cent of the respondents chose 'organizer' (83 per cent); 'learning companion' (81.4 per cent), 'guide' (78.4 per cent), 'knowledge provider' (73.6 per cent) and 'participant' (71.1 per cent) as roles they should play. Three of the roles are commonly related to learner-centredness ('guide', 'learning companion' and 'participant') and two are commonly related to teacher-centredness ('knowledge provider' and 'organizer'). It seemed that most teachers believed that they should play both learner-centred and teacher-centred roles.

Compared with the roles they believed they should play, fewer teachers rated themselves as performing these same roles well. However, the five roles that enjoyed the most votes in the 'should play' category also received the most votes for roles they felt they 'played well', though the percentage voting for the latter was lower. Nevertheless, the order of frequency of mentions slightly changed, with 'knowledge provider' (64.6 per cent) being the first, followed by 'learning companion' (58.8 per cent), 'organizer' (57.3 per cent), 'participant' (53.1 per cent) and 'guide' (49.3 per cent).

3.4 Confusions among teachers regarding learner-centredness

The survey also showed that quite a lot of confusion existed as to what learner-centredness should be taken to mean. To some teachers, it means:

- students enjoy absolute freedom in the learning process;

- centring teaching on the students no matter whether what they do is right or wrong.

- learning content should be determined by the learners;

- whatever happens in the classroom, whether it is right or wrong, the teacher has no say;

- it is mainly students' self-learning without the teacher's involvement.

3.5 Difficulties identified for implementing learner-centredness

Although the majority of the teachers were supportive of learner-centredness, they identified a number of difficulties that prevented them from implementing the approach. These included:

- a lack of support and understanding from society, school leaders and parents;

- the constraints of the school management/administrative system and the assessment system;

- the location of schools in the countryside, with low emphasis on English and a lack of positive learning environments;

- the lack of teaching facilities and resources;

- large classes;

- discipline problems;

- the old system and the new curriculum clash with each other;

- the low value attached to English as a school subject and the lack of teaching hours;

- perceived personal incapability;

- the lack of teaching staff and heavy workloads;

- the low level and lack of self-regulation on the part of students.

4. Features of classroom practice from good teachers

To find out what teachers actually do in classrooms, 18 teachers of good practices were observed, who were recommended by some local ELT advisers. All the lessons were audio-taped, transcribed and analysed. The following presents some typical features observed from classrooms.

4.1 Highly structured lessons with a variety of activities

Most lessons observed seemed to share some common structural features in sequencing, with a clear beginning phase, a substantial middle phase and a brief ending, despite the fact that they varied in types and order of specific activities. The beginning was most often typified by formulaic routine greetings between the teacher and the class, followed by some warm-up activities composed of daily exchanges, routine questions, a game or TPR activity to get pupils ready to learn English. The middle phase often consisted of one to three cycles of new language input and practice in which the teacher broke down the learning tasks into manageable smaller steps. This often lead to a stage of personalization, which included opportunities for children to use what they learned, however limited, to express things that were more personal and meaningful. Fourteen out of 17 new lessons moved to a stage of personalization. The ending of the lessons was signalled by homework assignments.

4.2 Classroom interaction patterns

A large proportion of class time (80–90 per cent) was spent on T-directed whole-class work in the form of a variety of activities and a much smaller proportion of time was spent on group/pair/individual work (10–20 per cent). However, whole-class activities were found in many different forms, which include: songs and chants, TPR activities, games, questions-and-answers, teacher's presentation of the new language, listening to the tape, repetitions and imitations, reading aloud, pair/group presentations and whole-class feedback.

4.3 Other findings

- Most classrooms (12 out of 18) were found in the traditional forms of lines and rows but these layouts did not seem to have affected how interactions took place in classrooms.

- There was a strong sense of collectiveness in the process of teaching and learning with teacher-directed, whole-class learning as the dominant form along with some pair/group work as well as individual work. There was a clear concern for common learning targets to be achieved.

- Teachers used a range of pedagogical alternatives – both learner-centred and teacher-centred, which are available for them to promote, engage and encourage every child to work towards the common goal.

- There were opportunities for children to develop skills for learning (learner training) in some classrooms.

- Teachers skillfully used demonstration and modeling to provide guidance and direction to children's learning and they functioned as guides, organizers, knowledge providers, models, and managers of time and order.

- Classroom atmosphere was overall well-ordered, active, supportive and encouraging.

5. Challenges facing the expansion of TEYL in China

Cao (2007) points out four main problems that feature in the expansion of TEYL in Chinese Primary schools:

- There is unequal provision between the east and the west of China and between cities and the countryside.

- EYL teachers' quality, both in terms of language proficiency and in EYL pedagogy, is low, and there is a serious shortage of teacher supply.

- Teacher effectiveness varies between different schools and in different regions.

- The provision of English in the country schools is even weaker, with no teachers and necessary resources available.

In addition, the transition from Primary to Secondary is beginning to encounter serious problems resulting from the unequal provision of English and the uneven quality of teaching in Primary schools.

Conclusion

TEYL in China is undergoing an important phase of expansion and innovation along with tremendous challenges characterized by uneven provisions between urban and rural areas due to the shortage of qualified teachers. The training of qualified teachers is obviously key to the success of TEYL.

Despite all the difficulties, a majority of Primary EFL teachers surveyed are overwhelmingly supportive of the new curriculum. In practice, teachers modeling good practice tried to mediate the learner-centred ideology in their own teaching contexts by integrating new teacher roles with their traditional ones. It is over-simplistic to label a teacher as 'learner-centred' or 'teacher-centred'. What is important is that teaching and learning activities should be fit for purpose (Alexander et. al.,1992), as well as fit for the contexts where teaching and learning take place.

Acknowledgement

I would like to express my appreciation to the British Council in Beijing for sponsoring me to attend the conference held in Bangalore, India, 3–6 January 2008.

References

Alexander, R.J., Rose, A. and Woodhead, C. (1992). Curriculum Organisation and Classroom Practice in Primary Schools: A Discussion Paper. London: DES.

Cao, Z. (2007). On the development of English Language Teaching in Schools. Speech given at the Basic Education Forum, The Fifth National Conference on English Language Teaching. Beijing: China. 19–23 May 2007.

Graddol, D. (2006). English Next. London: British Council.

Ministry of Education, China (2001). National English Curriculum Standards for Nine-Year Compulsory Education and Senior High School Education.

Ministry of Education (2001). On promoting English Language Teaching in Primary schools.

Wang, Q. (2003). New developments in Primary English education in China – opportunities and challenges. Journal of Basic Education 12 (2), 243-250.

Wang, Q. (2007). Primary EFL in China – Teachers' perceptions and practices with regard to learner-centredness. Unpublished PhD Thesis. The University of Warwick, UK.

Early Language Learning in Europe (ELLiE): A multinational, longitudinal study

Magdalena Szpotowicz, Warsaw University, Poland
Jelena Mihaljevic Djigunovic, Zagreb University, Croatia
Janet Enever, London Metropolitan University, UK

Introduction

This paper presents an outline of the research framework for a longitudinal, comparative study of early language learning (ELL) across seven European country contexts (Croatia, England, Italy, Netherlands, Poland, Spain and Sweden). In addition, two strands of evidence from the initial one-year scoping study are explored here, providing an early account of emerging findings and offering an indication of outcomes to be reported in the further three years of the research. Given the European priority for introducing early foreign languages in schools, there is now an urgent need for both qualitative and quantitative evidence on the precise nature and outcomes of ELL, as highlighted by the recent European Commission Report 'Languages for the children of Europe' (Edelenbos et al., 2006). This research aims to provide a much-needed body of data of sufficient scale to offer the kind of validity that previous studies have been unable to achieve, with the potential strategically to inform both future policy and practice.

Research framework

During the period 2006–07 an exploratory scoping study across six European countries (Croatia, England, Italy, Poland, Spain and Sweden) was conducted with the aim of exploring the viability of a longer study and establishing a data baseline. The countries selected reflect a cross-section of European contexts, including northern and southern Europe; 'older' European Union (EU) members and recent (newer) EU members; larger and smaller countries; the diverse linguistic roots of Germanic, Romance and Slavonic languages; contexts where the languages learnt in schools range across a continuum from the status of second to foreign language. The further three-year European Commission-funded study (European Commission, 2007) to be conducted from 2007–10 includes the addition of the Netherlands as a seventh country, while Croatia (as a European Union applicant country) is supported by an additional British Council research grant.

The central purpose of the study is to investigate what can be realistically achieved in second/foreign language learning in state schools where relatively limited amounts of curriculum time are allocated to such learning. In particular, the research explores the significance of the teacher's role in ELL and the impact of digital media on this process, both in and out of school. With the aim of developing a multi-faceted picture of how young children engage with foreign language (FL) learning the study design is essentially qualitative, while also incorporating quantative dimensions. Data sources include the learners, their teachers, the school principals and the learners' parents. Data was collected from a convenience sample of approximately 150 children aged 6–8 years in each country, amounting to a total sample of some 900 children. With the addition of a further 150 children from the Netherlands, the sample will increase to a cohort of 1,050 children, whose progress will be tracked as they continue through Primary schooling. During this process, the research team will gather qualitative data to construct a total of 250 learner profiles, 45 teacher profiles, and 45 school profiles, with the addition of quantitative data from the sample of over 1,000 children. Research tools include individual interviews, classroom observation and questionnaires, further supported by analysis of published local and national documents.

The following two sections of this summary present analysis of collated data on the learning environments experienced by these young learners, together with a full discussion of their developing attitudes and motivation towards FL learning. Together, these dimensions offer an insight into those early classroom experiences likely to prove crucial to the establishment of a foundation on which these language learners will build their confidence and competence as they progress in their learning.

Learning environment

The data on the learning environment was obtained from the interviews with foreign language teachers and from classroom observations. Information collected from each of these two sources was thought to complement the other and provided a summary of learning conditions in all the six countries (Croatia, England, Italy, Poland, Spain and Sweden) The sample comprised of 40 teachers (6–8 per country) who taught foreign languages to 6 to 8-year-old learners of the selected classes (approximately 150 per country).

The key areas of investigation included the classroom reality and the teacher's perspective on ELL. In scrutinizing classroom realities, we focused on how teaching was organized in different European contexts. The analysis of teachers' perceptions pinpointed their opinions on the role of language teachers of young learners, their views on the pupils' progress and their perceptions of how parents and other staff viewed ELL in their schools.

In this paper we have selected particular aspects of the classroom environment to focus on as most likely to be significant in their impact on learning. These include:

- the varying number of students per class;

- students' seating arrangements;

- teachers' talking time in the foreign language/mother tongue;

- teachers' reactions to learners' mistakes;

- teachers' opinions about their profession;

- teachers' perception of parents' and other staff's attitudes to ELL.

Due to limited space we have concentrated here on those similarities and differences that we found significant or of interest for further investigation.

The classrooms observed in the sample differed across the countries with respect to the number of students per group. The largest groups were observed in England where the number of students ranged from 28–32, and where only one school divided the class into two smaller groups for FL lessons. England was followed by Croatia, with classes containing between 22–29 students. In Poland and Spain, the classes were of similar size, ranging from 13–27. In Sweden and Italy, the classes under scrutiny did not exceed 24 children. The seating arrangement and the type of interaction in classrooms also differed. For example, in Poland and Italy, all the observed students were seated at desks, arranged in three rows, with one or two students per desk/table. In the remaining four countries, the seating was more flexible. The students were either seated in groups of 5/6 at tables, often changing their position to sit on a carpet around the teacher or board (an electronic whiteboard in England).

The amount of teacher talking time in the target language appeared to depend on individual teachers' preferred style, rather than anything pre-planned. However, it was noticed that the selected teachers in Spain used the target language to a greater extent (45–100 per cent of the time) than those of other countries. The lowest teacher talking time in the target language was found in Croatia (between 25 per cent and 60 per cent of the time). In England, Poland, Italy and Sweden the levels varied across schools but no country-specific differences were noted. These ranged from situations where almost no target language was spoken in class and most of the lesson was taught through the mother tongue, to classes in which the teacher exclusively used the foreign language.

Teachers' reactions to language mistakes made by the students while speaking in the foreign language during the lessons were also scrutinized. It appeared that in England, Croatia, Poland and Spain the teachers corrected, remodelled or prompted self- or peer-correction among their students almost immediately after the mistake appeared. The majority of teachers frequently used one of these techniques and only some teachers applied them rarely. It was interesting to note that the only teachers who were observed not to correct any language mistakes were the teachers from Swedish classes. The possible reasons for this difference need to be further explored.

Semi-structured interviews with FL teachers revealed that their opinions about the task of teaching a foreign language to young learners were mainly positive. Responses can be grouped into three categories:

1. very positive or positive;

2. stressing both enjoyment and the challenges of the task;

3. stressing the negative aspects.

The first category was represented by responses from almost 47 per cent of the teachers. They referred to their jobs as exciting/rewarding/fun/motivating/enjoyable. Another group, approximately 37 per cent, stressed that it was rewarding and challenging/difficult/demanding. Only 16 per cent claimed this job was mainly tiring/demanding/exhausting.

When asked to describe the methods they use while teaching at this level, teachers responded in a variety of ways. Many stressed their priority in teaching MFL was for communication, others focused on play and games or on exposing children to the target language. More precise answers were obtained when the question referred to the activities used most frequently in class. Almost all of the teachers listed games and songs, and many mentioned total physical response activities and acting out stories. Some said they often used storytelling, drawing or colouring. Only a few teachers referred to reading, writing or dictation.

The interview revealed considerable similarities across all countries in their perceptions of the types of activities that their learners enjoyed. All students were said to like games and songs; many teachers added acting-out and colouring. Some mentioned video films, stories and cutting-out activities.

As for the pupils' reactions to learning a foreign language, the teachers claimed that their students were either enthusiastic or moderately willing to learn and only a few teachers responded that the learners treated their FL classes indifferently. No negative responses were noticed by any of the teachers interviewed. Similarly, reactions of parents and other staff in school were perceived by the teachers as either positive or very positive. Only three teachers described some of the reactions as 'unsure'. No strongly negative responses were recorded by any of the teachers.

Our observations concerning the learning environments show that although the six European contexts differ in a number of aspects, the crucial elements of teaching foreign languages to children are very similar. Having analyzed the interviews with FL teachers and compared them with the data from classroom observations, we could draw the initial conclusions that teaching methods, the choice of activities and classroom management techniques do not vary significantly across all the researched contexts. The attitudes of all parties involved – those of the teachers, the students, the parents and other school staff – also seem to be positive across the sample.

Attitudes and motivation

Attitudes and motivation are considered to be among the key factors in early FL learning. Although there are quite a number of studies in this area, their results do not as yet build a coherent picture. Some (e.g., Nikolov, 1999) suggest that initially positive attitudes wane with time; others (e.g., Cenoz, 2003) show that motivation can be maintained over extended periods of time; while still others (e.g., Julkunen and Borzova, 1996) came up with mixed results. Possible causes of such conflicting findings may be twofold: different research designs and different contexts in which the FL was being learnt. In this study we wanted to remedy this complex situation by using the same research design in six country contexts and by taking into account the relevant contextual differences potentially impacting on YLs' attitudes and motivation.

In order to investigate YLs' reactions to FL learning the ELLiE team designed two instruments. A smiley questionnaire (ESQ – ELLiE Smiley Questionnaire) containing five items was constructed to elicit YLs' attitudes to five activities that were observed to be most commonly used in FL classes. The activities included: speaking, singing songs, learning new words, listening and using the FL while playing games. The second instrument was an oral interview carried out with a sub-sample consisting of six randomly chosen learners from each class. The interview elicited data on YLs' attitudes to the FL, to its native speakers and to classroom activities, as well as on motivational orientations and YLs' perception of parental support. The collected data was analyzed quantitatively and qualitatively. Due to space limitation, we present here only the major findings.

The level of motivation (M) of the whole sample (a total of 845 learners filled in the ESQ) was found to be high: M = 2.56 (max = 3), SD = .484. Girls were found to be significantly more motivated than boys (t = 5.447; p < .000). Significant differences in levels of motivation were also found among YLs in the different countries. YLs of French and Spanish in England were significantly less motivated than YLs in the other five countries. Croatian learners had a significantly higher motivation for learning EFL than the rest of the YLs. Spanish and Swedish young EFL learners showed significantly higher motivation than Polish learners, while Italian learners' motivation was of a similar level to that of the Polish, Spanish and Swedish cohorts.

Inspection of means for the individual five ESQ items resulted in very interesting insights. The highest mean (M = 2.72; SD = .57) was found for 'learning new words'. This suggests that already, at a very early school age, YLs associate FL learning with vocabulary building and perhaps prefer activities that can produce such concrete and measurable results. This may be considered as some sort of achievement motivation. Listening (M = 2.62; SD = .62) was the second most-liked activity, followed by speaking (M = 2.54; SD = .64) and singing (M = 2.54; SD = .72). Surprisingly, and in contrast to some other studies (Mihaljevic Djigunovic, 1993), playing (M = 2.42; SD = .77) turned out to be the least liked of the five included activities. This result is not easy to understand. Several possible interpretations come to mind. There are different conceptualizations of play that both YL teachers and

YLs themselves might entertain (Bruce, 2001). Also, designing and implementing a good play activity in an early FL class requires a very high level of competence in teaching young learners. Our future research efforts will include looking more closely into both teachers' and learners' conceptualizations of and attitudes to play as well as its implementation in the YL classroom.

Results of the oral interview were analyzed from a more qualitative perspective. For the purpose of this paper we will summarize and comment on findings obtained from two extreme sub-samples in terms of motivation: the cohorts from Croatia and England. It is interesting to note that, in contrast to Croatian EFL learners, the majority of whom chose English as their favourite school subject, only a minority of English YLs of French and Spanish selected their foreign language as a favourite subject. The two groups differed also in their motivational orientations. While YLs of French and Spanish in England thought it was good to learn French or Spanish in order to be able to use it when in the target language country and for communication with native speakers, Croatian YLs seemed to view their FL (English) as a global language and were more interested in using it for communicating with non-native speakers. Another interesting finding concerns the YLs' awareness and perception of native speakers. In England, a larger number of YLs had met native speakers of the FL they were learning, but they could not specifically comment on their perceptions of them. In Croatia, very few learners reported having met native speakers of English, but most of them expressed positive attitudes towards them. It is our assumption that this is the result of exposure to the FL through the media. Croatian YLs probably formed their attitudes on the basis of the numerous TV programmes they can watch on the national TV. These programmes are subtitled. In England there are few undubbed French or Spanish programmes on TV that would give YLs an opportunity to connect the language with characters as native speakers of French or Spanish. The different status of the FLs were also reflected in YLs' interest in learning other FLs: fewer Croatian YLs wished to learn other languages than YLs of French and Spanish in England. Apparently, Croatian YLs believed that English was the most useful foreign language. Parental support was perceived to be high in both cohorts, but more so in the Croatian sample. This may have been reflected in YLs' motivation too.

Our results suggest that young learners, generally speaking, react positively to FL learning. Their attitudes vary with the language studied, more specifically with its status and availability in YLs' lives. The impact of the contextual factors seems to be highly important too. We hypothesize that, among the numerous contextual variables, quality of teaching is of key importance. The follow-up to the study described in this paper will aim to test all these hypotheses.

Acknowledgements

This research has been conducted with the support of a European Commission, Lifelong learning framework grant: Project No. 135632-LLP-2007-UK-KA1SCR. An additional British Council grant supported the Croatian team.

References

Bruce, T. (2001). *Helping Young Children to Play*. London: Hodder & Stoughton.

Cenoz, J. (2003). The influence of age on the acquisition of English: General proficiency, attitudes and code mixing. In García Mayo, M. and García Lecumberri, M. (eds), *Age and the Acquisition of English as a Foreign Language* (pp. 77-93). Clevedon, UK: Multilingual Matters.

Edelenbos, P., Johnstone, R.M., Kubanek, A. (2006). The main pedagogical principles underlying the teaching of languages to very young learners. Languages for the children of Europe: Published Research, Good Practice and Main Principles. *Final Report of the EAC 89/04, Lot 1 Study*. European Commission, Brussels: Education and Culture, Culture and Communication, Multilingualism Policy. Available at http://ec.europa.eu.education/policies/lang/key/studies_en.pdf. Accessed 25 May 2008.

European Commission (2007). Early Language Learning in Europe (ELLiE). Agreement No. LLP135632-LLP-2007-UK-KA1SCR. EACEA:KA1 Policy cooperation and innovation. Available at http://eacea.ec.europa.eu/llp/funding/2007/call/index_en.htm. Accessed 25 May 2008.

Julkunen, K. and Borzova, H. (1996). *English Language Learning Motivation in Joensuu and Petrozavodsk*. Joensuu: University of Joensuu.

Mihaljević Djigunović, J. (1993). Investigation of attitudes and motivation in early foreign language learning. In Vilke, M. and Vrhovac, Y. (eds), *Children and Foreign Languages* (pp. 45-71). Zagreb: Faculty of Philosophy, University of Zagreb.

Nikolov, M. (1999). 'Why do you learn English?' 'Because the teacher is short.' A study of Hungarian children's foreign language learning motivation. *Language Teaching Research* 3 (1), 33-56.

Literacy development through the Integrated Curriculum Project: The Omani experience

Fawzia Al-Zedjali and Simon Etherton, Ministry of Education, Sultanate of Oman

Introduction

Education systems need to be continually reviewed, evaluated and developed in line with experience and current understandings. Education providers, particularly at the state level, have a responsibility to keep the provision of education up to date and effective in changing times. The Ministry of Education of the Sultanate of Oman undertook extensive education reform in introducing the concept of Basic Education – ten years of free schooling designed to help Omani children reach mastery and excellence in their learning, and to prepare them for effective participation in the ongoing process of comprehensive and sustainable social development.

After ten years of teaching the English Language curriculum in Basic Education, and with young men and women who began their education with the reforms in Grade 1 now completing their Basic Education in Grade 10, the Ministry of Education is reflecting on the Basic Education experience and making decisions about further development. The Integrated Curriculum Project is one initiative that is currently being explored and piloted in schools.

Basic educational reform in Oman

Changes to the education system

In 1998, the Ministry of Education introduced the Basic Education reform in line with educational principles outlined in United Nations Declaration of Human Rights. Basic Education in Oman has been defined by the Ministry of Education (2001: 6) as:

A unified ten-year education provided by the Sultanate for all children of school age. It meets their Basic Education needs in terms of knowledge, skills, attitudes and values, enabling them to continue their education or training based on their interests, aptitudes and dispositions, and enabling them to face the challenges of their present circumstances and future developments, in the context of comprehensive social development.

The reform includes:

- ten years of free schooling for every boy and girl divided into cycle one (Grades 1–4) and cycle two (Grades 5–10), which aim to widen the Basic Education base to provide learners with basic and necessary knowledge, skills, attitudes and values;

- two years of free post-basic education (Grades 11 and 12) consisting of both core subjects and electives;

- boys and girls in cycle one being taught together by female teachers;

- subjects continuing to be taught separately, with two new subjects: IT and Life Skills;

- English language being introduced at Grade 1 (not at Grade 4 as was the case previously);

- new curricula being developed according to current educational trends;

- continuous self-assessment;

- the introduction of Senior Teachers in schools.

These structural changes were aimed at supporting the development of Omani learners within the context of Islamic principles and values and an Omani cultural identity. Learners are expected to learn the basics of Arabic language and to be fully literate in Arabic. They are also expected to develop an understanding and appreciation of Omani, Arab and Islamic heritage. In addition to mastery of mathematics, science and IT, they are expected to develop competency as independent learners and in critical thinking, creativity and aesthetic appreciation. Proficiency in English is also an important goal of the reform.

Changes to the English language curriculum

A significant change through the reform has been the introduction of English language to children from Grade 1, not Grade 4 as before. Children are expected to study English for five 40-minute lessons a week. A new syllabus was designed, written and produced within the Curriculum Department of the Ministry of Education. This decision ensured that the classroom materials were appropriate for the Omani context and the content familiar and relevant for Omani children.

In line with accepted thinking at the time, a decision was taken to delay the introduction of reading and writing in English to the second year of schooling, as it was thought it might interfere with Arabic literacy development.

In the first year, the major focus is on the development of listening and speaking skills. In the second year, children will be helped to extend their range of oral/aural language, and taught to use it to help them to decode the written form of English at word and simple sentence level. In Grades 3 and 4, oral/aural skills are extended further, and reading and writing skills are introduced and developed (English Language Curriculum Dept., 1999: 17).

The approach to literacy development therefore focused mainly on developing sight recognition of words taught through the topics (usually content vocabulary) and developing top-down reading strategies, such as using visual clues, using memory of details of stories and chunks of language, using context clues and prediction. Teachers also taught children the names of the alphabet and to decode some words using initial letter recognition.

As the reform has unfolded, it has been recognized that children are not leaving the first cycle of Basic Education having developed the expected competencies in reading and writing. The decision to delay the introduction of reading and writing until Grade 2 was reviewed and an immediate response was to introduce a new skills book to introduce reading and writing in Grade 1. This new skills book introduced a focus on phonics that was largely absent from the original approach. Although this immediate response has been welcomed in the field, the Ministry recognize that the curriculum, and literacy development in particular, has to be developed further and a number of options are being explored. One option that has been developed and piloted is the Integrated Curriculum project.

The Integrated Curriculum Project

The rationale of the Integrated Curriculum (IC):

The Integrated Curriculum Project comes as a response to the ongoing evaluation of the Basic Education experience, especially regarding the need to further develop literacy skills in both Arabic and English languages. It aims to develop children's literacy skills in both languages through a holistic approach to learning. This holistic approach to learning is a key principle of the IC. Children engage with new knowledge, skills and information in an integrated way, rather than breaking them down into subjects. The following subjects are all learnt together through one book and from one teacher: Arabic, Islamic Studies, Social Studies, Life Skills, Maths and Science. Having one class teacher to deliver integrated knowledge and skills further develops the principles of child-centred learning. By taking responsibility for one class, the class teacher can get to know her learners much better and can create a much more appropriate learning environment and more effective formative assessment. In addition to the integrated Arabic book, children learn five other separate subjects. These include English, IT, PE, music and art. This reduction from 11 to 6 subjects also resolves the ongoing problem of the heavy school bag.

In addition to enabling the class teacher to understand her learners' needs more effectively, the integrated curriculum ensures that children develop an understanding of their world in a holistic and natural way. It also ensures that this understanding is developed though their mother tongue, Arabic. Cultural values and identity are closely linked to language, and an understanding of concepts is carried through the language they learn. For this project therefore, it is important that children learn about their world in Arabic.

The Integrated Curriculum Project was set up as a four-year project started in 2006/07 in Grade 1 and piloted in four cycle 1 schools in Muscat. The four schools were carefully selected from different areas of the capital region to provide as representative a sample as possible of cycle 1 Basic Education schools.

Development of the Arabic curriculum

In the first semester of Grade 1, children study an Arabic Preparation Book. This aims to provide the foundation for learning Arabic literacy. Children learn the letters of Arabic with both their long and their short vowels and their grammatical and orthographic signs ('sukoon' and 'tanween'). However, it is important to state that the children are also exposed to Arabic writing in longer texts where they develop their top-down reading strategies. In addition to developing literacy in the first semester, children also work at developing their basic numeracy through a Maths Preparation Book.

In the second semester of Grade 1, children continue to develop their literacy and numeracy through themes integrated with learning Islamic Studies, Science, Life Skills and Social Studies. There is now one integrated Arabic textbook to support this learning.

Development of the English curriculum

A number of significant changes have been introduced to English Language Teaching in the Integrated Curriculum Project. The first important change is that the teaching time has been increased (actually doubled) to 80 minutes per day. This follows the principle that very young language learners need more time to engage in English and to activate and utilize their natural language learning instincts and abilities. Space in the timetable has been created for this by integrating the learning of the six core subjects.

Another important area of change has been in developing the teaching materials. A decision was made to develop the existing curriculum rather than to buy or create a new one. This decision was partly based on practical issues such as cost, time available and limiting the amount of change imposed on teachers, and partly based on the view that the curriculum is of a high quality and is relevant to Omani children in an Omani context. However, it was also realized that important changes would have to be made to the materials to provide a greater focus on literacy development and to utilize the extended lesson time available.

Another reason for developing the materials has been to introduce a focus on maths and science through English. Although children develop their understanding of maths and science through Arabic in Grades 1–4 (in line with the rationale presented above), the Integrated Curriculum Project aims to prepare children to learn maths and science through the medium of English from Grade 5. This means that, in addition to building up core language competencies to enable children to learn their maths and science through English when they get to Grade 5, children also need to be fully numerate in English and to learn how to perform in English the basic mathematical operations they have already learnt in Arabic. They also need to develop the key terminology and specific language they will need to study maths and science through English in Grade 5.

There has also been development of the assessment procedures. Continuous assessment through profile charts is now based on learning outcomes. Self-assessment has also been developed, with children not just learning to assess how much they liked activities, but also how difficult or easy they found the work, how hard they worked on it and whether they completed it.

The teacher's book has also been completely rewritten and reorganized. Teachers had found the previous teacher's book to be quite prescriptive as lessons are laid out in steps with teachers attempting to cover as many of the steps as possible in the time available. The new teacher's book is organized into tasks that can usually be taught in an order teachers feel to be most appropriate for a particular class at a particular time. It has encouraged teachers to make more decisions in their planning and in their teaching.

These developments have all had a significant impact on the way children are learning English in the four Project schools, but the most significant change has been in the approach to literacy development.

Development of literacy in English through the Integrated Curriculum Project

An important change has been a focus on literacy development in English from Grade 1 alongside Arabic. Although it is expected that there will be some developmental confusion between Arabic and English, especially in areas of directionality and some letter recognition and formation, the evidence so far, based on classroom observations and feedback from teachers, is that children seem to 'code-switch' effectively in relation to reading and writing in English and Arabic. There are also important links between the way children are learning to read and write in Arabic and English that seem to ensure continuity of literacy development in both languages.

Children leaving the first cycle of Basic Education have often struggled to reach the required competencies in reading and writing. A number of key areas can be identified. Problems with handwriting are mainly attributable to lack of time given in class for handwriting development. Problems of reading can be related to the fact that children do not have a detailed or developed understanding of the relationship between sounds and letters of English; of the basic sounds of the letters of the alphabet, of vowel and consonant digraphs and of blends and clusters. They also are not able effectively to sight-read high frequency grammatical and functional words as they mainly learn to read content topic-based words (usually nouns). So a child could commonly read 'chocolate' as a whole word, but could not read 'the' or 'where'.

As a result, a new approach to teaching early literacy was developed for the Integrated Curriculum Project. Key differences are a focus on phonics (both synthetic and analytic), a focus on developing sight recognition of high-frequency grammatical and functional words; and the introduction of shared reading.

Children now learn the alphabet in Grade 1, developing their understanding of the sound of the letter, the name of the letter and the shape of the letter all at the same time. They use the shape, sound and name of something to recognize much of the world around them, from their family and friends to animals and objects, so this is not a difficult task for them. They then learn common consonant digraphs (th, wh, sh, ch, ck, ss, ll, etc.) and vowel digraphs (ee, ea, oo, ai, etc.) and blends (dr, cl, pl, etc.). In addition to building up knowledge of synthesizing sounds and letters, children also learn to use analogy to read words – using their knowledge of the rhyme patterns of words they already know to read and write unfamiliar words. Knowledge and use of onset and rhyme is an important focus of the approach to literacy development.

There is now an explicit focus on teaching of high frequency words, including grammatical and functional words. Teaching is through greater exposure to written text and by noticing and reading these words as they occur. These words are also taught and focused on through word cards, specific activities in the skills book, and through spelling. The focus of spelling in the Integrated Curriculum Project is on developing reading and writing, not only on remembering vocabulary. Children learn to practise spelling patterns as well as becoming familiar with and memorizing high frequency grammatical words.

Shared reading is now a built-in feature of lessons with children sharing reading a big book regularly in lesson time. Through the shared reading, children learn how to understand the meaning of texts by using a variety of top-down reading strategies modelled by the teacher. They also develop an understanding of the structure of texts and of genre. As children move to Grade 3, big books are replaced by graded readers that can either be read together and shared, or can be used for individual sustained silent reading.

The approach follows from the belief that effective readers use a whole range of strategies and skills to understand the meaning of a text and that children need to develop the confidence and the ability to utilize these strategies effectively. The unpublished external evaluation (Ambusaidi, 2007) conducted at the end of the first pilot year has clearly demonstrated that this approach seems to be working.

The initial evaluation of the project

The pilot year was extensively evaluated by an external team who investigated the pilot schools and compared the competencies of the children with those from similar schools in the same areas (Ambusaidi, 2007). In addition to comparing observational data and test results ('tests' were familiar classroom activities selected to show learning and ability), the evaluators administered a questionnaire for teachers and supervisors, conducted conference interviews with parents, and held discussions with headteachers.

The results of the evaluation have clearly identified a number of areas of success, as well as some areas that require further development. Children's literacy levels in both languages have shown significant progress in comparison with children in other Basic Education schools. As well as achievement in reading and writing, the evaluation has also identified significant progress in children's oral fluency and language knowledge.

Stakeholders (teachers, children and parents) have also broadly welcomed the changes implemented through the project. Generally, they appreciated the introduction of the class teacher as they felt their children's needs have been identified and followed up more effectively. In terms of English, they very much appreciate the new approaches introduced to literacy development (especially the phonics and the shared reading activities). They also liked the design and layout of the new materials and the introduction of more home-school links.

Future challenges for the project that have been identified through the evaluation include a greater emphasis on developing Maths in Arabic through the Maths Preparation book and more in-service training for teachers.

There will be another evaluation at the end of Grade 2 to follow up the progress of those children after two years of the project, as well as another evaluation of Grade 1. The materials are constantly being evaluated by the teachers, who feed-in to their development, both in terms of revisions and the development of future materials. Teachers do feel great ownership of the project as a result.

Conclusion

All education systems need to evolve and develop to keep up with the changing world and with changing understanding. Changes need to be informed by current theory, but they also need to be informed by experience; experience of what has been before and the experience of others. Change is also a risky business, because what might work in one context and culture might not work so effectively in another. As a result, change needs to be carefully planned, piloted and evaluated to ensure that it is positive and appropriate.

The Integrated Curriculum Project has certainly learned from the experiences of others and has been informed by those experiences. The project also aims to build on the education reform, not to provide an alternative. So far the evidence of the effectiveness of the project has been positive, but more experience will be needed before a final decision may be taken on whether to implement it in every cycle 1 basic school in the Sultanate of Oman.

The Integrated Curriculum Project has provided the means to explore a whole range of new approaches and methods. Many of the innovations will guide and inform future decisions, whether the project is implemented or not.

References

Ambusaidi, A. (2007). An Evaluation Study for the Integrated Curriculum of Grade 1 Children. Muscat: Ministry of Education.

English Language Curriculum Department (1999). English Language Curriculum Framework. Muscat: Ministry of Education.

Ministry of Education (2001). Basic Education in the Sultanate of Oman: The Theoretical Framework. Muscat: Ministry of Education.

Trainer training innovation: The trainer training programs in Taiwan

Chiou-lan Chern, Department of English, National Taiwan Normal University, Taiwan
Hsiu-ming Hsu, Chin-hsi Junior High School, Taoyuan County, Taiwan

Introduction

In Taiwan, the Primary in-service training programs organized by the Ministry of Education (MOE) have gone through a few phases of change. In 2003, a group of seed teachers were recruited and trained regularly to support local school teachers. In 2007, a three-tier structure of teacher trainers was officially implemented. The first tier is the overseeing planning group, whose jobs are to disseminate and implement government policies as well as trouble-shoot and organize training workshops for local consulting teams. The second tier is the local advisory group, whose teacher trainers are to visit schools in their districts and provide pedagogical advice and assistance. The third tier is composed of mentor teachers from local schools. The actual training sessions and activities that have been organized will be introduced and discussed in the paper. Goals and specific tasks for future projects will also be suggested.

Background of ELT in Taiwan

English is the major foreign language taught in schools in Taiwan (Crawford, 2003; Su, 2000); it is also the language used for wider communication in business and scholarly exchange. It had been traditionally taught at Year 7 until 2001 when a nine-year Integrated Curriculum was implemented and English was introduced to the Grade 5 curriculum (Chang, 2007; Chern, 2002). English instruction was further lowered to Grade 3 in 2005. The major reform relevant to ELT evidenced in the nine-year Integrated Curriculum includes:

- adopting one set of curriculum guidelines that allow multiple sets of textbooks;

- integrating learning subjects into seven learning areas, which puts English under Language Arts with Mandarin and other Taiwanese dialects;

- introducing multiple channels to teacher certification;

- adopting the Communicative Approach to English instruction; and

- replacing the annual achievement-based high school entrance exam with Basic English Competency Tests, which are proficiency-based and administered twice yearly.

These changes had a strong impact on teachers who had grown used to one standardized curriculum and one set of textbooks applied nationwide. To accommodate the need to disseminate information on this new system and new curriculum, different structures of teacher support system have been introduced since 2003.

Teacher support systems

From 2003 to 2005, two different support structures have been implemented to train teachers to cope with the reform in education. In 2003, the Deep Plowing Project was introduced and a group of experienced elementary and high school teachers, 'seed teachers', were recruited to help disseminate new information and familiarize teachers with the new curriculum (MOE, 2004). The seed teachers were appointed by local education bureaus and trained to be specialists to help local teachers. They received training on the latest teaching strategies and ideas and joined a Regional Instructional Consulting Team, which included school principals, master teachers and university professors, with the aim of visiting local schools, offering workshops, and sharing teaching ideas. Seed teachers were appointed from 2003 to 2006; their mission was to visit all schools in their region within this three-year timeframe and to report back to the MOE regularly. This was the first system introduced to ensure that all English teachers became familiar with the latest teaching methods under the Communicative Approach.

Of the many policies related to the nine-year Integrated Curriculum, the Deep Plowing Project, with the inclusion of seed teachers, was the most successful. Knowing the importance of having a bridge between central government and local teachers, the MOE put another support structure in place prior to the expiration of the term of seed teachers. Beginning in 2005, the three-tier instructional and consultative team structure was planned, experimented and officially implemented in 2007, to continue the work of seed teachers (MOE, 2007a). In this structure, the first tier, the MOE Curriculum and Instructional Consulting Team (also known as Central Advisory Team, or CAT), is at central government level; the second tier, the Regional Instructional Consulting Team, is at local government level; and the third one, composed of mentor teachers from various schools, is at school level. (See Figure 1.)

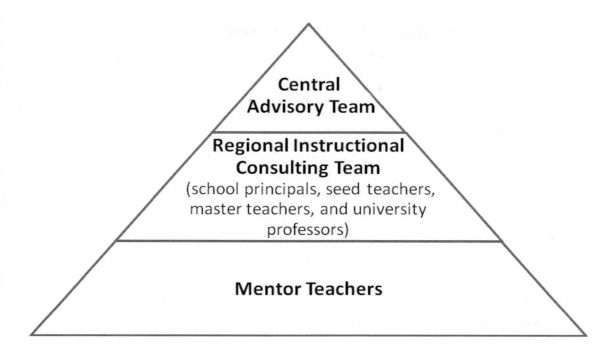

Figure 1: *The three-tier support system*

Like seed teachers, the MOE Curriculum and Instruction Consulting Team (referred to as CAT hereafter) is a national programme established to facilitate teachers' professional development. There are six school teachers on the team, three each from elementary and junior high school levels. CAT members are experienced teachers (the current CAT members have an average of 20 years of teaching experience) who work with central government to plan training courses. In 2007, the Regional Instructional Consulting Team was composed of a group of 266 master teachers, including 120 Secondary school teachers and 146 Elementary school teachers, representing 25 counties in Taiwan. Mentor teachers were those identified by the Regional Instructional Consulting Team from individual schools as active teachers who were willing to share ideas. In the future, when teacher appraisal schemes are officially introduced, mentor teachers will have to pass teacher professional development evaluation and certify themselves by attending MOE-sponsored training sessions. Though the teacher appraisal schemes have not been officially implemented nationwide, a project called 'Experimental Teacher Professional Development Evaluation' has been carried out since 2006.

The content of training courses

Two stages of training courses are offered to prepare teacher trainers. Beginning training courses (Stage 1 courses) are offered yearly to newly recruited Regional Instructional Consulting Team members. The training courses include topics on policies (e.g., new curriculum guidelines, ability benchmark and Basic English Competency tests) as well as those focusing on consolidating teachers' ELT professional background. More advanced courses (Stage 2 courses) are offered to returning Regional Instructional Consulting Team members in the second year to further prepare them to become trainers. The focus of Stage 2 courses is on the 'why' and 'how' of putting policies into practice, networking between central and local governments, as well as linking theories and practices in ELT. The mission of the Regional Instructional Consulting Team is to:

- demonstrate classroom/instructional techniques;

- advocate and implement policies; and

- provide a communication network between central and local governments.

By the end of 2007, 48 teachers had gone through Stage 1 training and 51 teachers completed Stage 2 training. The courses to be offered for Stage 1 and Stage 2 training in 2008 are listed in Table 1.

	Hours allocated	
Topics	Stage 1	Stage 2
Implementation and promotion of educational policies	3	3
(e.g., information from the MOE and regional education bureaus, e.g., nine-year Integrated Curriculum, High Quality Teaching Practice, Teacher Evaluation)	3	6
Curriculum and instructional leadership (e.g., how to organize professional development activities, like workshops, study groups, innovative teaching/learning projects)	3	6
Curriculum development and evaluation (e.g., design and develop school-based curriculum or teaching materials, evaluate courses/ curriculum and hot topics)	9	6

Curriculum innovation and resources/management/application (e.g., new ideas on teaching, teacher evaluation, assessments, learner achievement analysis, and use of technology)	9	6
Instructional assistance: theory and practice (e.g., professional dialogues/idea sharing, teaching demonstrations/observations, teaching portfolios)	9	6
Others (e.g., panel discussions with MOE representatives/ELT experts/CAT members to address hot topics, or topics chosen by regional mentors)	3	3

Table 1: *The topics for Stages 1 and 2 training courses*

The Regional Instructional Consulting Team members have the autonomy to decide, according to their particular teaching contexts and regional challenges, which projects to implement and which instructional goals should take priority. Trainers on this team meet regularly every year to choose crucial projects and topics for the subsequent years.

Facilitation of trainer training operation

As the three-tier trainer support system has been in place for over a year, some problems have surfaced. For example, some school principals were reluctant to release experienced teachers to participate in the project for fear of losing experienced teaching staff. At the same time, some teachers, not having their rights and obligations clearly defined, also felt reserved about being recruited to participate in the Regional Instructional Consulting Team. To further strengthen the system and ensure the participation of trainers, a new policy, called the 'Project for Construction and Implementation of Teaching Consultation Network Between the MOE and Local Government', was introduced in October 2007 to define and consolidate the structure of the local and central support team (MOE, 2007b). In the document, the specific rights and obligations of the team members are stipulated, which give master teachers 2–4 release hours and CAT members 10–18 release hours to do trainer training. It also allocates specific funds for local education bureaus to organize training workshops, with additional money allocated to remote areas for the Regional

Instructional Team to organize professional development activities. Schools with which the CAT members are affiliated also receive some subsidy to hire substitute teachers and additional funds (NT$50,000) to reimburse the school for releasing experienced teachers.

Conclusion

The latest educational reform in Taiwan started with the implementation of the nine-year Integrated Curriculum, which incorporated English into the elementary school curriculum. To ensure the success of this new policy, a range of teacher support systems have been instituted. First, seed teachers were recruited and trained to help local teachers cope with the latest policies in education. Then a refined three-tier support system was introduced to prepare trainers and mentors. These support systems flourished because the MOE, in a timely manner, infused resources into the projects and instilled a sense of achievement into trainers. Over the short period of time since the implementation of the project, the CAT members have grown in number, from six in 2006 to seven in 2007, and gained respect because of their devotion to their mission, which has expanded in scope from teacher training to policy piloting. The Regional Instructional Consulting Team and mentors in schools have also gained prestige as their work has been recognized. The institution that oversees the whole project, the MOE, has received both praise and criticism on the way, finally succeeding in putting the teacher training system in place.

From the implementation of the Deep Plowing Project to the stipulation of the 'Project for Construction and Implementation of Teaching Consultation Network Between the MOE and Local Government', all trainers (including those from central and regional consulting teams) are expected to practice processes summarized in 'SCAFFOLDS' – Systemize, Care, Administrate, Function, Facilitate, Offer resources, Listen, Devote and Support. Through the process of SCAFFOLDS, trainers initiate trainees to take their local teaching contexts and resources into consideration and thus develop 'high quality teaching provision mechanisms', which would enable them to automatically explore, construct and shape their own needs. When 'high quality teaching provision mechanisms' are fully put into action, we believe teachers will begin to thrive through professional development activities, and that more teachers in Taiwan will join the community of high quality teachers.

References

Chang, V.W. (2007). A brief sketch of Taiwan's English education at Primary level. In *Primary Innovations: Regional Seminar* (pp. 67-73).

Chern, C-L. (2002). English Language Teaching in Taiwan today. *Asia-Pacific Journal of Education* 22 (2), 97-105.

Crawford, J. (2003). Languages in the elementary program: A tale of two contexts. *English Teaching and Learning* 28 (2), 61-78.

MOE (2004). The Nine-year Integrated Curriculum Deep Plowing Project. MOE Document # 0920195655A. Available at http://www.nttues.nttu.edu.tw/cultivation/p01.htm. Accessed July 2008.

MOE (2007a). Guidelines for the Selection of MOE Curriculum and Consulting Team. MOE Document # 0960053021C. Available at http://www.edu.tw/eje/law_regulation_list.aspx?pages=3.

MOE (2007b). Project for Construction and Implementation of Teaching Consultation Network Between the MOE and Local Government. MOE Document # 0960150116C. Available at http://www.edu.tw/eje/law_regulation_list.aspx?pages=2.

Su, F-H. (2000). New goal orientation of English education for young EFL learners. *Proceedings of the Conference of ELT Curriculum for Young Learners in East Asia 2000*. Taipei: National Taiwan Normal University.

Beyond English: Primary plurilingual schools in Buenos Aires, Argentina

Leonor Corradi, Dr Joaquin V. Gonzalez, Instituto Superior del Profesorado, City of Buenos Aires, Argentina

Introduction

This paper aims at reporting on an innovative project in Primary schools in the City of Buenos Aires that was implemented in 2001 to provide equal opportunities to all children and to show that underprivileged children can achieve the same results as children from better backgrounds (Ministerio de Educación, 2003). Its positive results are the direct consequence of the main goal of the project: Education through English based on three pillars: social, linguistic and educational. The main constraints are related to two areas: society's views about learning English at schools and the tradition of English teaching, which considers grammatical accuracy to be the main objective to be achieved, and organizes syllabi following this objective.

In Argentina, English and other foreign languages have formed part of Secondary schools' curricula since the early twentieth century though they were not explicitly mentioned in the Education Acts that regulated education. The 1993 Education Act established that foreign languages should be a mandatory subject starting in Year 4 in the Primary school, and that within Foreign Languages, English has to be taught for at least six years. In the City of Buenos Aires, a foreign language has been included in the curriculum since the year 1968 in double shift schools and has formed part of the curriculum of single shift schools since 1996. In all these schools, learners study English from Year 4. In most of these schools, the approach to language is grammar oriented with learners completing their courses of study feeling that they only know a few grammar facts about English, which they cannot use to communicate. What happens in the private sector is completely different. There is a tradition of bilingual schools that excel in the teaching of English both at Primary and Secondary levels. There are also numerous private language schools, which teach the same students that attend state-run schools.

In 2001, the government of the City of Buenos Aires implemented the project of Plurilingual Schools (decree 140/03) so as to provide equal access to underprivileged children who would not have the opportunity of learning English outside school (Gobierno de la Ciudad de Buenos Aires, 2003). The term 'plurilingual' (CEF, 2005) was chosen because students learn English as a foreign language; they also learn a second foreign language – which can be French, Italian or Portuguese – and there is strong emphasis on Spanish, their mother tongue, as well. The project was started in 26 of the complete shift schools, which is 12 per cent of the schools. These schools were chosen for their population, which mainly consists of children from very poor backgrounds. Learners have English lessons four days a week, for two periods a day, thus doubling the number of lessons allocated to English in the rest of the schools.

Challenges

The first challenges to be faced were associated with the fact that there is no tradition of bilingualism in the area of state education, especially in EFL contexts. The second challenge was related to the rationale underlying the project; that of educating through English, thus emphasising the educational aspect of English, not only its instrumental value.

The rationale for the Primary plurilingual schools project

These schools are based on three pillars: social, educational and linguistic, each with its own aims.

Within the social domain, the main goals are:

- *Inclusion* into an educational system that should prepare children for the society they have to live in.

- *Acceptance of diversity* (to be distinguished from tolerance, which would result in having to live with differences).

- *Socialisation* – entailing children having to learn new codes and rules, the culture of the school and society.

- *The use of language to communicate* (as opposed to children having to resort to violence or aggression).

Educational objectives are divided into two cycles. The first cycle covers Years 1–3, while the second cycle covers Years 4–7.

The aims for the first cycle are the following:

- *The development of fine motor skills.* Many classroom teachers complain that children should master most of these, yet do very little when they see that children have not acquired them.

- *Space management.* By way of example, the following are some of the activities that focus on this aim: children are shown what bookmarks are for and how to use them; they should stick worksheets in their copybooks, making sure the title is not hidden; they have to figure out if the worksheet is too big for the page; etc.

- *Tidiness habits.* Many children's habits are different from what is expected at school and this is part of what teachers should teach.

- *Taking care of materials.* There is a tendency in environments of structural poverty not to take care of materials. This is because the idea of ownership is alien to some of the people living in this environment.

- *Accepting and following rules and instructions.* Children often find it difficult to follow the new rules at school, especially those which are never spelt out or are part of the hidden curriculum.

- *Respect.* This is emphasized in relation to teachers, peers and any person who forms part of the school community.

Growth of educational objectives

The first four objectives of the first cycle are transformed into organization habits for the second cycle, and the last two develop into conflict resolution and group awareness.

Apart from the three just referred to – organization habits, conflict resolution and group awareness – the following are further educational objectives for the second cycle.

- *Use of resources.* Children become aware of what resources they have available.

- *Autonomy and independent learning.* Children learn how to work autonomously and independently, and they know when and how to get help.

- *Rhythms and styles.* Children should become aware of the fact that there are different rhythms and learning styles and that no one of them is better or worse than the others. This also emphasizes the idea of diversity.

- *Role of mistakes.* Children realize they can learn from mistakes – both their own and others.

These educational objectives do not constitute a separate set of activities carried out in the classroom, but form an integral part of the teaching and learning of English. The belief is held that language cannot and should not be separated from education.

The third pillar, the linguistic one, includes the following objectives:

- Developing learners' awareness of how English works, which enhances their awareness of L1.

- Helping learners become aware that language is a means of constructing and understanding meanings as opposed to a set of grammar rules.

In order to achieve these objectives, a CLIL approach is used, combining features of EFL and ESL instruction. The setting tends to be natural in the first cycle, with teachers providing plenty of opportunities for children to acquire the language, while in the second cycle, elements from instructional settings are incorporated to help learners become aware of how English works (Ellis, 1994; Lightbown and Spada, 1999).

The curriculum that accompanies the project

The curriculum for these schools is based on the Curriculum for Foreign Languages of the City of Buenos Aires (Ministerio de Educación, 2001). The teaching points are organized into cycles around the following areas:

- the social practice of language materialized in the four language skills;

- areas of experience for the learners;

- use of English;

- reflection on the use of English.

The curriculum for plurilingual schools (Corradi, Cormick and Campagnoli, 2003) is more specific than the one just referred to and is organized according to years. It also includes educational objectives for each of the years of Primary schooling, cross-curricular links and expected levels of attainments expressed in can-do statements for each of the language skills (CEF, 2005). An example is provided below that exemplifies what has just been outlined. The list is not exhaustive, as indicated by the employment of ellipses.

Materials used

The same philosophy is used for materials as the one on which the project is based; that of integration. The three actors in the teaching and learning scenario interact and are integrated to allow for learning to take place (as shown in Figure 2), which means that the materials used should be in keeping with and at the service of learners and teachers.

Teachers use storybooks and readers, poems, songs, worksheets and their children's materials as well. There is a core of materials that have been created and compiled by the coordinator in collaboration with the teachers, which provides some common ground for all learners at these schools. Teachers are also encouraged to use other materials as they see fit or believe necessary, depending on their learners' needs and interests. When other materials are used, their value is then discussed at meetings and shared with other teachers.

Figure 1: *Organization of the curriculum*

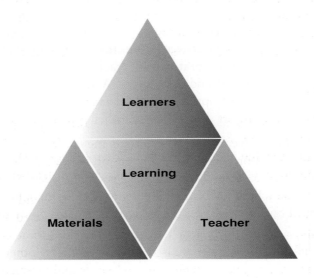

Figure 2: *Interaction and integration of actors in learning*

There is also a course book for each of the years, from 1-- 7. This course book provides a kind of backbone and gives teachers and learners a sense of wholeness and continuity. It is mainly used to help learners become aware of how language works after English has been presented to learners through other means closer and more related to their own experience.

The learners in the project

The project follows the principles of meaningful learning (Ausubel, 1968) and the natural cycle of learning (McCarthy, 1996). The main principle that underlies both theories is that the learner is an active participant in the learning process and therefore, he or she should be placed at the centre of the teaching and learning process. Teachers start from where learners are, and help them move on. Different learning styles and rhythms are catered for, with some activities designed for mixed-ability and mixed-level classes. Every learner knows what he or she needs to do to improve, to solve difficulties or to learn better. There is emphasis on self-evaluation, which learners engage in from Year 1.

The teachers in the project

Teachers need to do an entrance course in order to join the project. Most of the teachers are graduates from teacher training colleges or universities, though not all of them have a degree in Teaching English to Young Learners, hence the need for an entrance course with this focus.

In all the schools, there are assistant teachers who team-teach with the teacher in charge. They also work with children who may need extra support or who have special needs. As part of the project, there is a two-hour weekly meeting on Wednesdays, at which different topics are discussed, such as mixed-ability group teaching and learning, children with special needs, behaviour problems, and assessment. Activities and worksheets are shared and evaluated. Teachers also have opportunities for teacher development and action research, which makes this project different from other projects related to English.

Another aspect that is innovative about this project is the fact that teachers are permanently guided and supported by a coordinator, whose main job is to visit schools and classes, interact with learners and create links between teachers and the schools' authorities. Since the coordinator is part of the school's educational community, the guidance and support offered are not only theoretical but are based on the analysis of what is going on in schools.

Constraints

The main constraints are related to two areas: society's views about learning English at schools and the tradition of English teaching that considers grammatical accuracy to be the main objective, and organises syllabi accordingly.

With respect to the first area, after seven years, the educational communities have changed their attitudes towards the teaching of English in state schools because they see the results in the children, who can use English and enjoy learning it. As regards the second area, inspectors in the educational system believe that if students have eight periods of English a week, they should be much more grammatically accurate, this view is shared by many teachers in regular schools. They also complain that with so many periods of English, students should be learning more complex structures, such as third conditional sentences and the use of the passive voice. What they fail to see is that the approach in these schools is spiral and goes deeper, instead of being linear and covering a fuller range of grammatical points. Learners do use some complex structures, though they may not know these structures have a specific name and may not be able to work out a grammar rule for them. Children at plurilingual schools are far better prepared to communicate from the very beginning than children from regular schools. They are aware of what clues the context provides them with so as to understand messages and put meaning across. They have no problem understanding people speaking in English to them, which is not the case with other students. Though it is true that children still make grammar mistakes, as any human being would when learning a language, their level of awareness is much deeper when compared with students from regular schools; they understand why something is wrong, which means that eventually they will learn how to correct their mistakes.

Results after seven years

Students show a more positive and open attitude towards English and a high level of awareness. They know that languages are used for constructing meanings and they know what strategies to use to put meaning across: linguistic, metacognitive and social. They are aware of what life skills they have acquired. Most importantly, they enjoy learning.

References

Ausubel, D.P. (1968). *Educational Psychology: A Cognitive View.* Austin, TX: Holt, Rinehart and Winston, Inc.

Common European Framework of Reference for Languages (2005). Cambridge: Cambridge University Press.

Congreso de la Nación Argentina (1993). *Ley N° 24.195 Federal de Educación.*

Corradi, L., Cormick, S. and Campagnoli, L. (2003). *Diseño Curricular para las Escuelas Plurilingües.* Documento de circulación interna.

Ellis, R. (1994). *The Study of Second Language Acquisition.* Oxford: Oxford University Press.

Gobierno de la Ciudad de Buenos Aires (2003). Decreto 140/03. *Boletín Oficial de la Ciudad de Buenos Aires.*

Lightbown, P. and Spada, N. (1999). *How Languages are Learned. Revised Edition.* Oxford: Oxford University Press.

McCarthy, B. (1996) *About Learning.* Barrington: Excel Inc.

Ministerio de Educación del Gobierno de la Ciudad de Buenos Aires (2001). *Diseño Curricular de Lenguas Extranjeras.*

Ministerio de Educación del Gobierno de la Ciudad de Buenos Aires (2003). *Proyecto Escuelas Plurilingües.*

Curricular innovation: The Karnataka experiment

Gayathri Devi Dutt, S. Venkateswaran and Deepthi Sashidhar, Regional Institute for English, Bangalore, South India

Introduction

This paper attempts to examine the arguments that determined a new policy of English Language Education in the state of Karnataka (implemented in 2007), and discusses how this policy statement influenced the implementation procedures so that they responded to community aspirations.

English Language Teaching in India has been witnessing a number of changes in the areas of policy decisions, shifts of perspective, curriculum design and development, and reforms in testing and evaluation, with the changing perspectives of the government (and of the state governments in particular) at the centre. There is unanimity among the states on the teaching of English as a subject of study. This unanimity is on account of the changing economic scenario worldwide and the influence of global market forces. This is in addition to the potential of the English language for facilitating upward social as well as economic growth. All these have contributed to the changing perspectives in language policies. The public's realization of the need to gain proficiency in the language of the Internet (Crystal, 2004) and teachers' need to equip themselves to fulfill this demand for the language has also had an impact. A study by the Regional Institute of English South India (RIESI, 2003) reveals the need for an early introduction of English as a language of study in schools and the readiness of students to receive English language instruction. The National Curriculum Framework (NCF, 2007) document describes the situation as follows:

> The English teaching profession has consistently recommended a relatively late (Class 4, 5, or 6) introduction of English and this is reflected in spirit in policy documents. The dissatisfaction with this recommendation is evident in the mushrooming of private English-medium schools and the early introduction in state school systems. The level of introduction of English has now become a matter of political response to

people's aspirations. There are problems of systemic feasibility and preparedness, e.g., finding the required number of competent teachers. But there is an expectation that the system should respond to popular needs, rather than the other way round (NCF, 2007: 1).

The government of Karnataka favoured an early introduction of English in government schools under pressure from political parties, the public, parents and other stakeholders. It promulgated the policy in October to November 2006, announcing the introduction of English from the academic year 2007–08 from classes 1–4 simultaneously. A six-month period was made available to make adequate preparations.

The compulsory English language education in the state of Karnataka, in particular, and the country as a whole, needs to be analyzed diligently in order to arrive at the ground realities that foretell (allow for) the probability of English language learning taking place, irrespective of the policy introduction. Schooling is made compulsory for all those in the age group of 6–14 years of age. Though Shakespeare, in his 'Seven Stages of Man' (As You Like It, 1985) calls the second stage of the human life cycle the 'schooling' stage, this is not the case for all children in India. Lots of incentives have to be given to children to motivate them to attend school regularly.

There are about ten million children in the state and the policy requires that every child has access to a schooling facility within a distance of one kilometre from his/her residence. According to this policy, nearly 98 per cent of the villages are served with a Primary schooling facility with minimum infrastructure. There are about 52,000 Primary schools in the state but 40 per cent of the school-going population does not attend school regularly in spite of government interventions. There are a considerable number of children who drop out of school and this has caused concern. There are about 214,000 teachers working at the Primary level of education in response to the policy of sanctioning one teacher for every 50 pupils enrolled.

Even with this ratio there are only two teachers to manage four classes (Classes 1–4) and, in practice, it is a single teacher in many schools, at least, for some part of the academic year. In addition, teachers in Primary schools have to teach all the school subjects and often in a multigrade situation.

Teachers need to have a thorough understanding of the subjects they are handling. These teachers will have undergone 12 years of education, during which they will have studied English as a subject for only eight years. Two years of teacher education is compulsory for seeking employment. During this two-year period, content enrichment and principles of teaching were addressed in depth. In addition to this, regular, in-service training courses are arranged to upgrade the skills of the teachers.

The demographic profile of the classroom presents at least five variables: children can be categorized by region, caste, class, gender and ability. The school functions for 200–220 days in a year. The prescribed time for the English course is 200 minutes per week (five periods of 40 minutes each). In spite of 'English for All' being the policy, every child only gets about 100 hours in a year to study English. This varies from child to child, depending on the regularity of attendance.

The RIESI study (2003) found that the classroom practices do not really take into account the heterogeneity that exists in a classroom in terms of motivation, attitude, achievement, socio-economic status, levels of interest, social backgrounds, linguistic backgrounds (multilingual and bilingual), poor access to acquisition-rich language learning environments and learners with learning and physical disabilities. This study also reveals that the children have a stock of 200–250 English words before they come to school. Though children are quite capable of learning more than two languages at a time, the fact remains that there are limited opportunities for government schoolchildren to use the English language outside the classroom.

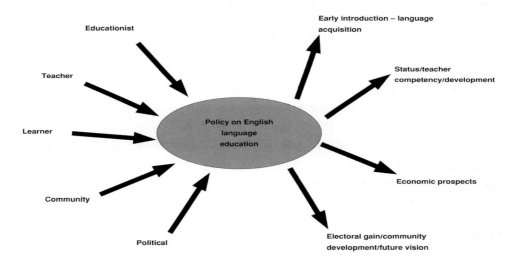

Figure 1: *Stakeholders and their expectations*

The curricular framework in Karnataka had to take into account the debate among policy stakeholders and their expectations of the returns anticipated from the policy, on the one hand, and the ground realities of students and teachers, on the other. The learners deserved priority; however, the expectations of other stakeholders could not be ignored.

One of the propositions made with regard to the ELT debate has been that if English is introduced from Class 1, it would be better to prescribe what the teacher can do and be realistic, rather than being idealistic and attempt impractical things. Therefore, the curriculum design, the content, and the training methodology not only had to be firmly grounded in the field realities but also had to be flexible and suitable to the socio-cultural ethos. There had to be some way in which the adversities had to be transformed into advantages. Based on this view, the curriculum committee for teaching English from Class 1, with Dr N.S. Prabhu as the Chairperson, designed the curriculum with the following objectives:

- to provide exposure to English language so as to lay the foundation for language acquisition;

- to develop learners' ability to comprehend the target language necessary for engaging in different activities;

- to develop the basic language skills orally before being introduced to literacy;

- to develop in the learner's mind a database of the new language through repeated effort at comprehension as well as through repetition of rhymes, dialogues, etc.

The justification for these goals is to provide the required amount of exposure to the target language given that the child has limited exposure to the language outside the classroom. Despite the short period available for learning a language, the principles of natural language learning are followed by emphasizing the development of oral skills for a considerable length of time before the literacy skills of reading and writing are introduced (Widdowson, 1990: 47). There is also a need to activate linguistic resources already possessed by the child and to enable them to relate and use this database to fulfil their communicative needs. In addition, children need to develop the confidence to use the language and to overcome the fear of its 'strangeness'.

The content adopted to achieve the goals mentioned above and the methodology suggested can be said to be well-directed efforts towards effectively addressing the hurdles in implementing the policy. The primary concerns in implementing the new policy to teach English from Class 1 are:

1. the heterogeneity among the learners;

2. teacher competence;

3. teacher profiles;

4. community pressures;

5. political expectations.

The curriculum framework suggests ways in which:

- the learners may be provided with a wide variety of means of exposure to the new language, considering the fact that they get only 40 minutes per day to listen to and speak English, and offers choices that cater to learners with differing learning styles;

- the teacher may be equipped with a set of conducive strategies to promote language acquisition in informal ways, with enough freedom to make responsible choices, with flexible options to transmit the curriculum based on learner needs, and with a new role as facilitator that compensates for any lack of competence and aids better confidence and professional development.

- the community and the public may be involved in the whole process, thereby facilitating the creation of a healthy language learning atmosphere in the home environment as well as in the classroom.

Instead of providing a textbook that is held sacrosanct by most teachers, and which thereby cripples their freedom in the classroom, there was a need for content that is 'learner friendly and accessible at all possible stages of teaching and learning in order to ensure unbroken, comprehensible input' (Tickoo, 2004: 15). The content was therefore presented in the form of a teacher's resource book and a learner's activity book. The teacher's resource book is a repertoire of stories, games, dialogues for practice, rhymes and songs, and Total Physical Response (TPR) activities. These activities ensure that the young children participate and engage in meaningful activities, in which they are constantly negotiating with each other and with the teacher to make meaning and in the process acquire the linguistic ability. The language-learning potential of each of these activities has been emphasized by several people (Wright, 1979; Philips, 1993) and they are being extensively employed across the world to teach language to young learners. The primary focus in these activities is on the listening and speaking skills in the initial years, moving on to reading and writing in Classes 3 and 4.

In the selection of the content, care has been taken to make it suitable to the different levels of learning. The nature of linguistic input was of primary concern since the focus is on the natural approach to language learning. The idea is to provide input that is comprehensible and interesting, without any strict grading. Stories ignite the learner's natural acquisition mechanisms, thereby helping them to process the information and in a natural sequence of development (Littlewood, 1984: 59 and 94). Gradation of rhymes, songs, TPR activities, dialogues and games has been done according to the level of the learners. A note on how to use the prescribed content forms a part of the teacher's resource book. The ultimate goal of the different activities suggested to the teacher is to facilitate learning by involving the learner and ensuring mutual participation in the process. The activities suggested in the students' activity book range from the use of simple outline drawings to the writing of a few words and simple sentences over a period of four years.

The chief beneficiary of such a curriculum design is primarily the teacher. The inbuilt mechanism of the curriculum design ensures that the teacher who is minimally qualified to teach English is empowered to make decisions that affect their classroom processes. Each teacher can choose from the vast repertoire of stories, rhymes, games and TPR activities based on the needs of the class and then conduct the activities. Apart from the confidence invested in the teacher, it is worth noting that the teacher has the freedom to make responsible decisions. This promotes teacher autonomy and furthers teacher development since the teacher is transmitting the content and is also a learner in the whole process. The teacher assumes the new role of a facilitator in practice – a role that requires basic language proficiency but assures maximum output from learners. Thus, the Primary school teacher, as Tharu (2005: 23) says, 'from whom a lot is demanded, [and who] is probably the functionary with the least professional autonomy in the world of education', is invested with greater autonomy through the new curriculum.

The inclusion of the activity book for learners is one of the strategies employed by the curriculum process to ensure community participation. The learner's activity book ensures that learning is continuous and reassures parents that children do get enough opportunities in the classroom to practise and reinforce what is being learnt.

Teacher orientation was a crucial phase in the entire process of policy implementation. Training programmes regularly provided to teachers were aimed at improving their language proficiency as well as their methodology. In this context, however, the primary objective of the training programme was to reach out to teachers across the state with a view to removing their fears/suspicions of the new language, reassuring them and instilling confidence in their own ability to teach what is a highly desirable and yet daunting language. A cascade mode of training was deemed unsuitable (for obvious reasons, including the fear of the dilution of the input) and hence an innovative strategy to reach out to more than 100,000 teachers across the state had to be designed. To make the orientation process more effective, two different kinds of training programme, with a total duration of six days, were planned. One was the centralized (satellite-based programme) for three days, which involved direct interaction with the curriculum designers and content developers, and the other was localized (face to face) for three days, conducted by the key resource persons trained by RIESI over the years as part of its capacity-building interventions. The training content included a session on classroom pedagogy, which involved a demonstration of how to transmit the content suggested (such as story narrating and preparing low cost teaching aids to support the less proficient teacher).

The response to training has been encouraging. To provide full support to the teacher, the supervisory staff were oriented to the new perspective so that they understood that formal testing and evaluation at the Primary level need not be a part of the process until such time as alternative practices could be put in place in relation to testing and the children feel confident enough to be evaluated.

To conclude, the innovativeness of the whole curriculum lies in the following characteristics:

- Content is not organized in grammatical sequence.

- It facilitates learning in the child and simultaneously the process enables teacher development.

- Learning is centred on comprehension and the focus is on oral work for a prolonged period before the acquisition of the literacy skills.

- Comprehension comes before production (i.e., listening comes before speaking). Meaning-focused activities, rather than language-practice activities, strengthen language learning.

- Building in room for teachers' to make their own decisions provides for effective language transmission and thus language acquisition by the learner.

- Access to continuous, in-the-field training is ensured.

- There is no formal testing, but rather progress indicators are suggested.

References

Crystal, D. (2004). *The Language Revolution*. Cambridge: Policy Press.

RIESI (2003). *English at What Stage and Why?* Bangalore: Regional Institute of English South India.

Littlewood, W.T. (1984). *Foreign and Second Language Learning*. Cambridge: Cambridge University Press.

NCERT (2003). *National Curriculum Framework*. India, New Delhi: National Council for Educational Research and Training.

Philips, S. (1993). *Young Learners*. Oxford: Oxford University Press.

Shakespeare, W. (1985). *As You Like It*. Oxford: Oxford University Press.

Tharu, J. (2005). Going beyond Whole Language to a Whole Child perspective. *The English Classroom*, Regional Institute for English, South India (RIESI), December 2004 – June 2005.

Tickoo, M.L. (2004). English in state-run Primary schools: Responding to programme-design and implementation problems. *English Classrooms* (RIESI) 6 (2), 13-21.

Widdowson. H.G. (1990). *Aspects of Language Teaching*. Oxford: Oxford University Press.

Wright, A. et al. (1979). *Games for Language Learning*. Cambridge: Cambridge University Press.

Teaching techniques: From listening to music to storytelling

M. Teresa Fleta, The British Council School of Madrid, Spain

Introduction

The teaching techniques presented in this paper are intended to create a rich linguistic environment; to improve the four skills in English as a Foreign Language (EFL); to stimulate the learner's imagination and creativity; and to develop learners' multiple intelligences.

In order to explore different approaches to EFL teaching, we refer to the teaching techniques presented to young learners in a bilingual school and how these teaching techniques were introduced experientially to a group of student teachers so that they could experience the methodology at first hand.

This paper is organized as follows. First, background information on child language acquisition and on the theory of the Multiple Intelligences (MI) are provided; then, the teaching techniques used with children and with student teachers are described; and, finally, some pedagogical implications are considered.

EFL learning at an early age at school

The pedagogical techniques described in this article are based on the idea that learning English as an additional language (L2) at an early age is a data-driven process that can be compared to the acquisition of the mother tongue. As MacWhinney (2004) puts it: 'The learning of finite grammars is a very conservative, data-driven process' (MacWhinney, 2004: 4).

Child learners, like native children, approach an L2 with no explicit instruction of the grammar rules and extract and abstract information (meaning, pronunciation and grammar) from the input data around them. At an early age (3, 4, 5 or 6 years of age) children learn languages in an unconscious and natural manner and they detect and internalize the grammar rules of the language they are learning by being exposed to it; first, they filter the input data and later, they create their own output data. As shown in Table 1, children who undertake an L2 start off with the innate language faculty and with the experience of having acquired a mother tongue:

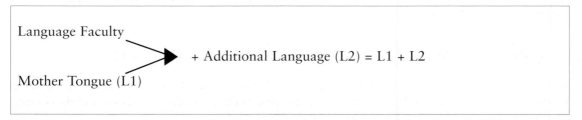

Table 1: *Child L2 acquisition*

Halliwell (1992) reports that young learners focus on the message they want to convey and that children approach new languages in class well equipped:

> Young learners do not come to language classroom learning empty-handed. They bring with them an already well-established set of instincts, skills and characteristics which will help them to learn another language. We need to identify those and make the most of them (Halliwell, 1992: 3).

Child learners who have access to English at school through different activities (routines, transitions, songs, chants, stories, drama or art) work on the target grammar and the classroom and the school become the language learning environment in which EFL teaching and learning take place. Moon (2000) states that the linguistic environment determines the amount of linguistic data children have access to and that the teacher, as language facilitator in class, plays an important role within this linguistic environment:

> The different contexts in which children can learn English affect the quality and quantity of language input which children get. In a foreign language situation, children will depend almost entirely on the school environment for input, so you as their teacher may be the only source of language, which makes your role in children's language learning very important (Moon, 2000: 14).

According to the MI theory developed by Gardner (1983), we are thought to possess at least eight different avenues for learning (linguistic, mathematical, spatial, musical, kinaesthetic, interpersonal, intrapersonal and naturalistic) and each individual is thought to possess a combination of these intelligences. The pedagogical techniques presented in this paper were designed to help each learner to develop their intelligences and learning styles. At an early age, the learning environment not only influences language development but also, as Gardner (1995) puts it, the development of the different intelligences; thus, using different teaching techniques favours the development of those learning styles:

We are not all the same, we do not all have the same kinds of minds, and education works most effectively for most individuals if ... human differences are taken seriously (Gardner, 1995: 208).

The pedagogical techniques considered here show how MI theory can be put into practice in the classroom and enable learners to work from the different strengths they all possess, and how by stimulating learners' different capacities, they can become creative and communicate in the L2.

Teaching techniques for child and for adult learners

The child and the adult EFL learners were engaged in story-making activities before storytelling. Table 2 presents information on both types of learners: the children from a bilingual school, and the student teachers from the Universidad Complutense de Madrid (UCM):

	Young Learners	Student Teachers
Place	The British Council School	School of Education, UCM
Number of participants	21 children	18 adults
Age range	7–8 years	18–38 years
Number of stories	21	6
Time	A semester	1 hour 30 minutes session

Table 2: *Information on EFL Learners*

Young learners

The 21 children taking part in the pedagogical experience were from the British Council School of Madrid (BCS). This bilingual school takes children from 3 to 18 years of age and 98 per cent of the students are native speakers of Spanish. All students are prepared for the UK and the Spanish University entrance and French is the main foreign language.

I developed the pedagogical experience together with my colleague, Elizabeth Forster, and the children taking part were from Ms Forster's class. The 7 to 8-year-old children were in Year 2 and had been learning English for four years. The entire experience took place over a period of six months during one academic year (from November to May) and the pedagogical experience was divided up into different phases.

Procedure

1. First, children listened to Grieg's piece of music 'In the hall of the mountain King'. They imagined a character and drew a picture of the character they had imagined. Since the initial stimulus was the celebration of Halloween, the characters and the vocabulary that came up were related to this theme (ghosts, witches, monsters, a headless man, a giant …). The purpose of this activity was to work on the musical, spatial and linguistic intelligences and to tap into children's imagination and creativity.

2. In the gym, children moved to the music by Grieg as they thought their character would move and used different types of movement (for levels: high, low and medium; for speed: fast and slow; for directions: backwards, forwards or sideways; and for movements: jumping, skipping or running). The purpose of this activity was to review the quality of movement skills, to reinforce vocabulary in English and to develop facets of the kinaesthetic and musical intelligences.

3. In the classroom, children worked individually, thinking about a story setting and a title, and made a list of adjectives and verbs corresponding to their settings and characters (some settings were castles, caves, forests or mountains; some adjectives: brown, green, white, purple, big and huge; and some verbs: fly, run, fight, eat or scare). The essential purpose of this activity was to work on the area of linguistic intelligence.

4. Later, children integrated all the information into a flow chart. The flow chart consisted of six spaces: one for the beginning of the story; three for the middle of the story, where the conflict or problem was indicated; and two spaces for the resolution of the problem. In pairs, children interacted with a peer and told him/her their story using the flow chart as a guideline. The purpose was to give children the opportunity to work on their interpersonal, intrapersonal and linguistic intelligences.

5. During another session, children transferred the information in the flow chart into a book format of six pages, with additional front and back pages. The book format was based on the fairytale structures and the six spaces of flow chart corresponded to the six pages of the book. Children transferred the pictures and described the action taking place in the written form, using the adjectives and verbs that had been chosen previously. They designed and decorated a cover page and wrote a blurb for the back of the book. The purpose of this part of the project was to work on the linguistic and spatial intelligences.

6. Children read their stories to different audiences and worked on storytelling skills (loud and clear voice; pausing for dramatic effect; showing the illustrations to the audience).

Student teachers

The adult learners who were introduced experientially to the EFL teaching techniques were from the School of Education at the UCM and they were enrolled in the pilot subject

'English Literature and its Didactics'. The idea of presenting the teaching techniques to future teachers came up during the preparation of three workshop sessions on story time, storytelling and story-making, with my colleague Dr M. Luisa Garcia Bermejo. The aim of the workshops was to provide students with tools for practical sessions at Primary and Infant schools and for their professional future.

The 18 students who experienced the methodology were in their first, second and third year of the degree and their age ranged from 18 to 38 years. They worked individually and in groups during an hour and a half session and time was allotted for each task.

Procedure

1. First, students listened to Grieg's piece of music 'In the hall of the mountain King'. They imagined a character, thought of a setting, drew a draft of the character they had visualized, and gave their character a name. For this part of the experiment, students worked individually and the amount of time allotted was ten minutes.

2. Then, in groups of three or four, students worked on brainstorming associations, talked about their characters and decided on one or more characters to write the story about. Students worked on the text and the illustrations, designed and decorated a cover page and wrote a blurb for the back of the book in approximately 35 minutes.

3. During the last 35 minutes, students presented their stories to the class.

The student teachers did not have a session in the gym and were not allotted extra time to work on specific language for their stories.

Discussion

As teachers of young learners know, children can learn words easily but they forget them easily, too; so there is a need for learning strategies that are memorable and that offer young learners the greatest possibility of remembering new words. The activities described in this paper were memorable and gave child learners the chance to create and to express their own messages in their stories. By doing so, the words they had been learning were easily retrieved from memory.

The pedagogical activities involved the understanding and the use of EFL in class and while carrying out these activities, the children were improving the four skills (listening, speaking, reading and writing) in English, and as Gardner (1994) reports, listening to and telling stories may have a great significance in the young child's life:

> ... story hearing and telling is a very special, almost religious experience for the young child, one which commands his absolute attention and seems crucial in his mastery of language and his comprehension of the world ... (1994: 203).

Young learners' imagination and creativity were also at work during the process and children were able to live their stories from the vantage points of the visual, kinaesthetic, spatial, interpersonal, intrapersonal and linguistic intelligences. From the early stages, learners were encouraged to create characters, places and situations in stories. By doing so, they were making connections and, as Wright (2006) points out:

> Making new connections is what creativity is! Wandering and wondering without clear goals is more important than linear thinking if you want to make new connections and to discover new things (2006: 17).

The student teachers experimented with the teaching techniques that had been initially designed for the young learners, in order to have a better understanding of the teaching techniques and to be better able to put them into practice in class. They worked individually and in groups, shared ideas and made decisions on which characters to choose, which materials to use to make up the story books, and also which student would tell the story to the class.

Pedagogical implications

As for what may be useful for teachers from these experiences, the study suggests that story-making and storytelling are very effective resources for teaching/learning EFL and to activate the different intelligences. The music stimulated the young and the adult learners' creativity, imagination and intuition. By being exposed to the musical stimulus, the young and adult learners developed visualization abilities and created a rich linguistic environment. Learning through music, movement and art involved learners holistically; language flourished in terms of input and output opportunities; and the ability to speak improved through interaction and practice with teachers and peers within this learning environment. Thus, the music that teachers consider adequate for each occasion and for each particular group of learners can become a teaching/learning resource and an important foundation for literacy.

By participating in the process of making books and telling stories to an audience, the young and adult learners were encouraged to interact and to do as much as they could by themselves, individually or in groups. For classes with large numbers of students, the idea of making a big class book might be contemplated.

Story-making and storytelling were excellent vehicles for the presentation of EFL in class and for the development of the four skills. From the linguistic point of view, young and adult learners moved from listening to the music, to the sentence level, in order to tell their stories in English. The 27 stories created by both types of learners reflected the way they had internalized EFL through activities specifically designed to bring their multiple intelligences into play.

Finally, it is interesting to note here that although the teaching techniques presented in this article were designed to teach EFL, they may also have applications in developing language and literacy skills in an additional language and the mother tongue.

References

Gardner, H. (1983). *Frames of Mind: The Theory of Multiple Intelligences.* New York: Basic Books.

Gardner, H. (1994). *The Arts and Human Development: A Psychological Study of the Artistic Process.* New York: Basic Books.

Gardner, H. (1995). Reflections on multiple intelligences: Myths and messages. *Phi Delta Kappan* 77 (3), 200-209.

Halliwell, S. (1992). *Teaching English in the Primary Classroom.* London: Longman.

MacWhinney, B. (2004). A multiple process solution to the logical problem of language acquisition. *Journal of Child Language* 31, 883-914.

Moon, J. (2000). *Children Learning English.* Oxford: Macmillan-Heinemann.

Wright, A. (2006). Being creative: Things I find useful. *Cats: The IATEFL Young Learners Publication Spring 06.*

Acknowledgement

I wish to thank my colleagues Elizabeth Forster and Dr M. Luisa García Bermejo. I also want to thank the audience at the Bangalore Conference for their comments and suggestions on some of the content of this paper.

English Language Teaching in Turkish Primary education

Yasemin Kırkgöz, ELT Department of the Faculty of Education,Çukurova University, Adana, Turkey

Introduction

In 1997, as part of a major curriculum innovation project in English Language Teaching (ELT), the decision to lower the starting age at which children learn English was taken in Turkey. At Primary level, the 1997 curriculum introduced a number of innovations. First, it extended the duration of Primary education from the previous five to eight years by integrating Primary and Secondary education. Secondly, English was introduced for Grade 4 and Grade 5 students as a compulsory school subject for all recipients of compulsory education. The curriculum (the Communicative-Oriented Curriculum; hereafter COC) was also innovative in introducing the communicative approach to teaching English within the Turkish context, where teaching is predominantly teacher-centred (Kırkgöz, 2006; 2007).

The Turkish Ministry of National Education (MNE) is responsible for centrally administering the ELT curriculum and the syllabuses of Primary and Secondary schools. With regard to the weekly teaching hours, initially, two lessons per week were allocated to the teaching of English for Primary Grades 4 and 5, and four lessons in Grades 6 through to 8, with each lesson lasting 40 minutes. Accompanying the curriculum innovation was the publication of a series of new textbooks, issued by the MNE, incorporating a communicative perspective. The state Primary schools are required to use the officially issued MNE-approved books.

This paper describes a case study concerning how Turkish teachers of English in state Primary schools approach the implementation of the COC innovation, their perceptions of the innovation, and the factors that impact on teachers' classroom practices. A questionnaire, observation and teacher interviews were used to collect data. Based on research findings, suggestions are proposed to ensure more effective implementation of the curriculum innovation.

The COC framework and its implications for teachers

The COC aims to raise pupils' awareness of a foreign language; to promote a positive attitude towards the learning of the English language; to increase pupils' interest and motivation towards the English language; to establish classroom situations in the context of games, setting up meaningful contextualized learning activities, and helping pupils to develop appropriate strategies (Kocaoluk and Kocaoluk, 2001). In its policy document, the MNE also makes it clear that the ELT curriculum should promote student-centred learning to replace the traditional teacher-centred view of learning, addressing students with different learning styles. Students are expected to take an active part in the learning process.

As pointed out by Carless (1998: 355), 'if teachers are to implement an innovation successfully, it is essential that they have a thorough understanding of the principles and practice of the proposed change'. The COC curriculum, with its emphasis on developing learners' practical communicative competence, encouraging active student participation in the learning process, has several implications for the teachers engaged in Teaching English to Young Learners (TEYL). First, the policy implies that teachers should be familiar with classroom practices deriving more from interpretation-based practices. Secondly, teachers are expected to make the professional adjustments to their existing beliefs to enable the proposed curriculum objectives to be achieved.

Teacher development opportunities

The nationwide implementation of TEYL initially exceeded the available resources, leading to a pressure on the system. To compensate for the initial teacher shortage, MNE recruited all available people with some proficiency in English, e.g., classroom teachers, former adult-only EFL teachers and non-ELT teachers.

In recognition of the training needs of the teachers, various teacher-training organizations attempted to facilitate diffusion of innovation to teachers. The MNE set up an In-service English Language Teacher Training and Development Unit (INSET). Collaborating with the MNE was a local association, the English Language Teachers' Association in Turkey (INGED), and two foreign associations, the British Council (BC) and the United States Information Agency (USIA), which organized local seminars for state Primary school teachers to help them keep up with new developments in ELT methodology.

The case study

This case study addressed the following questions.

1. What are the Turkish teachers' instructional practices?

2. What are the teachers' perceptions of the curriculum innovation?

3. What factors impact on teachers' implementation of the COC innovation in state schools?

Data was collected from more than 45 public Primary schools, situated in and around Adana, one of the major urban areas in Turkey, so that a representative sample of schools implementing COC might be taken over a period of three months.

Participants

Fifty teachers of English in different public Primary schools participated in the study. Twenty-seven of the teachers were graduates of ELT departments; 21 were graduates of the western languages, such as French; and two had BSc degrees in mathematics and biology. The 13 male and 37 female participants ranged from 25 to 48 years of age, with the majority in their 30s. Their teaching experience ranged from 2 to 16 years. Only seven teachers had received some local in-service training.

Survey instruments

The survey instruments used in the study included a questionnaire, interviews and classroom observation. Initially, a questionnaire was devised to find out: a) personal information about the teachers and their experiences in TEYL; and b) the teachers' classroom practices and methods they employ when teaching English. The questions required respondents to indicate their responses from a five-point Likert scale, on which 1 represented 'never', and 5 'always'. Also, each section included one open-ended question. The final section of the questionnaire asked teachers open-ended questions to elicit their opinion concerning the new curriculum.

Eighteen teachers volunteered to be observed so as to provide a more detailed picture of how the English language instruction is carried out. In addition, I conducted in-depth interviews with seven teachers to gain further insight into teachers' perceptions concerning various aspects of the curriculum innovation.

Data analysis

Data from the questionnaires were analyzed through the computation of descriptive statistics, except for any handwritten comments, which were subject to content analysis. Interviews were tape-recorded and then transcribed for further analysis.

Findings

Teachers' classroom practices

Once the findings obtained through the questionnaire and the observation data could be considered together, teachers could be positioned along the 'transmission-based' and the 'interpretation-based' continuum (as defined by Young and Lee, 1985, quoted in Wedell, 2003: 442). Ten teachers tended to be situated towards the transmission end of the continuum; a minority (eight teachers) tended to be positioned towards the interpretation end; while the remaining 32 were eclectic, and were, thus, positioned in between.

The teachers in the first category used a mixture of structural, grammar-translation techniques, putting emphasis on the delivery of knowledge about the language while ignoring the development of pupils' communicative abilities. Teaching in these classes was observed as largely teacher-centred. Despite the MNE's objective of developing communicative skills, such teachers remained unable to adequately translate these objectives into their instructional practices. These teachers were found to be skilled in delivering language to adults. However, they lacked practical experience on how to apply COC in their teaching.

In comparison with the transmission-oriented teachers, eight interpretive-oriented teachers applied CLT principles, adopting different approaches to address the varied learning needs of the pupils. Their style of teaching represented an innovative approach consistent with the COC principles. The pupils were actively involved in communicating and using the target language through games, songs and short dialogues established by the teachers. Taken as a whole, the lessons that were observed seemed to indicate that the teachers were able to put into practice a number of the main features of the COC. Interview data indicated that teachers' attitudes seemed to derive primarily from intensive two-week in-service training they received from the MNE. The remaining 32 teachers were found to combine features of the COC with that of the transmission approach to ELT.

Teachers' perceptions of the new curriculum innovation

Teachers expressed two positive aspects of the new curriculum. First, all teachers agreed that lowering the starting age had a positive influence on young learners' acquisition of English. Second, teachers mentioned that they found the textbooks well-illustrated; easy to implement (particularly for Grades 4 and 5); and easily available, as the books were provided free of charge.

Besides the positive aspects of the curriculum, several factors were identified that inhibited successful implementation of innovation, as illustrated in the following section.

Factors influencing teachers' implementation of the new curriculum

Teachers' understanding of TEYL and their background training

In the interviews, each teacher was asked what their understanding of teaching English to Grade 4 and 5 students was. Eight of the teachers described one of the aims of TEYL along the lines that it was intended 'to make learning more enjoyable through the use of games, songs and activities, to let pupils learn happily, to involve them in learning, but not highlighting the grammar'. These teachers believed that motivation is a key feature of TEYL and that the teacher needed to be 'active' in order to create a lively classroom atmosphere. In this respect, their beliefs were consistent with the current views of CLT and TEYL, and the official rhetoric. It has since been discovered that these teachers had previously received in-service training, which seemed to facilitate their implementation of the COC in their classroom.

As stated in the foregoing section, the remaining ten teachers were found to have previously taught adults and as a result were not familiar with teaching techniques at Primary level; they had received no training with regard to TEYL. The teachers' lack of experience in using practical communicative tasks as the starting point for language practice, their emphasis on grammar, and their background experience of teaching only adults seemed to reduce the extent of their implementation of communicative teaching in the classroom. With its communicative-oriented methodology, the new curriculum represents a major change for teachers more familiar with a traditional classroom in which the role of the teacher is to transmit knowledge to the students. These teachers admitted that they needed a reorientation to develop the skills necessary to teach at this level, in the way recommended by the MNE. The views of eclectic-oriented teachers were a mixture of the two.

Lack of guidance and the influence of textbooks

It has been found that the MNE textbooks did not provide teachers with clear guidelines on how to make use of the textbooks or understanding of their design and layout. Also, the ideas laid down by the curriculum document were not always reflected in the course books. While cultivating communication skills like speaking is emphasized by the MNE, the textbooks did not promote the listening and speaking components of ELT. Teachers stated that some activities were not contextualized in meaningful situations.

The teaching time available and class size

Insufficient time allocation to TEYLs was another factor that had an impact on teachers' implementation of COC. Teachers stated that the allocation of two hours of weekly lesson time was insufficient to complete the syllabus and carry out communicative activities. Besides the lack of time, the class size (an average of 40–50 students per class) was found to create difficulties in implementing the syllabus effectively.

Conclusions and suggestions

This article has investigated the introduction of TEYL and the structure of the COC in state Primary schools through a case study research design. Based on research findings, several suggestions can be made to establish a more effective implementation of curriculum innovation.

First, a greater emphasis needs to be placed on teacher development opportunities. Making cultural adjustments from a transmission-based to an interpretation-based paradigm requires practising teachers to alter their perceptions of learner-teacher roles and to develop appropriate classroom management techniques. Thus, in-service teacher development opportunities need to be increased for teachers engaged in TEYL, particularly those who are more accustomed to teaching English with older pupils.

Along with teacher education and teacher development, better provision of financial and materials resources, including a revision of the textbooks (which should include more guidance for teachers), would also contribute greatly to successful implementation of curriculum innovation. The teachers also require the physical resources to implement the changes.

Another suggestion concerns extending training facilities. As suggested by Fullan (1991) and Kennedy (1996), it takes years for change to spread throughout the educational system. Time is important so that the teachers can understand the principles and practical aspects of a curriculum innovation. However, if teachers are not given the support of information, adequate skills training, time and resources, their progress to the stage of the 'adaptation' of the innovation may not necessarily take place. Therefore, as suggested by Brindley and Hood (1990) and Wedell (2003), training needs to be ongoing, particularly during the first years following the innovation, and training provision must be offered to as many teachers as possible to ensure full implementation of the curriculum initiative.

Finally, a review of the intensity of the foreign language instruction is needed in order for measurable progress in the target language to be seen. The present teaching hours in early years (an average of 76 hours of instruction a year) in Turkish state Primary schools remains far below the minimum number of 200 hours of instruction per year recommended by Nunan (2003).

If these suggestions are put into practice, it is more likely that the process of ELT curriculum innovation will ultimately achieve its hoped-for outcomes in Turkish state Primary schools and that a complex, costly process will ultimately be worthwhile.

References

Brindley, G. and Hood, S. (1990). Curriculum innovation in adult ESL. In Brindley, G. (ed.), *The Second Language Curriculum in Action* (pp. 249-261). Sydney: National Centre for English Language Teaching and Research, Macquarie University.

Carless, D.R. (1998). A case study of curriculum innovation in Hong Kong. System 26, 353-368.

Fullan, M. (1991). *The New Meaning of Educational Change*. London: Cassell.

Kennedy, C. (1996). Teacher roles in curriculum reform. *English Language Teacher Education and Development* 2 (1), 77-88.

Kırkgöz, Y. (2006). Teaching EFL at the Primary level in Turkey. In McCloskey, M., Dolitsky, M., Orr, J. (eds), *Teaching English as a Foreign Language in Primary School* (pp. 85-99). Alexandria, VA: TESOL Publications.

Kırkgöz, Y. (2007). Language planning and implementation in Turkish Primary schools. *Current Issues in Language Planning* 8 (1), 174-91.

Kocaoluk, F. and Kocaoluk, M.Ş. (2001). *İlköğretim Okulu Proğramı* 1999–2000 [Primary Education Curriculum 1999-2000]. İstanbul: Kocaoluk Publishers.

Nunan, D. (2003). The impact of English as a global language on educational policies and practices in the Asia-Pacific region. *TESOL Quarterly* 37 (4), 589-613.

Wedell, M. (2003). Giving TESOL change a chance: supporting key players in the curriculum change process. *System* 31, 439-456.

The Teacher Development by Radio project in Nigeria

Felicia A. Moh, British Council, Maitama Abuja, Nigeria

Introduction

The issue of continuing professional development for teachers has been a worrisome one in Nigeria. Often, when teachers are certified, there is no ongoing training or support afforded them and the teacher is left alone to recycle whatever knowledge he/she had acquired at the training college/institution, completely oblivious to whatever research or practice might subsequently have been carried out in the field of study.

The Teacher Development by Radio project grew out of the need to supply professional development to Nigerian teachers in a cost-effective manner. There was the need to reach teachers without necessarily having face-to-face contact with them. The original programmes were drawn from the BBC Teachers in Action series, dealing with contexts very much like Nigeria's. Using these as a model, Nigerian producers and editors developed home-grown highly educational materials showcasing examples of good practice from Nigeria. Partnerships are secured with local radio stations who provide free airtime, free use of studio facilities, personnel such as producers and editors and who jointly drive for sponsorship with the British Council. The feedback indicates an enthusiastic response borne out in the quality and quantity of calls, text messages and e-mails. Teachers attest to its usefulness and other African countries are buying into the initiative. This paper attempts to capture these efforts to supply professional input to teachers via the medium of the radio.

Background

Although some colleges of education and universities offer in-service courses during holidays, due to the large number of enrolees, this has been grossly insufficient to meet the continuing professional development needs of the teeming population of teachers requiring them.

The result has been that teachers recycle obsolete knowledge using out-dated methodology. There has been a nationwide outcry about the falling standards of education as the products of the system demonstrate lower and lower proficiency in English as well as in other subjects taught in English.

It is against this background that the British Council in Nigeria conceived a project to meet the needs of professional growth in a cost-effective manner while reaching a wide audience. Teacher Development by Radio targets the teacher at the Primary and early Secondary level who not only teaches English, but also other subjects using English.

The overall aim of the project is to ensure that teachers throughout the country receive professional support through distance learning. We use this medium to reach audiences that may not have face-to-face contact with the British Council.

Origins of the project

Teacher Development by Radio is based on a Hornby School held in Kaduna, Nigeria, in 2004, to which eight different African countries sent teams of four delegates, representative of both media and educational interests and backgrounds. The school, which lasted for one full week, was run jointly by the BBC and the British Council. It trained the participants in the skills needed to produce radio programmes of linked and edited items to form an in-country balance with the BBC programmes on offer. The BBC component of the programme was 'Teachers in Action', a series of 24 programmes drawn from contexts like Nigeria's where English is a second language.

During 2004, several countries picked up on the initiative and developed offshoots of the concept back at home. Unfortunately none of them lasted, partly because the BBC refused to sign re-broadcasting agreements with African media partners due to a change in policy. This change was not reversed until 2005 when re-broadcasting agreements became possible again.

In February 2005, during a visit to London for another project, Gillian Belben and Colin Davis, accompanied by Dr Abdurrahman Umar of the National Teachers' Institute, a key stakeholder, were able to meet Andrew Bush, Director of BBC Learning, who assured them that re-broadcasting agreements would now be forthcoming and that they could use new programmes from the BBC archives to adapt to the Nigerian context. In the light of this, we set up a week-long refresher course in early May for the Nigerian team, held in Ahmadu Bello University, Zaria, and run by BBC Voices Kaduna. This led to some reorganization of the team and to a distinct plan to develop a series of programmes based on the BBC's 'Teachers in Action' series. In fact, the basic materials for the first two programmes were recorded during that week.

Nigeria put money into a refresher course with a new media and education team, retraining them in the skills first offered by the Hornby School – programme planning, interviewing, linking, editing, coordinating. Since then, the team has planned 24 programmes and has produced them based on the BBC series.

Objectives of the programme

- The programme aimed to work with teams in various parts of the country to produce home-grown educational materials.

- The first two series of programmes were intended to give important and topical inputs on the latest developments in Primary and early Secondary education.

- The programmes sought to put Primary and early Secondary teachers in touch with what is happening in different parts of Africa and the world, inviting them to take a fresh look at their own teaching.

- The programmes sought to encourage teachers to become active participants in the development process by joining in teachers' panels and by phoning in their views and questions to the studio guest.

Partners

In the pilot phase of the project, the British Council partnered with the Kaduna State Media Corporation. They sent in their producers and editors both to the Hornby School and for the refresher course. They produced and aired the first twelve programmes in Series One.

Officials in the state Ministry of Education collaborated in the project by providing the studio guests who answered questions during the phone-in sessions. The programme gradually assumed an important place in the radio corporation's understanding of its social responsibility. It was impossible to handle all the calls received from the enthusiastic and appreciative audience.

Due to the success of the Kaduna pilot, the British Council decided to produce versions for five other Northern states as well as versions for the South South and the South West parts of the country. Radio stations, Ministry of Education officials and the local English Language Teachers' Association were contacted and approval secured for the reproductions and for the broadcast. Currently, state versions of the programmes are running in about four Northern states.

In the process of securing a collaborative partner in the South, we approached the Federal Radio Corporation of Nigeria (FRCN), a federal agency that runs radio stations in each of the 36 states of Nigeria, including Abuja, the nation's capital. In a historic event, a Memorandum of Understanding was signed to broadcast not just 'Teachers in Action', but also other educational programmes that the British Council might design in the future on all the 37 radio stations owned and run by FRCN. A retraining programme was conducted for FRCN producers and editors who are producing a truly national version of all the 24 programmes.

The partner radio stations provide free airtime, which is funding in kind. They also provide personnel to be part of production, editing and broadcasting as well as jointly seeking sponsorship. Broadcast commenced in October 2006 and will run for a minimum of six months before the same programmes will be re-broadcast. It is estimated that seventy million people listen to this programme. (This is an FRCN estimate based on the spread of their stations. Outside a few towns like Lagos, Abuja and Port Harcourt, which have other competing radio stations, the FRCN enjoys a monopoly of broadcast in many parts of the country.) Outside the FRCN, it is anticipated that government and corporate agencies may also show interest in sponsoring the programme.

Benefits to the station/sponsor

- These programmes are highly educationally desirable and motivating for Primary teachers and for the general educated public interested in Primary education.

- They enjoy the full support of the Ministry of Education, who help in promoting them to reach the widest audience.

- They establish the sponsor as an important supporter of educational development in Nigeria.

- The station shares in the proceeds generated from sponsorship of the programme by corporate donors.

Project framework

In the following sections, some information about the framework of the project will be given to clarify how it was implemented.

Section 1: The production team

The Production team consisted of the following: the project manager, the team of producers and an editor. The responsibilities of each member of the team are detailed below.

The English Language Project Manager was the overall leader, providing direction, administering budgets, critiquing whatever was produced, securing viable and mutually beneficial partnerships, monitoring and evaluating the project. She was also the link person between the BC and the Ministries of Education, radio agencies and the teacher associations.

The five producers:

- participated in brainstorming for the content and structure of each programme;

- travelled to centres to make contacts with radio stations to explain the process required;

- worked with a local reporter and a British Council coordinator to conduct the interviews required for each programme;

- identified and carried out interviews relevant to other programmes as the occasion required;

- undertook a preliminary edit of the material and organized the files for each programme;

- discussed with the editor the final composition of each programme;

- took the final links back to the presenters to be recorded for each radio station.

The Programme Editor:

- participated in brainstorming for the content and structure of each programme;

- worked on the brainstormed material to produce a structure for each programme for the coordinator and interviewer to work with;

- collated and edited the material brought back by the roving interviewer;

- discussed with the producer/sub-editor (and the project manager, if available) the final composition of each programme;

- prepared the presenters' links for each programme and sent them to the project manager for vetting;

- transformed the recorded links and collated material into a finished programme.

Section 2: The format

The programme format is based on the BBC programmes from their series of the same name, but the commentary is given by a Nigerian rather than by a British voice. The BBC programmes take their materials from schools and systems all over the world, but particularly from South Africa. The Nigerian programmes keep these materials, but weave around them Nigerian inputs from schools, teachers and experts from the six geo-political zones of Nigeria. The programme material concludes with a 30-minute live phone-in during which teachers and the general public are encouraged to participate by contacting an expert studio guest.

Section 3: The pattern of the programmes

- The introduction, leading into a Nigerian section of 15 minutes, is based on the theme and ideas of the BBC programme, containing comments from the general public, teachers, trainers and administrators, classroom descriptions and extracts, children talking and panels of interested parties. Emphasis is placed on showcasing examples of good practice within Nigeria.

- This is followed by the BBC programme itself, lasting about 15 minutes, exploring the topic with examples and comments from South Africa, India, Bangladesh, Zambia, Brazil, etc.

- Finally there is a phone-in with a studio guest, during which the topic is discussed live with comments and questions from listeners. The studio guest is usually an education practitioner, an expert teacher or a senior official from the Ministry of Education who can competently handle the issues raised by the listening public.

Section 4: Monitoring and evaluation

The feedback indicates an enthusiastic response borne out in the quality and quantity of calls, text messages and e-mails. Teachers attest to the usefulness of the programmes and other African countries are buying in to the initiative.

We plan to have interactive forums with the Federal Ministry of Education and other stakeholders/corporate sponsors to raise media awareness for the programme. Occasional teachers' forum or focus group discussions will be organized to gauge reactions to the programme. We use PCMCIA memory cards to capture the quality and quantity of text messages sent during the interactive sessions. Basic cassettes are also used in recording live calls. There is a dedicated e-mail address to which people may send in reviews and feedback on the programmes. A cell phone line is also used in capturing text messages.

The local Ministry of Education promotes the programmes in the schools, encouraging teachers to listen and phone in. A questionnaire is administered to sound out teachers' responses using the teacher associations.

Prospects for teacher development by radio

The programmes could be used in other states and other countries either:

- as they are, with the introductory sections and links being re-recorded and edited in with a local link person and local information, retaining the Nigerian content and music, but using an in-country expert for the studio guest during the phone-in; or

- by keeping the format, but re-planning and re-recording the Nigerian material and music to suit the local environment, which would require recording and editing equipment and skills.

Already, Cameroon has commenced production and broadcasting by editing the materials sent in from Nigeria. Ethiopia intends to run a Hornby School on this and have asked Nigeria for personnel. They may kick-start theirs after this training.

As for equipment, the programmes can be produced with a mini-disk player/marantz recorder and a computer with editing software. It will be necessary to work with a producer for radio who is conversant with operating this equipment. Then a studio would be needed for transmission and mixing, which a radio station can supply.

The listing in this series follows the BBC format.

Titles for series 1:

1. What is an effective teacher?

2. The language of education

3. Curriculum change

4. How do children learn?

5. Using children's ideas

6. Planning flexible lessons

7. Imaginative resources

8. Working with the community

9. Homework

10. Assessment

11. Discipline

12. Joyful learning

Titles for series 2:

1. Lesson planning

2. Managing large classes

3. Group work

4. Teaching and learning in multi-grade classes

5. Motivation

6. Correction

7. Reading

8. Using the radio

9. Resources for teaching and learning

10. Parental and community involvement

11. Teachers' support groups

12. Change – children/teachers/methods

Conclusion

The Teacher Development by Radio programme has highlighted the enormous challenges faced by teachers in Nigeria and the impact that a little effort can make. In the phone-in sessions, I am often overwhelmed by the number of calls and text messages sent in from teachers from all over Nigeria. I had thought that English teachers would be the most enthusiastic of the listeners, but many Science teachers call to testify of the utility of the information and knowledge and its transfer value to their specific contexts. Many of the teachers call to express their appreciation for our contribution of a specific programme targeted to their needs. Those in the rural and semi-urban areas are often the most appreciative. These are usually the teachers with the least opportunity for teacher development.

The radio is an expensive medium for reaching large audiences of diverse background. It is the cheapest and most popular means of communication. Even nomadic tribesmen carry radios. It is estimated that about seventy million people tune in to 'Teachers in Action' every Tuesday night in Nigeria. These are people who otherwise would have been excluded from any formal training or courses. Taking workshops and seminars would have cost a fortune and would have been very time-consuming. Radio is faster and cheaper, and reaches a wider audience. Audience feedback is also immediate so that the task of judging its impact is made easier. Programmes like 'Teachers in Action' may well be the way to go for other developing countries looking at ways of improving the standard of their teachers.

References

The BBC materials referred to are BBC Teachers in Action Series 1 and 2 broadcast by the BBC in 2003 and 2004.

An EFL project for communication between Arab and Jewish children

Maureen Rajuan, Achva Academic College of Education & Hebrew University, Jerusalem, Israel
Orly Michael, Achva Academic College of Education & School of Education of Bar-Ilan University, Israel

Introduction

The setting of our project is that of a teacher's college in the south of Israel. In order to accommodate the diverse population of the college, as well as the geography of the area, the project attempts to reach out to and involve the local community. The project involves Jewish student teachers doing their fieldwork practicum in a Bedouin school.

The educational system of the Ministry of Education of Israel is divided into two main sectors: the Jewish sector and the Arab sector. This accommodates the language needs of the majority of Israel's citizens. Hebrew is the native language of Jewish children and the medium of instruction in the Jewish schools is Hebrew. Arabic is the native language of Arab and Bedouin children and the medium of instruction in the Arab schools is Arabic. In the case of Arabic, there exists a difference between spoken and formal, written Arabic, resulting in some difficulties in the instruction of the native language. In addition, Arab children are required to learn Hebrew as a second language in order to prepare them for participation in mainstream society, as well as for entrance into higher education, in which Hebrew is the dominant language. Both Jewish and Arab children are required to learn English according to the same curriculum of the Ministry of Education (English Inspectorate, 2001). However, English is a second foreign language for Jewish children and a third foreign language for Arab children.

The emphasis on English as a neutral language common to both Bedouin and Jewish children, as well as the medium of instruction for educational intervention by Jewish student teachers, served to neutralize the issue of language as a cultural barrier (Abu Raas, 2000; Akstein, 2000). English became the medium of communication between the Bedouin children and their Jewish student teachers, as well as a potential means of communication with Jewish children.

The Bedouins of the Negev are an indigenous ethnic group (Berry, 1990) that tries to retain its cultural heritage while moving to participate in the larger social network of Israeli society. As is the case with many minority groups, delayed educational, economic and political equality (Blai, 2006; Glaubman and Katz, 1998) often result in negative stereotypes that may be internalized by the group members themselves (Banks, 1981). For this reason, it is beneficial for children of minority groups to be helped to re-examine stereotypes about themselves, as well as about other ethnic groups, in order to increase their self-esteem.

The theory underlying the educational intervention of this project was based on the principles of Raviv, Oppenheimer and Bar-Tal (1999):

1. Developmental factors form the basis for concept formation. Children develop through the basic stage of concrete concept formation and egocentric viewpoints to more advanced stages of role-taking ability at an older age. For this reason, it is important that the concepts presented to young children be on an appropriate level of concrete concept formation. Friendship, as the main theme of the educational intervention, was chosen as an age-appropriate concept for young learners.

2. Children's understanding of life in different socio-cultural settings becomes meaningful when they are enabled experience in a practical way, relevant to their own lives. Interaction with Jewish student teachers and examples taken from Jewish children in neighbouring schools were common experiences for the Bedouin children in their own educational context.

3. External sources of information serve to enrich and change existing information. The educational intervention was based on presentation of materials designed to compare and contrast the Arab and Jewish cultures. Some examples include holidays, religious artifacts, traditional clothes, foods and customs, folk tales and legends taken from both cultures.

Stereotypes have usually been considered to be fixed and rigid. Webster's definition (1996) is 'a standardized mental picture held in common by members of a group that represents an oversimplified opinion, attitude or judgment of members of another group'. Cognitive psychological theories viewed stereotypes as fixed and rigid concepts stored in memory and activated automatically in order to categorize or evaluate people (Hilgard and Atkinson, 1967). However, the newer social view perceives stereotypes as inherently comparative, flexible and variable (Sani, Bennett, Mullally and MacPherson, 2003). Research has shown that children as young as five to seven have been able to differentiate between 'out groups' of variable degrees of difference from their own 'in group.' In the educational intervention, this principle was illustrated by the teaching about peoples from around the world. Bedouin children were given a worksheet about Japanese, Chinese and other nationalities. When discussing these cultures, Bedouin children came to view the similarities between Jews and Arabs as greater than before.

Method

Instruments

Two research tools were employed before and after the educational intervention:

1. an open-ended free-association task asking the pupils to complete the sentences 'Arabs are …' and 'Jews are …' in order to investigate their attitudes and stereotypes;

2. a task in which children were asked to make figure drawings of a Jewish person and an Arab person (with no gender specified).

Procedure

The research tools were employed by the children's Bedouin English teacher in the absence of the student teachers in order to obtain the most unbiased answers. In the free-association task, children answered in Arabic and their English teacher translated their answers into English after the completion of the task. The free-association descriptors were categorized as positive, neutral and negative.

The children were instructed by their Bedouin English teacher to draw two figure drawings, one of a Jewish person and one of an Arab person (with no gender specified), before and after the educational intervention. All the drawings were collected, analyzed with the help of a clinical psychologist and the relevant literature (Abraham, 1989; Koppitz, 1968; Wimmer, 2005), and each placed into one of four categories: pictures with signs of violence, neutral pictures, pictures with signs of friendship, and empty pages.

Results

Table 1 shows that negative descriptions of Jewish people in the pre-test made up more than half of the total list (57.0%). The negative descriptions decreased in the post-test to only 25.5%, showing a significant reduction in negative opinions and stereotypes. Further, positive descriptions increased from 22.3% in the pre-test to more than half of the total list (57.0%) in the post-test, evidence that information about and communication with another group yielded more positive opinions about members of that group.

Pupils' statements	Negative	Neutral	Positive	Total
Pre-test	102 57.0%	37 20.7%	40 22.3%	179 100%
Post-test	35 25.5%	24 17.5%	78 57.0%	137 100%

Table 1: *Comparison of distributions of frequencies and percentages of descriptors according to categories before and after educational intervention*

The descriptions were also analyzed qualitatively and yielded some interesting multicultural insights regarding the cultural characteristics of Bedouin children. Descriptions related to religion were dominant and included both positive and negative perspectives about Jewish people. The descriptor 'godless' was written 11 times in the pre-test and decreased to 7 times in the post-test, more than any other negative descriptor. This was an interesting finding in itself in terms of the great importance the Bedouin children place on religion (both positive and negative expressions) in comparison to the Jewish children who would place no, or very little, importance on an expression such as 'godless'. Descriptions relating to the religion of Jews, such as 'have a religion', 'have a different religion', 'respect their religion', appeared 12 times in the pre-test and only 3 times in the post-test. Similarly, 'respect the Arabs' religion' appeared five times in the pre-test and not at all in the post-test. A possible explanation for this is that religion became a much less important issue from the perspective of the Bedouin children after learning about the Jewish children, as expressed in the high number of times 'respectful' (seven times) and other positive personal qualities, such as 'honourable', 'loving', 'nice' and 'faithful' were written in the post-test.

Similarly, other lifestyle issues related to culture were expressed in the pre-test, but less in the post-test. Examples are: 'wear exposed clothing', 'interested in fashion' and 'drink alcohol', which were all based on principles important to Muslims. It appears that gaining information about Jewish children changed the focus of Bedouin children's attention from external appearances to internal characteristics.

We can observe a tendency on the part of the Bedouin children to find closeness and similarity in the post-test between themselves and the Jewish children in such expressions as 'cousins' (three times) and 'Semitic people' (used twice). Even the use of the terms 'Christians' (three times) and 'Druze' (once) in description may evidence not only the Bedouin children's misunderstanding, but also their desire to see the Jewish children as having a religion closer to their own, one to which other Arabs subscribe.

Friendship was the most frequently used concept evident in descriptions given in the post-test. It appeared in many forms: 'friends', 'friends of Arabs', 'believe in friendship', 'know the meaning of friendship', 'close friends', etc. for a total of 23 times as compared to only three times in the pre-test.

Another category of descriptions, dealing with war and peace, emerged. Phrases of reconciliation and connection, such as 'love and forgive', 'believe in peace', and 'like to get to know people' are found frequently in the post-test.

Language, as another barrier to connection, was listed nine times in the pre-test in phrases such as 'their language is not respectful' (once), 'have their own language' (once) and 'talk in Hebrew' (seven times). In the post-test, the same phrases, 'talk in Hebrew' (five times), 'don't speak' (once) and 'quiet' (twice) decreased in number, possibly showing the beginning of a bridge in communication through the use of English as a neutral language.

The results of the picture-drawing task support those of the free-association task in that signs of violence in the pictures decreased after the educational intervention. The pictures were of a neutral nature, both in the sense of containing less signs of violence, as well as in terms of their evidencing fewer cultural and national symbols depicting ethnic and religious differences. Table 2 displays the quantitative analysis of the picture drawings:

	Violence	Neutral	Friendship	No drawing	Total
Class	3 9.7%	7 22.6%	12 38.7%	9 29.0%	31 100%
Class	4 17.4%	8 34.8%	8 34.8%	3 13%	23 100%
Total	7 13.0%	15 27.8%	20 37.0%	12 22.2%	54 100%

Table 2: *Distribution of frequencies and percentages of children's drawings after the educational intervention according to categories*

Discussion

Our research findings point to three major conclusions. The first being that stereotypes are variable and given to change, as held by the newer social view, through educational interventions of a limited and focused nature. We have found that one effective strategy for the changing of stereotypes among young children is the strengthening of their own self-image. Another is the comparison of one's ethnic group with other 'out groups' of differing characteristics.

The second conclusion is that age-specific interventions are effective at the early stage of concrete concept formation. Children can relate to the concept of friendship in the context of their own lives when confronted by information and encounters with other ethnic groups.

The third conclusion is that learning English as a neutral language can bridge cultural, religious and ethnic barriers between native languages. English, when taught as a language of communication, is perceived by children as a tool for discovering the similarities they share with other children.

References

Abraham, A. (1989). *The Visible and the Hidden in Human Figure Drawings*. Tel Aviv: Reshafim.

Abu Rass, R. (2000). Learning strategies and second language learning. *English Teacher's Journal*, English Inspectorate, Israel Ministry of Education 53, 68-74.

Akstein, S. (2000). Whole language means a whole lot of things. *English Teacher's Journal*, English Inspectorate, Israel Ministry of Education 53, 99-102.

Banks, J.A. (1981). *Multiethnic Education: Theory and Practice*. Boston: Allyn & Bacon.

Berry, J.W. (1990). Psychology of acculturation: Understanding individuals moving between cultures. In Brislin, R.W. (ed.). *Cross-Cultural Research and Methodology Series*, Vol. 14 (pp. 232-253). London: Sage Publications.

Blai, E.W. (2006). *Bedouin Children in the Negev: Current Situation*. Jerusalem: Knesset Research and Information Center (Hebrew).

English Inspectorate (2001). *English Curriculum: Principles and Standards for Learning English as a Foreign Language in Israeli Schools*. Israel: Ministry of Education.

Glaubman, R. and Katz, Y. (1998). *The Bedouin Community in the Negev: Educational and Community Characteristics*. Ramat-Gan: Bar-Ilan University.

Hilgard, E.R. and Atkinson, R.C. (1967). *Introduction to Psychology* (4th edition). New York: Harcourt, Brace and World, Inc.

Koppitz, E. (1968). *Psychological Evaluation of Children's Human Figure Drawing*. London: Grune & Stratton.

Raviv, A., Oppenheimer, L. and Bar-Tal, D. (eds) (1999). *How Children Understand War and Peace*. San Francisco: Jossey-Bass Publishers.

Sani, F., Bennett, M., Mullally, S. and MacPherson, J. (2003). On the assumption of fixity in children's stereotypes: A reappraisal. *British Journal of Development Psychology* 21, 113-124.

Webster's New Encyclopedic Dictionary (1996). Cologne, Germany: Konemann.

Wimmer, M. (ed.). (2005) *Talking Drawings: Tools and Methods for Understanding Children's Drawings*. Tel-Aviv: Mentor Press.

Acknowledgements

The authors would like to express their appreciation to Aliza Ben-Menachem, Clinical Psychologist, for her expert analysis of the children's drawings and help with the relevant theoretical literature.

We also want to thank our student teachers, Limor Rozenbaum and Tal Brown, for sharing their materials, research data and experiences in the writing of this paper.

The EYL publishers panel: Supporting innovation and best practice in EYL: The role of publishing

Catherine Kneafsey, Oxford University Press
Kathryn Munt, Pearson Education
Atiya Zaidi, Ratna Sagar Publishers
Convenor, Shelagh Rixon, University of Warwick, UK

Introduction

Innovation involving the introduction of English at Primary school level or the lowering of the age at which children start English in the Primary school often starts at government level with political objectives often looming as large as educational objectives, as many of the presentations at this conference confirmed. The grand announcement of an initiative having been made, it is frequently the case that the practicalities of exactly how it is to be implemented are then left rather vague and for others to work out at Ministry or Local Education Authority level. Meanwhile teachers in their schools have day-to-day decisions to make about how best to meet the requirement to teach English to the children in their care. Many of these teachers may have found themselves compelled by events to adopt the role of English teacher in addition to their other duties and it may or may not be a role with which they feel immediately comfortable. With budgets and time for teacher orientation at a national level often limited, the contribution that appropriate teaching materials may make in supporting teachers in their efforts is extremely important.

Different countries differ in their approaches to the supply of materials and in the degree of freedom of choice that state-funded Primary schools are allowed in the teaching materials they use.

Three main approaches are found:

1. materials are *specially commissioned*, written to the specifications of a Ministry of Education or other educational authority, for example the textbook series entitled 'Elementary School English' currently used in South Korea;

2. materials originally published for a wider market (so-called 'glocal' materials) are adapted to local needs, for example, the internationally used Longman/Pearson

Education text *Gogo Loves English* being adapted to suit the requirements of some regions of China;

3. material is *adopted without modifications;* existing published materials, which seem to provide a good fit with the needs of a particular context are adopted, such as Oxford University Press's 'Happy House' material, which is used in Bahrain.

Beyond the day-to-day support that is given to teachers by simply putting something in their hands from which they can teach, published materials may play a direct part in teacher development. They may, for example, give the rationales and provide the resources for activities that teachers may not have had the opportunity or confidence to try before. An example of this is the Story Cards provided with the 'BUGs' series (published by Macmillan) with pictures of key moments in the story on the front for the children to see and a script of the story on the back to support the teacher telling the story. Materials may also become the focus and source of examples for seminars and training courses in Teaching English to Young Learners.

All of these possibilities, in optimum conditions, involve feedback from and consultation with representative teachers as well as teacher orientation to the new materials. That way the textbook or other course materials can truly become the 'agent of change' (Hutchinson and Torres, 1994).

The Bangalore panel on EYL publishing was set up to encourage communication and discussion between publishers and influential members of their constituency. There were two main aims.

1. First, the panel aimed to discuss the selection of teaching materials as reflected by each of the approaches described above and acknowledging these as powerful means in themselves of helping teachers become comfortable with innovation. Particular attention was paid to ways in which possibly unfamiliar classroom practices thought beneficial for children by writers and editors could be made both transparent and appetising to teachers using the materials.

2. Secondly, the panel sought to learn more about the roles which responsible publishers can play in their relations with particular teaching contexts, These efforts often go far beyond the processes centred around the ideation, design and production of a set of teaching resources intended to fit the needs of a particular situation, and extend into direct dialogue with practising teachers. Such dialogue may result in modifications to the materials themselves so they may more closely meet the concerns of teachers and the needs of the children, but may also result in teacher development interventions that inform and support teachers in implementing methodological or language focused aspects of existing materials that may lie outside their current experience.

The introduction to the session by the convener covered the general points mentioned above, as a framework within which the publishers could situate their contributions.

The main part of the session consisted of short presentations by the representatives of three publishing houses, all of them with major commissioning and editorial responsibilities in the area of EYL materials, but each representing on this occasion one of the three material-provision approaches discussed above. This was followed by questions and answers.

The first presentation, given by Kathryn Munt of Pearson Education, gave a picture of a highly developed version of the second approach described above. Kathryn described how a centrally developed corpus of material that contributed to the EYL course 'English Adventure' was moulded to produce parallel editions to suit different contexts. Adjustments were made in areas such as cultural content and activity types through a process of drafting and re-drafting guided by feedback from teachers and consultants worldwide.

The second presentation, by Atiya Zaidi of Ratna Sagar Publishers, represented the first approach described above. Atiya described the interactive feedback and consultation process that took EYL materials designed to fit the needs of an Indian EYL context through several successive editions, with revisions being made for each edition in response to teachers' observations and requests.

Catherine Kneafsey of Oxford University Press represented the third approach described above. Catherine showed how a publishing company could provide practical training support to teachers in a particular context – in this case in Bahrain, where existing EYL materials, entitled 'Happy House', had been adopted without adaptation because they were seen by the authorities to be a close fit with local needs. Teachers, however, were felt to need support and orientation in order to make the best use of the resources provided. This was achieved over a four-year period through teacher-development workshops and seminars provided by a teacher educator appointed by Oxford University Press.

References

Hutchinson, T. and Torres, E. (1994). The textbook as agent of change. *ELT Journal* 48 (4), 315-328.

Applying multiple intelligences for teaching ESL to young learners

Kalyani Samantray, Department of English, Saila Bala Women's College, Utkal University, Orissa, India

Introduction

Multiple Intelligences (MI) as a teaching strategy has not yet got a foothold in ELT in India, though it has two very powerful applications at the Primary level:

1. paving the way for long-term success in ESL by keeping young learners motivated to learn rather than just filtering information through the linguistic intelligence;

2. transforming the role of teachers, who typically rely on mandated curriculum, materials and approach.

A small-scale project was undertaken to validate the premises mentioned. The project involved nine teachers of English (teaching at the Primary level) reflecting upon and identifying their less-developed MIs, and noticing the correlation between their strong MIs and their teaching approaches. During the project, the teachers identified their own stronger intelligences as well as the intelligence patterns of their students, and used inputs in a variety of ways for better ESL learning outcomes.

The concept of multiple intelligences

Gardner (1983) proposed the concept of MIs wherein human cognition is considered to be multifaceted as opposed to the traditional theories (Spearman, 1904; Tolman, 1932; Thurnstone, 1938) of intelligence. These theories are characterized by two fundamental assumptions: that human cognition is unitary; and that individuals can be adequately described as having a single, quantifiable intelligence.

The theory of MI looks at human potential in its broadest sense, which is a significant development on the existing paradigm. Instead of positing intelligence as *monolithic*, MI regards intelligence as *multifaceted*, and, rather than intelligence as whole, specific facets of it are regarded as being as more developed than others in different individuals. This implies that some intelligences are better developed in individuals than other intelligences. The theory also suggests that one form of intelligence is not better than another; each one is equally valuable, viable and valid.

When applied to the area of learning, MI helps in identifying individual learners' basic personal characteristics, traits, behaviours and preferences for each of the nine intelligences put forward by Gardner (1993; 2000).

MI in India

With all its potential, the concept of MI has not yet got a foothold in early childhood education in India though it has two very powerful applications in the Indian context. MI, first of all, has the potential for helping more learners succeed by keeping them motivated to learn. When teachers offer different pathways for learners to learn – rather than just filtering all information and learning through the linguistic and mathematic intelligences – more learners can find success in school. Secondly, it can offer a continual process of teacher development through reflective practice by teachers on their own strengths and weaknesses, and offering opportunities to them to improve on their weaknesses. It can transform the role of teachers who typically rely on mandated curriculum, materials and approach.

A project based on the MI principles

With this background, a three-month, short-term project was undertaken with the participation of three Primary schools in Bhubaneswar to experiment with the MI principles.

Eighty-five learners of Class 5 from the three Primary schools, and nine teachers participated in the project.

Of the nine intelligences described by Gardner, eight were used in this project.

The assumptions of this project

The assumptions underlying this project were that:

- Teachers have to first, identify their own less-developed strengths and intelligences in order to make them aware of their unconscious teaching biases.

- With such awareness, teachers may then begin to notice the patterns and correlations between the strengths they employ in providing input in ESL teaching and the approaches they are less comfortable with and, therefore, don't use.

- With such awareness, they may plan lessons and input in the classroom using eight different intelligence modes to provide a holistic approach to teaching ESL.

- This in turn will allow for greater learner autonomy through self-motivation, since learners would find their personal intelligence types match with the input provided and would not have to adjust to the linguistic and mathematical intelligences alone.

In order to offer multiple pathways for learners to learn, teachers have to reflect upon and identify their less developed strengths and intelligences because we naturally rely on and use teaching strategies that match our strongest intelligences. The project was expected to help teachers in reflecting upon and identifying their less developed MIs, and to notice the correlation between their strong MIs and their teaching approaches. They would thus identify learners' *highs* (their personal intelligence patterns) and *lows* (intelligences that are not well developed), and use inputs for better ESL learning, motivation and outcomes.

The questions investigated

The questions investigated through the project were the following:

- Are the learners' strengths the same as the teacher's or are the learners most intelligent in ways the teacher is least so?

- Do learners use intelligences that are different from the ones their teachers use?

- Will teachers notice that they were unaware of or have avoided using the teaching strategies best designed for developing all the different intelligences in learners?

Procedures

Stage 1: Establishing the MI profiles of the teachers

To help the teachers to become aware of their unconscious teaching biases, it was fundamental for this project to define the MI contours of each participating teacher using class observation, an MI test and a structured interview.

- **Class observation:** The classes of the nine participating teachers were observed and extensive notes taken by the researcher to establish their pathways for input, which in turn revealed each teacher's dominant intelligence types.

- **MI test:** The teachers took the MI test, analyzed their responses in order to codify their strengths, and discovered for themselves the blueprint of their dominant intelligences.

- **Teacher interview:** Using a structured set of questions, the teachers were interviewed so that the nature of ESL input they provided to their learners and the explanation of their preferred pathways for input use were gathered. When asked if they would use input in the class for ESL teaching in some other ways, they seemed quite uncomfortable to adopt new pathways.

The teachers were quite surprised to see their test results match with the classroom observation results and the outcome of the interview. Some acceptance of the idea of multiple pathways to ESL learning emerged following the triangulation results. The teachers also felt quite convinced that there exist pathways for learning other than the ones they typically use in their ESL classes.

This triangulation ascertained the dominant intelligence types of the teachers: linguistic, mathematical and musical. The way they preferred to deliver input for ESL matched with their *stronger* intelligence types, and their unconscious teaching biases.

Testing learners for their MI

As it was not possible get the MI profiles of all 85 learners, a randomly chosen sample of 20 learners took the MI test to figure out their individual intelligence profiles (Armstrong, 1993 and 1994).

It was not very surprising that their MI profiles illustrated their most developed intelligences to be kinesthetic, musical, naturalistic and visual-spatial.

Outcomes of Stage 1

Teachers were more surprised at the MI profiles of their learners than their own profiles. It was a revelation for them that learners actually prefer to learn differently from the way(s) the input was presented to them. They also realized to a great extent that they prefer verbal-linguistic and mathematical intelligences to the other modes.

This led to a degree of acceptance by the teachers of the idea of there being multiple pathways to ESL learning.

Stage 2: Lesson planning using eight intelligences

Once the teachers had been sufficiently convinced of the utility of imparting input in a number of ways to accommodate the different intelligences of their learners, they agreed to use prepared lesson plans on an experimental basis. Nevertheless, they were involved in the process of planning the lessons.

Linking the learners to the activity types

It was then essential to introduce the learners to the idea of planning lessons differently since they were also equal stakeholders in this procedure, and without their cooperation the teachers could not be expected to carry on with most of the activities.

The learners were more than excited at the opportunity to do things in a variety of ways rather than just using reading and writing to learn English.

'Activity Centres' were created in the classrooms, each focusing on one type of 'intelligence'. Learners got acquainted with the names of the centres and what they were expected to do at each centre. They could work according to the requirement of each centre.

The following table shows the association created between each of Gardner's intelligence types and the matching activity centre.

Gardner's identified Intelligences	Center Name
Linguistic Intelligence	Reading Centre
Visual-Spatial Intelligence	Art Centre
Kinesthetic Intelligence	Building and Activity Centre
Mathematical-Logical Intelligence	Math Centre
Musical Intelligence	Music Centre
Interpersonal Intelligence	Working Together Centre
Intrapersonal Intelligence	Personal Work Centre
Naturalistic Intelligence	Adventure Centre

Table 1: *Gardner's Intelligence types and the matching work centres*

A sample lesson plan

- At the **Reading Centre,** the learners read a story entitled *In the Town*, which depicted a young girl from a village exploring the interesting places of a town with her friend.

- At the **Building Centre,** the learners actually constructed the town in a box referring to the text.

- At the **Math Centre,** each group worked with geometric concepts of square, angles, circles, height, length and breadth, etc. using different objects. They also created shopping lists with a budget to buy articles from the shops/supermarket.

- The **Music Centre** provided a listening/spelling activity. The learners listened to music while studying the spelling of words that occurred in the text, such as town hall, library, foot-bridge and beach. They also learnt the syllabic structure of words by beating the rhythm and clapping.

- Work at the **Art Centre** involved cutting out paper in different sizes, which the learners coloured, pasting and labelling them to identify the different areas and zones of a city.

- The **Working Together** (interpersonal) **Centre** had a cooperative learning activity where the learners had to read a fact sheet on the town and jointly answer questions.

- The learners were engaged in a fantasy writing activity on the subject 'Things you would take with you on a journey to a future city' at the **Personal Work** (intrapersonal) **Centre.**

- At the **Adventure** (naturalistic) **Centre**, the plan was to visit a local museum/library, and prepare a report on the visit.

Classroom implementation

Creating eight different 'work centres' relating to the eight MI pathways was not possible in the classrooms due to lack of space. The walls of each classroom were used to show eight spaces each dedicated to one of Gardner's eight intelligences.

The learners work at each centre for 30 minutes everyday. On Saturdays, they chose two centres as it is a half school day. In this way, the learners 'visited' each of the eight centres every week.

Changes perceived

Although lesson planning still remained a big challenge for the teachers at the end of the project, there was a marked acceptance of the idea of different intelligences by the teachers. Transformations were perceived in the earlier teacher attitude of fixity with regard to the pathways for ESL input. Teachers subsequently focused on the development of the intelligences that are traditionally neglected, such as musical, kinesthetic and naturalistic.

In addition, there was distinct improvement in learner attitude towards learning English. English did not scare the children as much as it had done before. It became rather fun for them to accomplish things using English.

Assessment of ESL learning

The assessment that was planned to record the progress of the learners in their ESL achievement was quite unconventional. A chart was prepared with the names of the learners and the name of each activity. Using a colour code, the learners were assessed for their attainment levels: green for 'competence', yellow for 'working on', and red for 'underachievement'. It was very heartening to see 46 per cent of the participating learners demonstrating competence in all the work centres, with nearly 100 per cent completing each activity on their own without abandoning any. Only 8 per cent were under-achievers in the writing and math activities.

Problems in implementing MI

Teacher reluctance was the major problem in implementing MI. Even though they realized the potential of using multiple pathways for initiating input in their ESL classes, the teachers were not keen to leave the beaten track. This was partly due to there being no incentive for innovation. If anything did not work out with the new scheme, the teachers feared reprisal from the school authority.

Discussion with the school administrators and parents about the long-term benefit of the MI approach did not make them acquiesce to the MI approach. Though the discussions were quite short, the focus of the school administrators on short-term gains and test results for their learners was quite obvious. They did not care much for long-term learning and were therefore not very supportive of such work by their teachers.

Neither did parents seem to recognize the value of an MI methodology since they were also very much concerned with the immediate test marks of their children and were not so interested in the 'long-term' gains of MI for their children as presented to them.

Conclusions

Extensive awareness and a supportive curriculum are the minimum requirements for implementing a new approach like MI. It may safely be concluded that applying multiple pathways for input can forestall cognitive narrowing in learners. MI also has the potential to lead to continuous teacher development.

References

Armstrong, T. (1993). *7 Kinds of Smart: Identifying and Developing Your Many Intelligences*. New York: Plume.

Armstrong, T. (1994). *Multiple Intelligences in the Classroom*. Alexandria, VA: Association for Supervision and Curriculum Development.

Gardner, H. (1983). *Frames of Mind: The Theory of Multiple Intelligences*. New York: Basic Books.

Gardner, H. (1993). *Multiple Intelligences: The theory in practice*. New York: Basic Books.

Gardner, H. (2000). *The Disciplined Mind: Beyond Facts And Standardized Tests, The K-12 Education That Every Child Deserves*. New York: Penguin Putnam.

Spearman, C.E. (1904). 'General intelligence' objectively determined and measured. *American Journal of Psychology* 15, 201-293.

Thurstone, L.L. (1938). *Primary Mental Abilities*. Psychometric Monographs 1. Chicago: University of Chicago Press.

Tolman, E.C. (1932). *Purposive Behavior in Animals and Men*. New York: Century.

An impact study of a TEYL innovation project in Beijing, China

Wang Qiang, Beijing Normal University, PR China
Sun Lin, Beijing Institute of Curriculum Innovation, PR China
Ma Xin, Beijing Normal University, PR China

Research background

In 2001, China initiated a nationwide curriculum innovation in Primary and Secondary schools. At the same time, English was added to the Primary curriculum starting from Grade 3 with a time allocation of 80 minutes a week. As Beijing is the political, cultural and economic centre of the country, and is increasingly internationalized, with high parental demand for more effective English education, the government of Beijing, guided by the national English curriculum, lowered the provision of English for schools from Grade 3 to Grade 1 (age 6). However, there had been very little research in China on teaching English to young learners (TEYL). As a result, a well-justified programme based on systematic research is needed for a better provision of TEYL in Beijing.

Under such circumstances, PECI was initiated. PECI is a six-year piloting project (from 2003–2009), under the Beijing municipal government's tenth 'Five-year strategic research project' on social sciences, and headed by the Centre for Foreign Language Education and Teacher Education, Beijing Normal University, in collaboration with a private non-profit-making educational institute in Beijing. It involves seven non-key Primary schools with approximately 1,500 pupils and 30 teachers as participants. The research team consisted of over 20 members with consultants, university researchers, course designers, material developers and a number of research assistants and administrative staff.

The goal of the project is to find ways to improve the effectiveness and efficiency of teaching and learning English in Primary schools so as to make the process of learning a foreign language a fruitful and motivating experience for children, contributing not only to their significant language development, but also to the development of their interest, confidence, learning strategies and their ability to think and to study other subjects. The project aims to achieve its goal through:

1. developing innovative teaching approaches;

2. selecting appropriate materials and teaching methods;

3. developing resources;

4. implementing new ways of assessment;

5. exploring effective approaches to teacher development;

6. discovering factors that influence curriculum change and exploring solutions to solve the problems;

7. building up a holistic framework for innovative TEYL in more developed cities, such as Beijing.

The theoretical basis for PECI includes: holistic approach, learner-centredness, whole person development, whole language approach with integrated skills development, motivated experience, multiple intelligences, task/project-based and formative assessment.

Specific innovative aims of the project include:

1. Introducing English from Grade 1 (6 years old) to Grade 6, with five 40-minute lessons a week.

2. Offering the course in three interrelated formats: Comprehensive English (three periods/week), Reading (one period/week) and Video-Audio-Oral (one period/week).

3. Increasing the effectiveness and efficiency of teacher training and promote teacher autonomy through a variety of activities.

The research project is formative by nature. It follows an interactive process of designing, constructing, implementing, evaluating, monitoring, redesigning and restructuring, leading to step-by-step improvements. This spiral model ensures the validity and practicality of the research project.

This paper reports on the impacts of PECI in the first four years on pupil development, including the learning of other subjects, teacher development and school development.

Research design

Research questions

The main research questions for this study are:

- What impact has PECI had on pupils, teachers and schools? Specifically:

  - In what aspects have pupils changed over the four years (linguistic, affective, metacognitive and cultural awareness)?

- Has the learning of English had any effect on pupils' learning of other subjects?

- How have teachers changed during the project?

- What is the impact of PECI on schools?

Data collection

Since 2003, a variety of data have been collected systematically. The main types of data include interviews with teachers, pupils, parents and school principals (once a year), pupils' work, test results (of English, Chinese and Maths, once a year), videoed lessons (four times a year in each school), teachers' reflections, stories, lesson plans and achievement certificates (twice a year), and school reports (once a year). The following presents the main findings based on the data collected.

Major findings

Impact on pupil development: Linguistic development

Based on the analysis of the pupils' writings and their annual English test results, we found that pupils had made significant progress in listening, speaking, reading and writing at each grade level and their abilities by the end of each year from Grade 1 to Grade 4 are illustrated in Table 1 below.

	Grade 1	Grade 2	Grade 3	Grade 4
Listening	Pupils can understand cartoons on familiar topics. The utterances of the cartoon are composed of simple and repetitive sentence structures.	Pupils can understand cartoons at the speed of approximately 50 words/minute. The utterances in the cartoon are composed of more varied repetitive sentence structures and related to familiar topics.	Pupils can understand videos at the speed of approximately 90 words/minute. The utterances in the videos are composed of varied and more complex sentence structures, and the topics of the videos are not limited to what they have learned about in class.	Pupils can understand videos with familiar topics at the normal speed and with more complex utterances. They can understand the main ideas and key information of the videos.

Speaking	Pupils can understand most of the questions about personal information (such as name, age, family members, likes) and respond correctly with little support.	Pupils can understand questions about familiar topics such as personal information, family and relatives, likes and dislikes, daily life and activities, animals, etc. They usually respond promptly and most utterances are expanded.	With the support of pictures, pupils can tell a story with the words and sentence structures they have learned in class, either independently or with their partners. They can clearly express their personal ideas and opinions.	They can initiate and keep conversations going. They can exchange ideas, opinions and comments in group discussions. They can present stories or posters individually or cooperatively.
Reading	Pupils can read stories they have learned in class; they can understand the main ideas and key information of a picture story with approximately 30 words.	Pupils can read picture stories with 60 words, either under the guidance of the teacher or independently.	Pupils can read picture stories with 100–200 words, either under the guidance of the teacher or independently. They start to use some reading skills such as phonic skills, predictions, using the clues of the pictures to guess the meaning of words or sentences. They can outline the structure of stories with a story chart.	They can flexibly use more reading skills to read picture stories with 300–500 words independently.

Writing	Pupils can make picture dictionaries; they can copy the stories they have learned.	Pupils can write picture stories with captions. Their writings are more creative in that they can use varied repetitive sentence structures. They can write on more topics.	Pupils can write from single sentences to short passages. They can write stories with increasing vocabulary and clear story lines. They can write on a variety of topics.	They can use English to accomplish different writing tasks, such as stories, summaries, outlines, book or movie reviews, diaries, and reports.

Table 1: *Pupil's linguistic development*

Affective development

The results from the questionnaire given to pupils of the first three cohorts showed that pupils from Grade 1 to Grade 3 developed and kept a high level of interest, strong motivation, self-confidence, and positive attitudes towards English. From the interviews with some parents and teachers, we found that parents were very pleased with their children's willingness to learn English. Teachers of the experimental classes found that these pupils were more confident and not afraid of making mistakes or talking with foreigners. It is also found that these pupils gradually developed cooperative awareness. From classroom observations we found that pupils from Grade 1 were less willing and effective when working in groups. With more practice and guidance from the teachers, children gradually got used to working in groups. By the time they entered Grade 4, they could divide roles among themselves, decide on the procedures of working efficiently, and could employ a number of problem-solving strategies to accomplish their tasks within the time allowed.

Learning strategies and thinking skills

The results of the questionnaires on learning strategies revealed that pupils from the experimental classes employed learning strategies more frequently in learning. These strategies include: previewing and reviewing; using flashcards; imitating; guessing; switching to the mother tongue; paying attention to what others are talking about; encouraging themselves; working with partners; and asking questions. With regard to thinking skills, compared with non-experimental classes, children from the experimental classes were more curious, imaginative, quick-witted. They were more willing to probe into facts. They were also more creative and logical in thinking. The following are some of the comments made by the teachers of other subjects:

> They have a strong desire to learn. When I ask one question, they will raise more related questions. They are more capable of doing independent reading outside the class. They've achieved more in the learning of Chinese (T6, a Chinese teacher).

While teaching both the experimental and non-experimental classes, I have to prepare different lesson plans. This is because I have to set higher targets for the experimental classes for pupils in those classes are more active thinkers and they can complete a lot of tasks by themselves (T21, a Maths teacher).

The pupils in experimental classes are brave in asking questions, and they ask more questions than pupils in non-experimental classes (T57, a Science teacher).

Cultural awareness

Along with the project, children have significantly developed their cultural awareness. It was found that these pupils showed great interest in learning about other cultures and liked to participate in the activities related to different cultures, such as performing classical plays in English, drawing, and talking about Christmas, Halloween and other festivals.

Impact on the learning of other subjects

As there has been quite a lot of debate on whether the introduction of English from age six may affect children's learning of other subjects, especially Chinese, test results of Chinese, Maths and English were collected yearly to compare children from experimental and non-experimental classes. The results showed that English had a positive effect on the learning of Chinese as children from the experimental classes scored distinctively higher than children from non-experimental classes in the same grade. No effect on the learning of maths was found. Interestingly, from the interviews with the teachers of other subjects, it was found that the learning of English has also promoted the learning of Arts, Music, Science and sports. The following are some comments made by these teachers:

Learning English can promote the study of other subjects. For example, they have a lot of opportunities to draw pictures. This is good for learning coloring and picturing in arts course (T31, Art teacher).

They (students in experimental classes) have a strong sense of cooperation and high level of participation in my class. For example, when I'm organizing group work activity, even if the group members haven't worked as a group before, they can cooperate very well. They have the awareness of cooperation. They have the basic ability of cooperation (T2, a Chinese teacher).

Impact on teacher development

PECI has developed a variety of activities to promote teacher development and they are found to have effectively promoted teacher autonomy. These activities include writing teaching reflections, analyzing teaching cases, getting feedback on lessons, attending seminars and observing and discussing videoed lessons, Teachers participating in the project seemed to have gone through four major stages of development:

1. resistance to new ideas and continuing to teach based on past experience;

2. relating theories to practice and trying new methods;

3. developing reflective awareness;

4. developing autonomy with personal teaching styles.

Typical features for each stage of teacher development were identified based on the data collected through teacher interviews, their self-reflections and our lesson observations. At the beginning, when these teachers first joined in the project, there were clear conflicts between the new ideas and their past experiences. Teachers showed resistance because the project required them to put in extra time and to be observed with suggestions for improvement given by curriculum developers and course designers. As a result, they found it painful to change. At the second stage, they increased their confidence little by little with the progress of pupils' language development, parents' approval and school support. At the third stage, they became more amazed and fascinated by the progress they made in teaching and their children's achievement in learning. They began to get awards from teaching competitions and enjoyed the gains the project brought them. Meanwhile, they became more self-critical about their own teaching. At stage four, teachers formed their own teaching styles. They were more willing to be observed and share their experience with other teachers, Some of them are now leading teachers in their respective districts and are often invited to give public lessons. More significantly, all of them have enhanced their love and devotion to teaching English to children.

The findings also suggest that teacher development in the Chinese context has unique characteristics:

1. The top-down approach to curriculum change has a positive role to play in promoting teacher development.

2. Some teacher-development activities commonly found in the Chinese context, such as observing public lessons, talking through lessons, case analysis and reflections, etc. are found to be particularly effective in scaffolding teachers in their professional development.

Impact on school development

From the interviews with the eight school administrators, we found that the schools involved in the project were very thankful as it had positively promoted whole school development. It promoted not only the development of English teachers but also dramatically increased interactions among teachers of different subjects, resulting in joint efforts to improve the overall quality of teaching. More importantly, with children's achievement and teachers' development, the reputations of these project schools were dramatically enhanced, which won a lot of parental support. Finally, the project provided an effective model for school reform.

Conclusion

This research has clearly shown that change is a lengthy, complex and gradual process. We need to allow time for change to take place, with good planning, support and resources made available throughout the process. Teachers also need to be well supported with pedagogical skills. Through practice and reflection, they gradually develop ownership and become autonomous. The research has shown that evidence of good progress in pupil development seems to be the most important driving force for both teacher and school development, which in turn enhances further pupil, teacher and school development over time. Change management needs to adopt a holistic approach to facilitate sustainability. In this process we need to take care that children attain both linguistic and non-linguistic targets if we are to maintain long-term motivation in language learning.

Successful change needs collaborations among curriculum developers, researchers, schools and teachers. Factors that are crucial for the success of PECI include: adequate time and intensity; appropriate course structure; focus on both linguistic and non-linguistic goals; good materials development; effective teacher training and development; strong school and parental support.

Implications and reflection on the research process

The length of the project poses enormous difficulty for managing systematic research with respect to changes in the personnel involved in the project. The rich amount of data collected over a period of four years has meant that we have been unable to process and analyze all of the data. To implement the piloted project on a large scale, we need national policy to allow the use of materials and resources. With the growth of the project, the research team also gained a lot of experience of working with schools and school teachers. We have developed expertise in designing the courses, selecting materials, innovating teacher methods, conducting teacher training and development workshops, and in designing assessment tools and research skills.

Acknowledgements

We would like to thank all those who have contributed to the project, especially the children and teachers from the seven participating schools.

Interactive teaching styles with CD-ROMs: Malaysian perspectives

Aizan Yaacob, Universiti Utara, Malaysia

Sheena Gardner, School of Education, University of Birmingham, UK

Introduction

Politicians in many countries have decreed that Information and Communication Technology (ICT) should be used in Primary schools in the belief that it will enhance learning, help produce a forward-looking generation well equipped to contribute to a rapidly changing technological world, and contribute towards realizing national goals, such as, in the Malaysian context, the aspiration to be a fully developed nation by 2020:

> The government will give priority to improving facilities and infrastructure and intensifying the use of ICT in all schools and institutions. Greater emphasis will also be given to raising the standard of the teaching and learning of Mathematics and Science and foreign languages (Economic Planning Unit, 2001: 25).

Governments have therefore invested large sums of money placing computers in schools and supporting their use. While familiarity with technology is in many ways beneficial, the evidence from research that ICT leads to improved learning in school is mixed, and politicians' hopes are not always well founded (BECTA, 2007).

ICT in Primary English in Malaysia

Laptop computers and sets of CD-ROMs for English, Mathematics and Science were provided to all Primary schools in Malaysia, starting with Year 1 in 2003. English teachers were encouraged to use the CD-ROMs in their daily English Hour, which (modelled on the British Literacy Hour) starts with shared reading experience and then moves into related language work. The aim was to expose students to greater opportunities to use English in an IT-rich environment and provide the basis of literacy in the English Language (Curriculum Development Centre, 2003).

The six Year 1 English CD-ROMs comprise 36 units organized around three major themes: World of Family and Friends, World of Knowledge, and World of Stories. The World of Stories units taught during our study contain stories told through simple sentences spoken and written below cartoon-like animation.

Studies of ICT and reading

Studies on the classroom use of ICT proclaim positive effects, particularly on students' interest and motivation, though critical reviewers caution that the evidence base of many of these studies is weak (EPPI, 2003; Plowman and Stephen, 2003). CD-ROM story reading does enhance learners' comprehension and vocabulary, though less so than teacher reading (Segers et al, 2004), supporting the dangers of 'set it and forget it' syndrome in whole class teaching (Miller et al., 1994: 190). Overall computers are viewed as a benign addition (Cuban, 2001), which can be fun, but may not transform teaching.

Studies of interactive storybooks have shown that the help features available in the computer-mediated text can influence reading comprehension (Reinking, 1988) and comprehension increases when manipulation of the text is controlled by the children (Reinking and Schreiner, 1985), particularly for intermediate and poor readers. Similarly, Miller et al. (1994), examining repeated reading of CD-ROM and hard-covered storybooks, reported CD-ROM storybooks with assistance features enhanced children's reading performance; while Edwards et al. (2000) found additional language awareness benefits with bilingual multimedia storybooks.

Other reading ICT materials involve drill and practice type activities, which have been criticized by Paterson et al. (2003: 178) as benefiting low-level skills but not higher-level experiences: 'many of these systems stressed assessment of measurable, fractionalized behaviours emphasizing content rather than process, and the mechanical rather than the meaningful'. Thus CD-ROMs have potential benefits in motivation, reading comprehension, vocabulary development and drilling practice for our whole-class EFL in northern Malaysia.

Our study

In observations of 26 Year 1 English Hour lessons by nine teachers in four schools, three teachers used CD-ROMs in their whole-class teaching (Yaacob, 2006). We noticed that while children were generally happy at the prospect of 'watching' CD-ROMs in the classroom, there was variation in how teachers used the CD-ROMs. Here we analyze this variation through differences in teaching style described in terms of classroom interaction, supplemented by teacher and student comments.

Extract 1: Passive viewing

CD: ONE DAY MOTHER SAYS TO MING AND LING: 'CHILDREN, HERE IS SOME MONEY. GO AND BUY SOME NEW CLOTHES.' *(A picture of Ming, Ling and their mother appear on the screen.)*

LING SAYS, 'BROTHER, LET'S BUY SOME NEW CLOTHES FOR MOTHER.'

'YES,' MING SAID. MOTHER WOULD BE VERY HAPPY. MING AND LING ARE VERY HAPPY. THEY RUN. THEY RUN TO THE SHOP THAT SELLS CLOTHES.

PING! PANG! 'OH NO!' LING IS AFRAID. SHE DROPS A VASE. IT'S BROKEN.

'BROTHER CAN WE GO HOME NOW?' LING ASKS.

[…]

'WHAT HAPPENED?' THEIR MOTHER ASKS.

MING TELLS THEIR MOTHER WHAT HAPPENED. MOTHER IS HAPPY. SHE TELLS HER CHILDREN: 'YOU HAVE DONE THE RIGHT THING. THAT IS THE BEST PRESENT FOR ME.'

T: OK, finished. OK, we will listen again. *(Teacher sits by the computer and replays the CD.)* Alia pay attention! OK. Listen one more time.

Extract 1 shows an absence of interaction during the CD-ROM reading: the students and teacher watch passively, as at the movies, without making comments. Given this lack of encouragement for active viewing it is perhaps not surprising that the teacher felt some of the students did not always pay attention to the story:

for students who … there are certain students who are not interested and we have to attract their attention by calling their names repeatedly then only they watch the LCD. Sometimes they appeared to be watching but their minds were elsewhere (Teacher C).

Extract 2: Teacher-assisted viewing of CD-ROM

T: OK. 'Z'. 'Z'. Today we're going to hear a story about 'Ahmad cries wolf'. Ok. Hear the story first. Look at the picture carefully. Look at the picture and listen to the story. What happened? OK. Listen.

CD: SHE IS AHMAD'S SISTER, SITI.

T: OK, This is Siti. This is Ahmad. They are brother and sister. (points to pictures)

CD: HE IS AHMAD'S FATHER.

T: OK, this is their father.

CD: She is Ahmad's mother.

T: This is mother.

CD: THIS IS A FARM.

T: OK This one we call farm. OK. Daniel!! So many animals. OK, what animals are there? What it is?

This one is duck, goat, chickens, duck and goats. *(Teacher explains the pictures shown in the story.)*

Extract 2 shows the interaction between Teacher A and the CD-ROM as they teach together. The lesson follows the CD format, with the teacher contributing by drawing students' attention to salient features in the story (e.g., pointing out main characters) and of the pictures (e.g., talking about the animals in the picture of the farm). Here the children are encouraged to be active viewers.

The interaction is between the teacher and the CD-ROM. Together they provide multi-modal, interactive comprehensible input using English (L2) and no Malay (L1).

Extract 3: CD-ROM led drill and practice

CD: HE SEES THE RIVER.

T: Come on! Read! HE SEES THE RIVER.

SS: *(a few students follow)* HE SEES THE RIVER.

CD: HE IS VERY HAPPY.

SS: HE IS VERY HAPPY.

T: HE RUNS TO THE RIVER. (Teacher reads from the screen.)

CD: HE RUNS TO THE RIVER.

SS: HE RUNS TO THE RIVER.

This drill and practice continues to the end of the story. Teacher B tells the students to repeat the phrases from the CD-ROM. There is minimal interaction between the teacher and students and the CD-ROM takes the teacher's role in the traditional drilling and repetition practice. This allows the teacher to take a back seat:

… it is true it's very interesting … you don't have to say you just put it on and ask them to read the sentences in the CD-ROM (Teacher B).

Extract 4: Teacher-led drill and practice

T: We start again. Listen again. Listen and you repeat.

CD: HASSAN HAS A MANGO TREE.

SS: HASSAN HAS A MANGO TREE!!!

T: OK. Next. Second sentence. (Pause.)

CD: NAZRI LOOKS AT THE MANGOES.

T: NAZRI …

SS: NAZRI …

T: LOOKS …

SS: LOOKS …

T: AT …

SS: AT …

T: THE …

SS: THE MANGOES.

T: OK. Look at the next sentence.

CD: DO YOU LIKE TO EAT MANGOES?

SS: DO YOU LIKE TO EAT MANGOES?

This extract shows that the CD-ROM is used by the teacher for drilling practice. The teacher controls the pace, stopping and starting the computer by pausing whenever necessary to correct students' pronunciation. She also jumps around the text selecting sentences for practice.

> … with LCD we ask students to see from the big screen xxx it's useful in a way that it's lighter (teaching load) if not we end up doing everything, talking and showing this and that and do more talking especially with children it's very tiring but with the LCD it's a bit lighter … (Teacher A).

Extract 5: Teacher-led phonics practice and vocabulary development

CD: NOW IT'S TIME TO LEARN SOME NEW WORDS. NEW. OLD. CLEAN. DIRTY. BUY. SELL. SHIRT. DRESS.

T: OK. Now we look one by one. What is this? Can you say it? (Reads from the screen:) New.

SS: NEW.

T: Again.

SS: NEW.

T: OK. What's the meaning of 'new'?

CD: NEW.

T: NEW.

SS: NEW.

CD: NEW. (Teacher clicks on word.)

SS: NEW.

CD: N.E.W. (Teacher clicks on phonics. The word is sounded out/ne/eh/wu/.)

SS: N.E.W. (Students repeat the pronunciation.)

CD: THIS IS MY NEW BOOK. (Teacher clicks on the sentence.)

T: OK shining. Buku ba^ [ru [new book]

SS: [ru

T: Buku ba^ ru new is ba^ [new book. New is]

SS: Ru!!!! [new]

T: Ha. This book is new. New clothes, huh? Shirt, huh? No. OK.

CD: THIS IS MY NEW BOOK.

T: THIS IS MY NEW BOOK. OK, read everyone.

SS: THIS IS MY NEW BOOK.

T: Again.

SS: THIS IS MY NEW BOOK.

T: Very good. Let's look at another word.

Here the teacher controls the computer and uses the resources on the vocabulary pages to practise the word in isolation, the pronunciation and spelling, and the word in the context of a sentence. This ability to move about the computer screen and elicit the pronunciation, or a picture of vocabulary items, is one the advantages of the CD-ROM materials.

… yes really effective, especially when teachers don't know how to draw and when pictures to explain the meanings of the key words are difficult to get for example when we teach adjective – sad we can show our facial expression but they'll be more excited when seeing the cartoon character feeling sad. Besides they will remember better (Teacher D).

Extract 6: Student interest and motivation:

Interviewer: What do you like about your English class?

Nicky: **Hmm tengok tu** movie **dalam cerita tu macam tengok wayang**
[watch a movie or story like watching a movie (in the cinema)]

All: Ha. (Everybody agrees.)

Interviewer: Why?

Nicky: **Sebab syok sangat boleh nyanyi.** [Because it's so much fun (we) can sing

Interviewer: Can you tell me a bit more?

Nicky: **Sebab ada boleh nyanyi lepas tu boleh tengok macam cerita.**
[Because there's a song can sing after that can watch the story (movie).]

This extract is typical of student reaction: they like the stories, and like to be active, as when they sing the alphabet song at the beginning of each CD.

Conclusions

1. CD-ROMs were infrequently used, but generally viewed positively. Teachers claimed that CD-ROMs were interesting, useful and made their teaching easier; learners claimed that they were 'fun'.

2. Teachers used CD-ROMs in very different ways, with different results:

*   Passive viewing of CD-ROMs (Extract 1) was associated with negative comments from the teacher about students' lack of interest and wandering attention.

*   Student repetition of CD-ROMs (Extract 3) reinforces the drill and practices teaching interaction patterns.

*   When teachers scaffold learning through the CD-ROM, they can provide rich multi-modal comprehensible input (Extract 2) and promote active viewing in L2.

*   When teachers control the CD-ROM, they can manipulate vocabulary features (sounds, phonics, images, words) effectively in context (Extract 5).

*   There was no evidence of teachers using the CD-ROMs as a springboard for discussion of the content and values of stories with the children – the kind of interaction desired by the Ministry of Education.

Implications

ICT approaches work if they are precisely targeted (Brooks et al., 2002) as seen when the teachers took charge of the CD-ROM and could click on pictures, sounds and phonics/spellings as needed.

ICT alone will not transform practice:

> most of the literature points to ... ICT [having been] brought into educational environments as a useful supplement ... school teachers ... continue with their existing teaching styles rather than use the introduction of new technologies as an opportunity to examine and transform existing practice (Becker and Riel, 2000, in Plowman and Stephen, 2003: 149).

Malaysia is not alone:

> With the benefit of hindsight, it is clear that what explains the paradox of greatly increased provision combined with less than necessary utilisation is probably our inability to provide clear guidelines about how to use ICT ... Knowledge for teachers about 'what works' has been lacking (BECTA 2007: 5).

This study points to options teachers may choose to meet their specific purposes, be they providing comprehensible input, providing drilling practice with a proficient model input, or providing vocabulary enhancement. As discussed in greater detail elsewhere (Gardner and Yaacob, forthcoming), different interaction patterns will be needed to develop reading strategies and discussion of texts through shared reading.

Transcription key

S	student
SS	students
T	teacher
CD	voice on the CD-ROM
CAPS	reading aloud
...	text missing
<bold>	native language elements in dialogues
[ ]	translations in square brackets
[	overlapping speech
^	rising intonation and pause (teacher expects students to complete)
(*italic*)	notes

References

Becker, H.J. and Riel, M.M. (2000). *Teacher Professional Engagement and Constructivist-Compatible Computer Use. Report 7*. Center for Research on Information Technology and Organizations (CRITO), Irvine, CA: University of California.

BECTA (2007). *Becta Report: Primary Schools – ICT and Standards: A Report to the DfES on Becta's Analysis of National Data from OFSTED and QCA*. Coventry: British Educational Communication and Technology Agency. Available at http://www.becta.org.uk. Accessed 20 October 2007.

Brooks, G. and the National Foundation for Educational Research (2002). *What Works for Children with Literacy Difficulties: The Effectiveness of Intervention Schemes*. London: Department for Education and Science.

Cuban, L. (2001). *Oversold and Underused: Computers in the Classroom*. Cambridge, MA: Harvard University Press.

Curriculum Development Centre (2003). *English Language Year 1 Teaching Courseware*. Kuala Lumpur, Malaysia: Ministry of Education.

Edwards, V., Monaghan, F. and Knight, J. (2000). Books, pictures and conversations: Using bilingual multimedia storybooks to develop language awareness. *Language Awareness* 9 (3), 135-146.

Economic Planning Unit (2001). *The Third Outline Perspective Plan 2001–2010*. Kuala Lumpur, Malaysia: The Prime Minister's Department.

EPPI (2003). A systematic review and meta-analysis of the effectiveness of ICT on literacy learning in English (pp. 5-16). Available at http://eppi.ioe.ac.uk/EPPIWeb/home.aspx?page=/reel/review_groups/english/review_two.htm. Accessed 20 October 2007.

Gardner, S. and Yaacob, A. (forthcoming) *CD-ROM Multimodal Affordances: Classroom Interaction perspectives in the Malaysian English Literacy Hour*. Language and Education.

Miller, L., Blackstock, J. and Miller, R. (1994). An exploratory study into the use of CD-ROM storybooks. *Computers Education* 22 (1/2), 187-204.

Paterson, W.A., Jacobs Henry, J., O'Quin, K., Ceprano, M.A. and Blue, E.V. (2003). Investigating the effectiveness of an Integrated Learning System on emergent readers. *Reading Research Quarterly* 38 (2), 172-207.

Plowman, L. and Stephen, C. (2003). A 'benign addition'? Research on ICT and pre-school children. *Journal of Computer Assisted Learning* 19, 149-164.

Reinking, D. (1988). Computer-mediated text and comprehension differences: The role of reading time, reader preference, and the estimation of learning. *Reading Research Quarterly* XXIII (Fall), 4.

Reinking, D. and Schreiner, R. (1985). The effects of computer-mediated text on measures of reading comprehension and reading behaviour. *Reading Research Quarterly* XX (Fall), 5

Segers, E., Takke, L. and Verhoeven, L. (2004). Teacher-mediated versus computer-mediated storybook reading to children in native and multicultural kindergarten classrooms. *School Effectiveness and School Improvement* 15 (2), 215-226.

Yaacob, A. (2006). Malaysian literacy practices in English: 'Big Books', CD-ROM and the Year 1 English hour. Unpublished doctoral dissertation. University of Warwick.

Notes about contributors

Fawzia Al-Zedjali: Ministry of Education, Sultanate of Oman

Fawzia Al-Zedjali has worked as a teacher, senior teacher, supervisor and teacher trainer with the Ministry of Education in the Sultanate of Oman. For the last two years, she has been a curriculum officer and has worked on developing the course books for the Integrated Curriculum project. Her main academic interest is initial literacy and teacher education.

Yuko Goto Butler: Graduate School of Education, University of Pennsylvania, USA

Yuko Goto Butler PhD is Professor of Language and Literacy in Education at the Graduate School of Education, University of Pennsylvania. Her research interests are primarily associated with the improvement of second and foreign language education among young learners in the US as well as abroad in response to the diverse needs of an increasingly globalizing world. Her most recent project examines various issues that have arisen in conjunction with the introduction of English language instruction at the elementary school level in select Asian countries, including Taiwan, Japan and Korea.

Chiou-lan Chern: Department of English, National Taiwan Normal University, Taiwan

Chiou-lan Chern holds a PhD in Education from the University of Queensland in Australia and is currently chair of the Department of English at National Taiwan Normal University. She teaches language skill courses and TEFL methodology at undergraduate level and conducts reading research seminars at graduate level. She has participated in various teacher-training projects and given presentations and workshops at Secondary and Primary schools in Taiwan.

Leonor Corradi: Dr Joaquin V. Gonzalez, Instituto Superior del Profesorado, City of Buenos Aires, Argentina

Leonor Corradi holds an MSc in Education (Surrey University, UK). She is a tenured lecturer in Methodology, a coordinator of city government plurilingual schools and co-author of the Curriculum Design for FL in Argentina. She has presented at national and international conferences, and is an ELT author. She has extensive experience in teacher development and TEYLS.

Gayathri Devi Dutt: Regional Institute for English, Bangalore, South India

Gayathri Devi Dutt has recently retired from the post of Director of the Regional Institute for English, South India (RIESI) based in Bangalore where she managed administrative and academic work. She began her career as an English teacher and moved vertically to different levels in the Education sector. Her academic experience includes teacher training (including satellite mode) and material production in ELT and other school subjects. She has specialized in gender issues having done a course at the University of Sussex and is interested in studying the implications of gender in achieving appropriacy while learning English as a second language.

Jelena Mihaljevic Djigunovic: English Department, Faculty of Philosophy, Zagreb University, Croatia

Jelena Mihaljevic Djigunovic is Professor of the TEFL Section at Zagreb University. She holds a PhD in Applied Linguistics and has published extensively on affective factors in MFL learning and on teaching young learners. She has authored two books (on affect and foreign language anxiety) and co-edited several volumes. She has participated in several international projects on language learning and teaching.

Janet Enever: Institute for the Study of European Transformations, London Metropolitan University, UK

Janet Enever (EdD) has taught at Primary, Secondary and Tertiary levels in England, Poland, Latvia and Hungary. She holds a doctorate in Education specialising in early-start FL Policy (Bristol, UK) and is currently a member of the Research Institute for the Study of European Transformations at London Metropolitan University. Her research and consultancy interests include Primary foreign-language policy and practice and the effects of increased globalisation on language provision. She is project director of a multinational European research study Early Language Learning in Europe (ELLiE).

Simon Etherton: Ministry of Education, Sultanate of Oman

Simon Etherton has worked in teacher education with the Ministry of Education in the Sultanate of Oman for the last eight years, having previously taught at Exeter University, in the South Pacific and in Europe. He has also worked on the Omani Integrated Curriculum Project for one year.

M. Teresa Fleta: The British Council School of Madrid, Spain

Teresa Fleta PhD is an English teacher and teacher educator. She has worked and carried out research studies in the British Council School of Madrid. Currently, she collaborates with the School of Education (UCM) and teaches the module: 'Teaching Young Learners' on the MA programme for 'TEFL' in Alcalá de Henares University.

Sheena Gardner: School of Education, University of Birmingham, UK

Sheena Gardner is Reader in Educational Linguistics and a member of the MOSAIC Centre for research on multilingualism at Birmingham University (UK), having worked in ELT/ESL teacher education/Applied Linguistics in North America, South East Asia, Africa and Europe. Her research interests in the use of language(s) across the curriculum include investigation of classroom-based assessment of English as an Additional Language across the curriculum among Year 1 learners in England, and a genre-based corpus study of assessed university student writing.

Mrinalini Mukund Ghatage: SNDT Womens' University Arts and Commerce College for Women, Pune, India

Mrinalini Mukund Ghatage holds an MA (English) and MPhil from University of Pune, Maharashtra State, India. Her area of specialization is ELT. She is NET- (National Eligibility Test) qualified and holds a Post Graduate Certificate Course of Teaching of English (PGCTE) at Central Institute of English and Foreign Languages (CIEFL), Hyderabad, India. She is now studying for a Post Graduate Diploma in Teaching of English (PGDTE) at CIEFL, Hyderabad. She has recently presented papers in Islamabad, Pakistan and Chennai, India. She has been working as an English lecturer for the last nine years in Maharashtra, India, where she teaches at undergraduate level.

Telma Gimenez: Universidade Estadual de Londrina, Brazil

Telma Gimenez is Associate Professor at Universidade Estadual de Londrina (UEL) and holds a PhD from Lancaster University. She supervises undergraduate students during their teaching practice and supervises MA and PhD students doing research on foreign language learning and EFL teacher education. She has worked as a consultant for the State Secretariat of Education in the state of Paraná, Brazil and is an active member of ELTeCS Latin America and many other professional networks.

Shamsul Hoque: BRAC University Institute of Educational Development, Dhaka, Bangladesh

Shamsul Hoque is an ELT Consultant at BRAC University Institute of Educational Development, Dhaka, Bangladesh. His main specialities include teacher training and materials development. He is a former ELT Adviser at Bangladesh Open University and former Chief Editor, National Curriculum and Textbook Board. He holds a Diploma in Education from Exeter University, a Certificate in TESOL from London University Institute of Education and an MA in English from Dhaka University.

Hsiu-ming Hsu: Chin-hsi Junior High School, Taoyuan County, Taiwan

Hsiu-ming Hsu is an English teacher at Chin-hsi Junior High School in Taoyuan County, Taiwan. She has served as a seed teacher and is currently a coordinator for the MOE Curriculum and Instruction Consulting Team.

Dilek I.nal: Department of English Language Teaching, Istanbul University, Turkey

Dilek İnal PhD holds the post of Assistant Professor at the Department of English Language Teaching at Istanbul University in Turkey. She received her MA in ELT and a PhD in American Culture and Literature. Her areas of interest are TEYL, teacher training and development, and literary studies.

Richard Johnstone: University of Stirling, Scotland

Richard Johnstone OBE is Emeritus Professor at the University of Stirling in Scotland. He has conducted extensive teaching, publication and research at national and international levels on of the early learning of additional languages. He was Director of the independent evaluation of the national pilot projects which introduced modern foreign languages at Primary school in Scotland; a member of the group of six which in 1999 conducted the first EC-funded survey of research on ELL across member states of the European Union, and a member of the group of three which in 2006 completed a follow-up EC-funded survey which included not only research but also professionals' views of good practice and the key principles of ELL teaching. Currently, he is Director of the UK's first project on early partial immersion in a foreign language and also Director of the independent evaluation of the national early bilingual education programme in Spain which is run under the joint auspices of the British Council in Spain and the Spanish Ministry of Education and Culture. He was commissioned by the Council of Europe to write the publication on early language learning in their languages policy publication series.

Kirti Kapur: National Council of Educational Research and Training, New Delhi, India

Kirti Kapur (BA, BEd, MA, MPhil, PhD) has a total of 20 years' experience in the areas of English Language and literature. She has taught in various schools and colleges across India and since her appointment at NCERT has been working in the areas of curriculum, syllabus and textbook development, evaluation, training, research and consultancy.

Yasemin Kırkgöz: ELT Department of the Faculty of Education, Çukurova University, Adana, Turkey

Yasemin Kırkgöz currently works as a lecturer at the ELT Department of the Faculty of Çukurova University, Turkey. She has published on language policy, curriculum design and innovation management, teaching English to young learners and using computers in ELT.

Kuchah Kuchah: Ministry of Basic Education, Yaounde, Cameroon

Kuchah Kuchah is the National Pedagogic Inspector for bilingual education in the Ministry of Basic Education in Cameroon. He is also Secretary General and Chief Convenor of the Cameroon English Language and Literature Teachers' Association. He has co-authored course books for English in French-medium Nursery and Primary schools in Cameroon.

Won Key Lee: Seoul National University of Education, Korea

Won Key Lee is currently Dean of Academic Affairs at Seoul National University of Education, Korea. He has been one of the forerunners in implementing Primary ELT in Korea, playing a leading role in creating the national Primary ELT curriculum, carrying out Primary English teacher training, and writing the national Primary English textbooks including CD-ROMs.

Samúel Lefever: Iceland University of Education, Reykjavík, Iceland

Samúel Lefever is an Assistant Professor in ELT at Iceland University of Education. He has taught English at various school levels and is currently involved in teacher training and educational research. His main research interests focus on English teaching and learning, including: classroom practices, language assessment, program development and English skills of young learners.

Rama Mathew: Department of Education, Delhi University, India

Rama Mathew is Professor of Education in the Department of Education, Delhi University, Delhi, having previously taught at the CIEFL, Hyderabad. She was Project Director of the CBSE-ELT Curriculum Implementation Study (1993–98). Her current interests include TEYL, language teacher education and qualitative approaches to curriculum inquiry. She is presently working on two projects: coordinating a project in mentoring in collaboration with the Open University, UK, under the UKIERI scheme, and developing an end-test for the proficiency course being offered to students of Delhi University, based on ALTE's can-do statements.

Ma Xin: School of Foreign Languages and Literature, Beijing Normal University, PR China

Ma Xin (MA, PhD candidate) is an English teacher and teacher trainer at the School of Foreign Languages and Literatures, Beijing Normal University, PR China. Her research interests include in-service and pre-service teacher training, teacher change, ELT methodology, and English textbook writing. In recent years, she has participated in a number of projects of teacher development and textbook writing.

Orly Michael: Achva Academic College of Education & School of Education of Bar-Ilan University, Israel

Orly Michael holds a PhD from the Hebrew University in Jerusalem, Israel. She is a senior lecturer at Achva Academic College of Education and a lecturer at the School of Education of Bar-Ilan University in Israel. She specializes in and publishes articles on teacher training, pedagogical instruction, multicultural education, mentoring and tutoring projects and distance learning in multicultural environments.

Felicia A. Moh: British Council, Maitama Abuja, Nigeria

Felicia Moh PhD has fourteen years' experience as an English language teacher trainer. She also taught English Language and Literature briefly at Secondary school level. She joined the British Council as the English Language Projects Manager for Nigeria.

In addition to Teacher Development by Radio, she piloted and still runs a supported open learning course for teacher trainers, the Continued Professional Development Course. She introduced the course in other African countries like Kenya and Cameroon and continues to monitor it.

Jayne Moon: Primary ELT and Teacher Education Consultant, Leeds, UK

Jayne Moon is currently a freelance ELT Primary consultant and teacher educator, formerly a lecturer in the School of Education, University of Leeds. She has extensive international experience of curriculum development and teacher education in Asia, Europe and elsewhere. She is author of *Children Learning English* (Macmillan) and joint editor of *Research into Teaching English to Young Learners*. Her research interests include the professional development of Primary teachers/trainers and the development of children's writing in the L2. She is currently the main consultant for a YL trainer training project as part of the British Council Primary Innovations Project in South East Asia.

Marianne Nikolov: University of Pécs, Hungary

Marianne Nikolov PhD is a Professor of English Applied Linguistics at the University of Pécs, Hungary. Her research interests include early learning and teaching of modern languages, assessment of processes and outcomes in language education, individual differences and language policy. She has published widely on early programmes, including classroom studies on young learners and their teachers.

Susmita Pani: English Language Teaching Institute, Bhubaneswar, India

Susmita Pani is a teacher educator at the English Language Teaching Institute, Bhubaneswar, India. She was a core member of the CBSE-ELT Curriculum Development Study team and also worked for the CBSE-ELT Curriculum Implementation Study project. She is currently involved in the Hornby South-East Asia project for developing teacher-training materials. Dr Pani's areas of interest are reading strategies, and teacher development. She has presented papers in these areas at international conferences and published in *ELT Journal* and *TESL E-Journal*.

N.S. Prabhu: ELT Consultant, India

N.S. Prabhu read English and Linguistics at the Universities of Madras and Reading, and taught English and ELT in India and Singapore. He worked for many years as the British Council's English Language Officer in southern India and in that time conducted a five-year experiment of task-based English-teaching in Primary Schools, which has been widely discussed in the literature as the Bangalore Project.

Maureen Rajuan: Achva Academic College of Education & Hebrew University, Jerusalem, Israel

Maureen Rajuan PhD is a teacher trainer at Achva Academic College of Education and an EFL teacher at Hebrew University, Jerusalem, Israel. She recently received her doctorate in teacher education from the Eindhoven School of Education, the Netherlands. She edits and translates academic manuscripts from Hebrew to English and has published articles in teacher education in international journals.

Uma Raman: ELT Consultant, Chennai, India

Uma Raman is an ELT consultant based at Chennai, India. She has taught English for many years at senior Secondary level and headed schools at the Primary and senior Secondary level. She currently produces materials for teaching English at Primary and middle schools and is also a teacher trainer.

Shelagh Rixon: Centre for Applied Linguistics (CELTE), University of Warwick, UK

Shelagh Rixon is an Associate Professor in the Centre for English Language Teacher Education at the University of Warwick where she coordinates the MA in the Teaching of English to Young Learners. Previously she was a career officer with the British Council, working in many countries including Italy, China and Israel. Shelagh has published teaching materials for children as well as research-based work on TEYL.

Kalyani Samantray: Department of English, Saila Bala Women's College, Utkal University, Orissa, India

Kalyani Samantray has been a teacher educator and classroom teacher at the university level in India for 18 years since completing an MA (TESOL) at the University of London, MPhil (Linguistics), CIEFL and PhD (Phonology). Her current interests are learning styles, materials production for ESL, teaching methodology and stylistics. She has a number of publications in her areas of interest.

Deepthi Sashidhar: Regional Institute for English, Bangalore, South India

Deepthi Sashidhar is a teacher trainer at RIESI with experience in teaching from primary to tertiary levels. She has participated in several ELT courses conducted by the British Council and others and specializes in teaching, training and material production for young learners. Her interests include the application of technology for teaching young learners and exploiting the potential of the satellite mode for teaching and training.

Magdalena Szpotowicz: Centre for Foreign Language Teacher Training, Warsaw University, Poland

Magdalena Szpotowicz is a senior lecturer at the University of Warsaw Centre for Foreign Language Teacher Training where she teachers EFL methodology and Young Learners' methodology. In her PhD research, she studied children's vocabulary acquisition in English as a Foreign Language. She has co-authored course books and curricula for young learners of English. Recently she has been involved in a multinational research study ELLiE (Early Language Learning in Europe).

Sun Lin: Beijing Institute of Curriculum Innovation, PR China

Sun Lin graduated with an MA in Education Studies. She has worked as a college English teacher, researcher and teacher trainer for nearly 16 years. Since 2003, she has been involved in a six-year Primary English curriculum innovation project in China. Her current interests are curriculum development, second language acquisition, classroom discourse analysis and teacher training.

S. Venkateswaran: Regional Institute for English, Bangalore, South India

S. Venkateswaran PhD has been a teacher trainer at RIESI for nearly two decades, training English teachers from primary to tertiary levels. He has also taught English to students at these levels. As a teacher trainer, he has involved himself in content development, course designing and training programmes. His interests are classroom pedagogy, action research and material production. He has authored a few course books for young learners.

Wang Qiang: Centre for Foreign Language Education and Teacher Education, Beijing Normal University, PR China

Wang Qiang (MA, MEd, PhD) is Professor and Head of the Centre for Language Education and Teacher Education, Beijing Normal University. She is also a research fellow at the National Research Centre for Foreign Language Education, China. Her research interests include: curriculum change, pre-service and in-service teacher education, action research, TEYL and ELT methodology. In recent years, she has co-headed the National English Language Curriculum Design Project for Chinese Schools and published quite widely in those areas of her interest.

Aizan Yaacob: Universiti Utara, Malaysia

Aizan Yaacob is a lecturer at Universiti Utara, Malaysia. She has worked in ELT/ESL Teacher Education for nearly 15 years. Her research interests include English for Young Learners, applied linguistics and bilingualism.